GLOBAL AYAHUASCA

SP SPIRITUAL PHENOMENA
TANYA LUHRMANN and ANN TAVES, Editors

GLOBAL AYAHUASCA

Wondrous Visions and Modern Worlds

ALEX K. GEARIN

Stanford University Press • Stanford, California

Stanford University Press
Stanford, California

© 2024 by Alexander Donald Gearin. All rights reserved.

No part of this book may be reproduced or transmitted in any form or by any means, electronic or mechanical, including photocopying and recording, or in any information storage or retrieval system, without the prior written permission of Stanford University Press.

Printed in the United States of America on acid-free, archival-quality paper

Library of Congress Cataloging-in-Publication Data
Names: Gearin, Alex K., author.
Title: Global ayahuasca : wondrous visions and modern worlds / Alex K. Gearin.
Other titles: Spiritual phenomena.
Description: Stanford, California : Stanford University Press, 2024. | Series: Spiritual phenomena | Includes bibliographical references and index.
Identifiers: LCCN 2023057987 (print) | LCCN 2023057988 (ebook) | ISBN 9781503636576 (cloth) | ISBN 9781503639836 (paperback) | ISBN 9781503639843 (epub)
Subjects: LCSH: Ayahuasca—Therapeutic use. | Ayahuasca—Psychological aspects. | Visions—Comparative studies. | Hallucinogenic drugs and religious experience.
Classification: LCC BF209.A93 G437 2024 (print) | LCC BF209.A93 (ebook) | DDC 615.7/883—dc23/eng/20240313
LC record available at https://lccn.loc.gov/2023057987
LC ebook record available at https://lccn.loc.gov/2023057988

Cover design: Michele Wetherbee
Cover painting: "Ila (Arbol Magico)" by Pablo Amaringo, reproduced with permission from the book *The Ayahuasca Visions of Pablo Amaringo* by Howard G Charing, Peter Cloudsley, and Pablo Amaringo

CONTENTS

	List of Illustrations	vii
	Acknowledgments	ix
	Introduction	1
1	Colonial and Postcolonial Roots	37
2	Global Shamanic Tourism in Peru	62
3	Wonder and Healing on Retreat	96
4	Natural Medicine in Australia	131
5	Becoming Modern in China	167
6	Integration and Society	190
	Conclusion: Visionary Contexts	220
	Epilogue	235
	References	241
	Index	265

LIST OF ILLUSTRATIONS

FIGURE 1.1 Watercolor illustration by Spanish bishop Martínez Compañón   45

FIGURE 1.2 Image in American fashion magazine *Elle*   59

FIGURE 2.1 Shipibo family of healers at Pachamama Temple   72

FIGURE 2.2 Pachamama Temple, Peru, winter 2019   80

FIGURE 2.3 Shipibo *chaman*'s healing utensils   81

FIGURE 2.4 Inside the ceremony *maloca*   81

FIGURE 3.1 Carlos leading a boat tour into the Yarinacocha lagoon   115

FIGURE 3.2 Pachamama Temple attendees on boat tour   116

FIGURE 3.3 Integration discussion with Pachamama Temple attendees   124

FIGURE 4.1 Australian ceremony facilitator Darpan   133

FIGURE 4.2 Ayahuasca ceremony space and environment   135

FIGURE 4.3 Integration ceremony with participants discussing their ayahuasca experiences   135

FIGURE 5.1 Mandarin translation of the American cult book *Plants of the Gods*   172

FIGURE 5.2 Antidrug propaganda about ayahuasca   175

FIGURE C.1 Opening talks at Psychedelic Science 2023 conference   221

ACKNOWLEDGMENTS

This book, which delves into ethnographic research across three continents, has been shaped and supported by numerous individuals and institutions. To start chronologically, my research in Australia from 2011 to 2014 greatly benefited from the team at Entheogenesis Australis (EGA) and their eclectic conferences and educational events. One of the most inspiring things about studying psychedelic use in a place like Australia was the social diversity of people it attracted. I'm grateful to Des Tramacchi, Erik Van Keulen, Kathleen Williamson, and Jonathan Carmichael for broadening my psychedelic perspectives while grounding them in place and society. My understanding of the evolving ayahuasca practices in Australia was deepened with the assistance of Steve McDonald from Psychedelic Research in Science and Medicine. The gonzo-journalism and ethnographic connections of Rak Razam were invaluable, as was the hospitality of Myz Guidance at the Rose Road Mystery School in northern New South Wales during my fieldwork. I owe much to the unwavering support of my PhD supervisor Sally Babidge, including across years of academic mentorship when psychedelic users faced greater societal stigma—including in academic contexts—than they do now. I'm grateful to Fernanda Claudio and Yancey Orr for supervisory input, and to the dedicated staff at the University of Queensland's School of Social Science. In addition, thanks go to my colleagues for providing feedback on my Australian-focused research, including Sebastian Job, Nese Devenot, Graham St John, Robin Rodd, and Vince Polito, and to my intellectual friends who helped me to see things in other ways, including Roozbeh, Terry,

ACKNOWLEDGMENTS

and Angela. The Brisbane-based store The Book Merchant Jenkins provided inspiring texts about psychoactive ethnobotany and underground psychedelia. A heartfelt thanks to friends and family for helping to keep me grounded during fieldwork. Finally, I am incredibly grateful to the hundreds of ayahuasca drinkers in Australia who shared their practices and stories with me and to the retreat facilitators for welcoming me into their healing spaces.

In winter 2019, the Pachamama Temple was a beacon of support and exchange. Maestra Rosa Pinedo Vaquez and her family welcomed me to research their work, providing invaluable perspectives and insights on administering ayahuasca to foreigners and locals. Dominik Janus was integral in linking me to the temple and shedding light on the complexities of co-running an ayahuasca tourism business in Peru. Mateo Norzi's efforts in forging relationships with the Shipibo healers' union ASOMASHK was greatly appreciated, while Sonia Lunceford's contribution to interviews at the temple was deeply valued. I owe a debt of gratitude to our dedicated team of translators: Sandro Marquez Sanchez, Jessica Bertram, Sven Perlberg, Maria Riega, and Michael Stanley, who meticulously translated Shipibo or Spanish interview content into English, several with a keen view of local shamanistic terminology.

I'm thankful to Oscar Calavia Sáez, Daniela Peluso, Glenn Shepard, and David Howes for their thoughtful engagement on my research into Indigenous Amazonian lifeworlds and ayahuasca neoshamanism. Bernd Brabec de Mori offered useful guidance before my fieldwork in Pucallpa, Peru. The charitable organization International Center for Ethnobotanical Education, Research, and Service (ICEERS.org) in Spain significantly aided my research, particularly through their World Ayahuasca Conferences, where I initially connected with key interlocutors from China, South America, and elsewhere. Special thanks to author and filmmaker Jerónimo Mazarrasa for enriching conversations on ayahuasca's global expansion. Michael Scott's generous insights, especially on wonder and ayahuasca, were very useful, as were Rupert Stasch's feedback on ayahuasca and the primitive stereotype. I'm especially grateful to my wife, Emily Yu Zong, for her deep and steady intellectual contributions to this book, particularly regarding the enigma of ayahuasca in society. I'm thankful to the staff at Xiamen University's Department of Sociology and Anthropology for helping with the Peru fieldwork.

Conducting fieldwork in mainland China posed challenges due to the

ACKNOWLEDGMENTS xi

dangers of researching an illegal activity in a place with stringent antidrug policies. While there are many individuals I wish to express gratitude to, some have opted for privacy and cannot be named here. I extend heartfelt thanks to the ayahuasca drinkers in China who generously shared their experiences with me. Appreciation goes to Cleo Peterson, Emily Yu Zong, Erika Dyck, Chris Elcock, and David Palmer for feedback on the Chinese ethnographic chapters. Thanks go to my Xiamen University research assistant who chooses to remain anonymous.

In an odd turn, I should acknowledge the educational and accumulative presence of tryptamine plants in my body, thinking, and perception. While hundreds of plants are known to have large concentrations of psychedelic "DMT" alkaloids, some of these plants also contain other molecules that can inspire different responses in humans. I'm grateful to *acacia obtusifolia, acacia acuminata, acacia confusa, psychotria viridis, mimosa hostilis, banisteriopsis caapi,* and *peganum harmala* for showing me beyond the edges of what was possible and for helping me to encounter different social worlds.

Numerous colleagues have influenced the ideas in this book, either through email exchanges or discussions at conferences. These include Evgenia Fotiou, Nicolas Langlitz, Carlos Suárez Álvarez, Jeremy Narby, Dena Sharrock, Jeff Guss, Martin Fortier, Kenneth Tupper, Dennis McKenna, Danny Nemu, Erik Davis, Gordon Matthews, Vince Polito, Paul Liknaitzky, Gayle Highpine, Adam Aranovich, Ido Hartogsohn, David Dupuis, Jules Evans, Tehseen Noorani, Chan Kai Tai, Howard Charing, Daniel Perkins, Wouter Hanegraaff, John Morton, Xavier Francuski, and Eric Swenson. I'm thankful for the copyediting expertise of Adele Wilkes, Patrick Farrell, and Justin Dyer, and for the constructive feedback from SUP editors Tanya Luhrmann and Ann Taves. Last, my gratitude goes to Vivian Lin, Julie Chen, and the staff and friends at the Medical Ethics and Humanities Unit at the University of Hong Kong for their support during this book's concluding writing phase.

An earlier and shorter version of Chapter 5 is published in the volume *Expanding Mindscapes,* edited by Erika Dyck and Chris Elcock, which I am grateful to include in an expanded version in this book.

An earlier and much shorter version of Chapter 3 was published in the *Journal of the Royal Anthropological Institute* in 2022, which I am grateful to expand upon in this book.

GLOBAL AYAHUASCA

INTRODUCTION

Twelve strangers sat in a large hut listening to the Shipibo healer Maestro Juan talk about the curative properties of ayahuasca. They had come to the edge of the Peruvian Amazon during the winter of 2019, arriving from Europe, North America, Southeast Asia, and New Zealand on a pilgrimage to transcend the modern world and find healing with an Indigenous psychedelic brew. Juan, wearing a t-shirt with an illustration of angels circling heaven by the nineteenth-century French artist Gustave Doré, was smoking a thick wad of hand-rolled *mapacho* tobacco while passionately telling us about tiny, invisible people who live deep in the rainforest, protecting an area where the powerful *noya rao* medicine plant grows. When its miraculous seeds fall into the river, fish quickly eat them and jump into the air, becoming colorful birds. "Ayahuasca is similar. It's not as powerful as *noya rao*, so you can drink it," he explained, adding, "Ayahuasca brings you into a new dimension where you can transform."

As we sat in the large *maloca*, where we would all drink ayahuasca that evening, I noticed a thin layer of dirt covering the floor which had drifted in through the transparent mosquito netting. At the center of the *maloca* was an old tree trunk that towered some twenty-five feet and helped to hold up the thatched roof. During the evenings, the tree framed the guests' ayahuasca experiences as a potent symbol of nature stretching out across the ceiling. Sitting at the base of the tree, Juan continued to captivate us with stories. He was highly respected among the hundreds of annual guests to the center.

Across the twenty-six ceremonies I attended there, many regarded him as its most powerful healer. His songs carried an unmistakable passion and joy, and guests frequently reported stronger visions when receiving an *icaro* song from him.

After listening to Maestro Juan's stories of healing and plant dieting, one of the guests asked how she could heal herself with ayahuasca. He responded in Spanish, relayed through a live translator into English:

> If your spirit is too polluted, then you will not see visions, or you will only see horrible, scary visions. The plants teach us special songs when we diet them. When we drink ayahuasca, our songs transform us into birds, plants, many things, and we clean your body so you can see beautiful things.

During the next three ceremonies at the retreat, all the healers and guests drank ayahuasca as usual, including Juan, but he stopped singing healing songs to each guest. Instead, staying alone in the middle of the *maloca*, he sang protective songs to fortify the space so the other healers could safely work on the guests without needing to defend themselves from external sorcery attacks. Given that Juan was a favored healer, many guests were disappointed and found themselves tuning in to his *icaros* even when a different healer was directly in front of them providing a one-on-one curing song.

Singing in the middle of the *maloca*, dressed in a full-length, white *cushma* robe, covered in the rainbow colored patterns that many see on ayahuasca, Juan was encountering a challenge that was remarkably foreign to the guests. The social dimensions of Shipibo sorcery are a cosmos apart from the "ego dissolution" and "becoming one with nature" narratives that their guests tended to share about their ayahuasca experiences. Indigenous approaches to the brew, in turn, are equally foreign to the mystical experience depicted by Gustave Doré on Maestro Juan's casual t-shirt.

Juan remained in the middle, but his protective songs had distinctly changed in a manner that generated confusion among the guests. His emotional and vocal tones dropped from a confident and loud cadence to one that was distressed, quivering, and weak. He breathed heavily between verses as if the air filling his chest was thick with affliction. Each song descended into a realm of agony and despair and then slowly returned to an assured beauty and grace. It resembled how healers in the Putumayo region drank *yagé* (ayahuasca) and sang songs that were "stimulating and soothing turmoil at one and the same time" (Taussig 1987:440). Juan was being almost consumed by distress, breathing in strength and singing to guard against the attacks of an overbearing force. His brother-in-law left the guests on the outer perimeter to sit with him and sing an *icaro* to boost his spirit. But the struggle continued across several ayahuasca ceremonies.

The guests spoke privately between the evenings, wondering what was wrong with Maestro Juan. They never asked him directly. I did not feel comfortable explaining what was happening. Later, Juan described to me the sorcery he had experienced during those ceremonies.

> The visionary attacks arrived in storms, teeth, spikes, many things. . . . They try to weaken us to make the visitors [*pasajeros*] think we are not strong healers. But I showed my power [*koshi*]. I swallowed tobacco smoke and my body turned into a boat. I threw a net over the dark energy and returned it to the sorcerer.

When confronted by grotesque or malicious visions, the healers responded by attempting to "dominate" (*dominar*) them through songs, spirit helpers, aromas, and, most important, a vital and destructive energy called *nihue* in Shipibo. The goal was to overpower and banish the malevolent energies or challenging visions. Juan later told me that he was struggling during those ceremonies because jealous rival healers outside the center had been magically attacking him. The other healers at the retreat corroborated his story. It was the same sorcerers who were telepathically spying on the retreat center and who had directed criminals to physically rob Juan. Several weeks earlier, he was driving on the dusty roads between the retreat center and the city to transport a reasonable sum of cash to the local bank, only to be confronted at gunpoint and mugged.

Financial instability and ambient poverty were the norm where Juan and the other healers lived in the sprawling urban landscape surrounding the retreat center. He resided in a dilapidated wooden dwelling. And, like the other healers at the center, Juan was motivated by the Shipibo ideal of *onanya joni* or "wise person," which involved an ability to guarantee food, safety, and wellbeing for children and generosity and care to extended family and outsiders (Espinosa 2012:458). For Juan, this meant earning enough money to send his children to local universities and to buy small dwellings or plots of land. When we met, his sole means of earning money for several years was by drinking ayahuasca and performing healing songs to hundreds of international guests annually.

Eventually, these ceremonial sorcery attacks stopped, and Juan reverted to his usual upbeat performances revered by the visitors. The guests typically did not believe in sorcery and often ignored any sign of it. They came to heal themselves, learn about their own spiritual interior, and transcend "modern" problems with shamans seen to be relatively uncorrupted by the ills of civilization. The guests never learned about the thieves or Juan's struggles with *brujeria* during those ceremonies. Instead, some of them benefited therapeutically from his visionary descent into an affective underworld by interpreting how the vocalizations in his songs shaped their own ayahuasca experiences.

Mark, a social worker from New York, said that Maestro Juan's struggling songs inspired an awareness of how he himself lacked emotional vulnerability due to the physical and psychological abuse to which his father had subjected him. During Juan's sorcery defense songs, Mark was confronted with surreal visions of insects and angry images in his childhood bedroom. He described experiencing an "ego death" after surrendering to the darkness and allowing the pain in, which included purging into a bucket and finding relief in "letting go of the past."

In contrast with the Shipibo healers' approach to "dominating" challenging or afflictive visions, the guests usually attempted to "let go" and permit disturbing experiences, which sometimes landed them in overwhelming territory. Expressions of distress were common in the ceremonies. Along with vomiting, other types of purging and externalization included crying but rarely screaming. The "let go" approach reflects the wider psychedelic therapy maxim which suggests that healing is achieved not by resisting but instead by moving in and through the darkness, however terrifying (Richards 2016:35; Pollan 2018). Mark described receiving healing by surrendering to Juan's musical journey—letting go into pitch-shifting vocalizations that cycled through an affective landscape of suffering, strength, and tranquillity.

While Juan was singing in a visionary realm that is experienced as social among local healers and sorcerers, Mark was experiencing a private inner world of psychological symbolism that required decoding and integrating into daily reality afterwards. At ayahuasca shamanic tourism, different ontologies sit side by side, sometimes interacting in a therapeutic relationship, other times unable to reach across the vast differences that separate them.

FINDING THE GROUND

Juan and Mark's different yet entangled relationships to ayahuasca captured my attention and created a rare sense of ethnographic astonishment that left a lasting impression. Such ethnographic contradictions, however, would appear relatively unimportant from the perspective of a historically popular approach to studying ayahuasca experiences. Psychologists, scientists, anthropologists, and others have fiercely pursued universal and shared aspects of ayahuasca reports at the expense of appreciating their remarkable specificities. This has resulted in a number of grand theories that define the visionary worlds as displaying, among other things, universal geometries and animal figures (Naranjo 1973); the fundamental structure of DNA (Narby 1998); the ecological wisdom of natural evolution (McKenna 2005); and the monistic views of perennial philosophy (Shanon 2002:164). In the 1970s, pioneering anthropologist of ayahuasca Michael Harner generated a list of "common denominators" of Indigenous visions induced by the plants. These included the soul separating from the body; visions of snakes, jaguars, demons, and deities; visions of distant persons and places, including cities and landscapes; and visions of unresolved crimes and sorcery attacks (Harner 1973:158–172). Reflecting broadly, he concluded with a call for more comparative studies to elucidate the "nature of the yagé-induced experience" (173). Similarly, while considering research about Indigenous and non-Indigenous ayahuasca experiences, the writer Peter Stafford concluded, "[T]he near-universality of many *yagé* images suggests that the *B-carbolines* are a good deal closer than other psychedelics to being a 'pure element' in a Periodic Table of Consciousness" (1992:351). What is important and astonishing, according to these researchers and writers, are the transcultural commonalities or universally shared aspects of ayahuasca experiences. But as a trained anthropologist, I cannot help but ask, What about *all* the differences? What about how ayahuasca can take vastly different forms mixed across varied ontological points of view, including animal, plant, machine, and humanoid?

First, this research quest towards universality is a feature of the global psychedelic therapy renaissance, which can be traced to its religious roots in the perennial philosophy (Richards 2016:10–11; Langlitz 2013:16). A multifaceted version appears in a brilliant study of ayahuasca by cognitive psychologist Benny Shanon (2002) published at the turn of the century. In *The Antipodes of the Mind: Charting the Phenomenology of the Ayahuasca Experience*, Shanon eruditely presents a wealth of insights about the cognitive nature of ayahuasca. But he is highly critical of those anthropological studies and social scientific arguments that demonstrated visionary experience shaped by society, history, or culture. What appears interesting about his discomfort is precisely its nuance. Shanon was partial to how the mind is developed in cultural and social contexts, but he nonetheless quickly criticized anthropological analyses and their apparent distortions of the *real* questions about ayahuasca.

Apparently, before he had learned of Indigenous ayahuasca visions, his own visionary experiences replicated them. Shanon's desire to focus on commonalities of ayahuasca experiences at the expense of differences is both personal and disciplinary when he argued that "the real mysteries of ayahuasca pertain to the mind, not society or culture, and hence they primarily pertain to the province of psychology—more specifically cognitive psychology . . . not anthropology" (319). Outside its brilliant and treatise-like contributions, perhaps the most striking flaw in Shanon's book is the claim that biographical materials are virtually absent in ayahuasca experiences.

As demonstrated in *Global Ayahuasca*, the biographical side of life has appeared, quite routinely, across ayahuasca narratives in Indigenous Amazonia, neoshamanic Australia, and corporate China. This includes vivid scenes of mundane elements at home and work; seeing neighboring cities, streets, and family scenarios; purifying the senses for a successful hunt or visualizing a new model of the self to bring tact to business decision making. But this ocular refraction of the ordinary is accompanied, most significantly, by widespread reports of extraordinary experiences of colorful otherworlds, strange dimensions, and more than anyone can imagine. Such wondrous expansions beyond the imagination have summoned a scientific quest for recognizing coherence in the alternate worlds of ayahuasca, but awe and wonder can also be humbling; not simply towards the mystery of ayahuasca, but also the so-called parochial qualities of social and cultural life that it embodies, displays, and brings to light.

Leaving aside how to measure the relevance of ayahuasca to psychological studies compared to anthropological studies, there is reason to unsettle an analytic focus on commonalities in the visionary experiences. A very large and diverse array of ayahuasca experience reports have now emerged across the planet. While there are similarities in how the brew modulates the brains and minds of individuals from different societies, to foreground this similitude at the expense of the cultural and historical contexts that also "modulate" its "effects" risks ignoring the details that are especially important to most ayahuasca drinkers. The brew's capacity to shapeshift to place-based ontological worlds is partly why it has become so compelling. Darpan, a pioneering Australian facilitator, explained during a retreat in 2012, "The brew takes on the mythological templates of the person who holds the cup." When the visionary experiences include features of the lifeworld and cosmology of the drinker, then they can take on special meaningfulness or even healing potency. However, there is a sense among some perennialist researchers that ayahuasca experiences shaped by social and historical context are somehow less significant and less "ultimate" compared to the intense, ego-dissolving mystical experiences of clinical books.

The naturalistic philosopher Chris Letheby (2021:221) asked whether Shanon's claims of cross-personal and cross-cultural commonalities in ayahuasca visions were false and *simply* the result of cultural transmission and interpretive bias. But searching for the fundamental nature of the visionary experience beyond the so-called "prosaic explanation" of culture (221) is but another iteration of diminishing attention to the relational meaningfulness that ayahuasca embodies and lives *with, through*, and *as*—including when ayahuasca is encountered as a caring plant spirit or as an odd disclosure of the naturalistic universe. Ayahuasca has attracted people from distant corners of the planet precisely because of its adaptive ontological capacities.

This inverted focus of moving away from universalist notions and towards the thick world of particulars not only throws into relief the infinite complexity of ayahuasca experiences, it also allows us to better understand the impulse to locate universal features. Healers, shamans, priests, and psychonauts have all attempted to define ayahuasca's miraculous worlds. Scholars, too, strive to identify their common elements. However, I argue, this effort can never be simply intellectual or objective. When researchers demonstrate the "common denominators" of ayahuasca experiences, they work to cultivate a shared mythos that can locate the self's interiority in a broader and sometimes planetary vision of humanity. If religion or spirituality is the glue that binds the social (Durkheim 2001), an evolutionary cognitive system to promote human cooperation (Watts and Turner 2014), or an antistructure and critical reaction against social norms (Turner 1995), then any attempt to define the perennial aspects of ayahuasca experiences is a social and political project as much as it is phenomenological. My approach, however, is less ambitious and more ethnographic. It veers away from the essential to consider the rich specificities of ayahuasca experiences and their unique refractions within different social and ontological worlds.

The perennial philosophy and its shuffle towards universality has profoundly informed psychedelic science and psychedelic therapies. But as Nicolas Langlitz indicated (2013:16), twentieth-century social scientists and humanities scholars demonstrated an opposing thesis. Anthropologists showed how contexts, beliefs, languages, and histories had an impact on the experiential properties of consuming ayahuasca (Langdon 1979; Luna 1986; Taussig 1987; Reichel-Dolmatoff 1997); peyote (Wallace 1959; Calabrese 2013); iboga (Fernandez 1982); and psychedelic chemicals in laboratory settings (Langlitz 2013). Writing with the Peruvian artist and shaman Pablo Amaringo, Luis Eduardo Luna concluded in *Ayahuasca Visions* that "cultural traditions play an important role not only in interpreting and imprinting meaning upon visions but also in shaping visionary experience" (1999:43). From living among the Siona in Putumayo Colombia, Esther Jean Langdon suggested that cultural meaning can provide the necessary grounds for navigating visions well:

> The *yagé* experience is not one of individual random visions or free association of the unconscious while under the drug's influence. It is, rather, an ordering of the induced visions into culturally meaningful symbols and experiences, thus gaining increasing control over the visions and events occurring. (1992:53)

Ayahuasca experiences can be many things. The experiences, like the person who undergoes them, are not cast outside society's worlds but can refract what is at stake on the ground in these contexts. A *vegetalismo* shaman who serves ayahuasca to global visitors in Iquitos Peru described to Evgenia Fotiou how some foreigners are disappointed when they do not have shamanistic experiences typical of Indigenous Amazonian peoples; however, "the spirits will come and teach you through the metaphors and dreams that you [already] know well," the shaman explained (2014:167). The Shipibo healers I met near Pucallpa were well aware that ayahuasca means something quite different to them compared to the international guests they treated. Enhancing social perceptions, whether analogically or relationally, is an interesting feature of ayahuasca practice. This includes among the "horizontal" social dimensions of ayahuasca shamanism (Hugh-Jones 1996) but also among the different long-term ayahuasca drinkers I encountered across the planet. By contrast, scientists were more likely to arrive with entrenched perennialist-mystical views—whether from biology, psychology, Huxley, or Eliade's shamanism research. Therefore, they could perhaps especially benefit from appreciating how ayahuasca experiences entangle different places and social worlds, precisely because this entanglement is where life becomes meaningful.

Scholars in the psychedelic humanities have demonstrated how intercultural features can shape the contents of psychedelic experiences, sometimes in quite sharp ways (Roseman et al. 2021; Roseman et al. 2022). David Dupuis undertook an ethnography of a shamanic tourism center in remote Peru that is run by a French physician cum Catholic priest working in collaboration with Indigenous healers. Dupuis illustrated how the visiting participants from France, North America, and elsewhere learned to perceive the sensory and affective dimensions of their ayahuasca experiences as "demon infestation" (2022a). Considering how beliefs from Catholic theology and Amazonian shamanism combined together within an ayahuasca ritual setting—which included icons of Christ, The Virgin, and Saint Michael, along with aromatic perfumes, tobacco smoke, holy water, salt, and exorcism prayers—Dupuis examined what he termed "the socialization of hallucination." Contextual and religious features helped participants navigate visionary experiences of fear, guilt, disgust, relief, joy, and appeasement as tensions between good and evil. These social factors, he suggested, educated attention in ways that informed the experiential properties of ayahuasca experiences. "The symbolic knowledge acquired by the participants, the iconographic elements surrounding the

GLOBAL AYAHUASCA

visionary experiences, as well as verbal and ritual interactions appear to be the main operators of a 'socialization of hallucination'" (634). Dupuis has also undertaken research on ayahuasca experiences in contrast to how patients navigate psychosis and schizophrenia (2021b). As ethnographers and theorists, however, we should be sensitive to the medico-pathological language of "hallucinations," given that many ayahuasca drinkers would find it inappropriate; some would find it offensive. While the medicalization of ayahuasca is a remarkable and valuable endeavor, it is just one register.

Opting to stay closer to the grounds of my participants, I approach their ayahuasca experiences as special kinds of seeing, hearing, smelling, touching, thinking, feeling, and encountering. This seems more accurate to what they mean when they describe their "song-paths," "visions," or "journeys." Keeping medical terminology in check also enables a more granular appreciation of how ayahuasca takes on a life of its own in the broader social worlds of those who consume it. In my research, notions of ayahuasca visions and journeys were crucial concepts for understanding the presence and absence of ayahuasca in the everyday lifeworld.

Thus *Global Ayahuasca* finds itself in much longer anthropological traditions. Moving beyond studying "traditional" societies or "urban subcultures" as if they were bounded by their own differences, it grapples with place-based, visionary frictions and intersections in the commercial expansion of ayahuasca across the planet. During the two decades since Shanon published *The Antipodes of the Mind*, the brew underwent a dramatic global flight to very different social contexts, particularly across South America, Europe, North America, and Australasia, but also in parts of Asia and Africa. These contexts provide a vast novel terrain of empirical perspectives on the experiential properties of ayahuasca usage. If Clifford Geertz (2000) is correct when calling anthropologists "merchants of astonishment," then we should expect anthropology to have an equal if not greater purchase—compared to cognitive psychology or any other discipline—at grasping the wonder of ayahuasca.

OTHER WORLDS

Ting Ting related to me how drinking ayahuasca in mainland China (at a first-tier city) had helped her overcome family trauma and advance her career. She grew up in a small rural city and moved to a large city in her early twenties with the hope of making a successful IT career. But this was not the only thing urging her to the metropolis. Before she left home, her father had been diagnosed with a terminal disease and given less than two years to live. "I went to [the city] for work," she said, but also admitted, "Deep down I knew I was leaving because I couldn't bear the situation." A decade after her father died, she drank ayahuasca in a group setting in China, trying to heal what she described as the deeply embodied shame and sadness of neglecting her family during those difficult years. During the ayahuasca session, she cried for several hours and vomited a few times. "My body had been carrying a massive emotional burden," she later explained. "After all the crying and the insights during the process, I felt so light in my jaw and neck and that's usually where the stress is centered."

Ting Ting had many visions the first few times she drank ayahuasca. They included seeing the inside mechanism of clocks working at a fixed pace with black and yellow snakes swarming in unison with the cogs; being a soldier in Ancient Egypt and ready to fight against demons; seeing dozens of red lanterns floating up to the sky, each with a face on it of someone she loved or someone she despised; and swimming free in a cosmic pool and gazing at the wondrous horizons of life. The recounting of these experiences each finished with her describing a comparatively mundane interpretation of how the vision provided psychological insight. She related to her visions like cryptic texts that needed to be decoded. The snakes, she explained, were, like her, "sensitive to changes, sounds, and disturbances" and were "alert and ready"; being a soldier was a sign of her "resistance towards facing the pain"; the vision of lanterns taught her to "let go of other people's opinions easier"; and she emerged from the cosmic pool "a new person, without armor or weapons. I felt reborn, confident, and ready for anything." Overall, she sensed that her ayahuasca sessions helped her forgive herself—and that this had positive repercussions for her job as a manager in a big IT company. "What I learned from my father's death is that you will not feel shame if you try your best to take care of someone or do something good." Reflecting on her aya-huasca sessions, Ting Ting added, "After releasing the pain from my body, I became more comfortable with myself. My colleagues appeared more open to my ideas because I can manage my body language and expectations better now." Healing her spiritual body with ayahuasca, she explained, improved her management techniques.

Using the Amazonian brew to improve workplace abilities and status was shared by other participants at the retreats Ting Ting was attending. The organizer of these sessions described his approach as secular, therapeutic, modern, and different from the Indigenous traditions of the Amazon rainfor-est. The evenings of drinking ayahuasca were not ceremonies or rituals but were specifically called "sessions" and "processes" to express a secular mind-set. A large portion of those who attended the mainland China retreats were young Chinese entrepreneurs and corporate managers. Some purchased expensive packages in which the sessions were accompanied by parallel workshops, including coaching, breathwork, ecstatic dance, and meditation events.

The activities were led by an energetic European man, let's call him Luke, who has a background working in the Chinese corporate sector and embodies its smooth style, slick appearance, and rational confidence. He had been drinking ayahuasca for sixteen years and been on more than ten trips to Peru and Brazil to learn from Indigenous specialists. His approach to serving the brew is shaped by a corporate coaching philosophy he developed called Bridging the Gap. Here, healing and enlightenment are pursued through trying to bring a coherence between an inner self, called the Monk, and an outer self, called the Suit, thus forming an enlightened "Suited Monk." Aya-huasca sessions helped the participants discover and perceive their "blind spots" and the emotional barriers and attitudes that were stopping them from achieving personal and professional goals and, ultimately, a more unified self.

During the morning before an ayahuasca retreat in China, I accompa-nied Luke in his car to buy vegetarian food for the guests. The restaurant was on the other side of the large (first-tier) city, so we had ample time for an in-terview. We were weaving through a shiny labyrinth of new roadways, many of them suspended off the ground, while passing opulent business towers and a city rapidly under construction. With one eye on the road, the other on the

GPS system, and his mind sharply on his ayahuasca business, he said the Amazonian brew was not a holy savior but a powerful tool that worked best for his clients when integrated with other healing and coaching modalities. A truck passed by hauling an expensive sports car. "Check it out. It's an Aston Martin," he said. We sped up to get a better view. "It's the model James Bond drives," he added. Later on during our drive, he described the challenge of designing ayahuasca sessions for his clients in China.

> To bring the plants [ayahuasca] to the modern world, sometimes it needs to be translated. If you start talking to a manager from a company who is very square-minded about power animals and *mariri*, he is going to think you are crazy.

The next day, shortly after the retreat had finished and everyone had left, Luke sent a message to the attendees: "Dear All. Just a reminder. Today payments have to be settled!" while sharing a video of his co-facilitator, a psychotherapist from New York, standing in an expensive hotel lobby and walking backwards in slow-motion while flicking money, 100 RMB red notes, into the air. When I asked Luke how much money he made from his special business, he pointed to the fact that he drove a cheap car. He embodied an authentic passion for the brew and for helping others that seemed to be facilitated by his own ayahuasca drinking.

Whereas the guests who were attending the Shipibo ceremonies with Juan in remote Peru were searching for a break from the stresses of modern life, the ayahuasca sessions in China were directed at cultivating an enlightened self that is equipped to excel in a competitive capitalist world. The Indigenous Amazonian brew had been reinvented into a nominally secular practice that aligned with the values and mindsets of clients in corporate China.

Several years beforehand, I was conducting a large study in Australia on the uses of ayahuasca among neoshamanic and New Age spirituality groups. Towards the end of interviewing an Australian, I asked a range of quantitative questions as usual, including his level of income, but this time it triggered discomfort. He replied, "Why do you want to know my income? That goes completely against the spirit of aya." When I told this story to Luke in China, his response highlighted a vastly different image of ayahuasca. He replied, "Money is a tool. It's not good or bad. It's neutral. It can be used in positive or negative ways. . . . Ayahuasca is also a tool. It can be used for good or for bad." To many Australian drinkers, such an instrumental and depersonalized view of ayahuasca as somewhat similar to money would be profane and sacrilegious. In Australia, ayahuasca is a sacred nature spirit *who* has an awkward relationship to money. Emails that request payment for a retreat often avoid words such as payment, bill, cost, or fee but instead include wording such as "the exchange for this ceremony is $250," "donations starting at $200 are welcome," or "an investment of $1,600 will gift you this remarkable opportunity." Some retreat services only required a donation to attend. But they were rare. Conducting the retreats was typically not a lucrative enterprise in Australia. Only a few of the twelve ceremony facilitators I spoke with managed to earn above the average national salary doing this. Here, the spirit of ayahuasca and Indigenous wisdom were perceived to transcend the disenchanted world of money, materialism, and modern life. Similar to New Age depictions of Gaia, ayahuasca is a sacred plant spirit *who* dwells in a pristine world of nature beyond the many ills of civilization.

The strict visa and travel restrictions of Australian society have made it difficult for Indigenous healers to visit from places like Peru, Brazil, and Colombia. This has promoted a relatively insulated space of ayahuasca creativity in Australia when compared to the historical flow of Amazonian healers to Europe or North America. The retreats in Australia attracted people interested in New Age spirituality and wellness, nature and environmentalism, mental health science and therapy, and the arts. At the turn of the century, in the early years of the movement, it was mainly just "psychonauts" who embodied a critical view of mainstream society that was amplified by the inner radiance of taking different psychedelics. Embodying this critical edge, during the year 2012, the most prolific ceremony facilitator in the country, Darpan, described ayahuasca's mission to me. His description mirrors a broader style of speaking that he and others took to microphones at psychedelic music and arts festivals and on local podcasts such as Rak Razam's "In A Perfect World" show designed to "anchor the vision and spark the new paradigm alight." Darpan said,

> We've become so specialized and compartmentalized in this rational, logical Western dreaming that we have become disconnected from our

larger multidimensional self, and ayahuasca is about reconnecting us. . . . Ayahuasca has come out of the jungle into the Western psyche to invite the Western psyche back into the garden. Come back into Gaia, back into Eden, back into oneness, back into connectivity and symbiosis and synergy with the plants, with Mother Earth. So, that's what I feel she's coming to the West to do.

Terence McKenna, the American countercultural icon of psychedelics in the 1980s and 1990s, not only provided Darpan with his initiatory ayahuasca bottles but also inspired his critical cosmological views of society. In McKenna's influential rap, "culture is not your friend" (St John 2024) and Amazonian shamans, with the help of ayahuasca, can pull the curtain aside to see beyond the mirage of culture. These attitudes were widespread among those who were first to explore ayahuasca sessions into Australia.

The retreats grew in popularity and became increasingly more mainstream during the 2010s, attracting people unfamiliar with Terence McKenna and words like "psychonaut." While the practice turned primarily into a healing phenomenon, the view of ayahuasca as a powerful spirit that resides beyond the problems of society persisted and maintained its critical potency. For those in Australia—and certainly in other non-Indigenous contexts— their mental, physical, and spiritual sicknesses were perceived to have resulted from conditions of modern life and its spiritual rupture from nature. Ayahuasca bridged the restless urban spirit through inner worlds of natural purification and visionary wonders. Sarah, a white, forty-year-old ayahuasca drinker, explained to me in the hills of northern New South Wales,

My first ayahuasca experiences were really painful. My spirit was trapped, hidden, in work routines and so many empty days, weeks, years; back when I was chasing a salary or a better job with a higher status. I was actually depressed then but I didn't realize it until ayahuasca ripped it all away and showed me divinity.

Sarah told me how ayahuasca inspired her to quit her high-paying job in the finance sector to become an artist, so she could "give to the world instead of taking from it." Profound experiences with the brew can have an enduring quality. Drinkers in Australia usually cherished a few key visionary experiences which they continually shared with other confidants over the years. Describing her most treasured experience, Sarah commented, "The vision was so fine and pure. I had to let go of so much social programming that was inside me, then *she* lifted me to see the beauty of the rainforest, the music and smell of nature held me, they were inside me." In Australia, ayahuasca and the spirit of Mother Nature embodied pure benevolence. The natural purification of ayahuasca and *her* capacity to inspire vivid visions provided an antidote to Sarah's disenchanted world of "social programming" and corporate work.

What can we make of these three very different ethnographic vignettes of ayahuasca in Peru, China, and Australia? The examples demonstrate a set of different relationships to ayahuasca that also depict different tensions regarding money. Maestro Juan's encounters with sorcery and invisible thieves during his difficult ceremonies cannot be separated from the broader challenge of fulfilling his family obligations and achieving *onanya joni* or "wise person." In his urban context—which is subject to scarcity and ambient poverty—money can easily become a measure of envy and invite risks of sorcery. The ambiguous nature of ayahuasca opened Juan to perceiving sorcery attacks from local *curanderos* connected with armed thieves, but it also provides him with the means to protect himself from such pathological incursions.

In the Australian example, ayahuasca invigorated meaning for Sarah to counter the depression and disenchantment of "chasing a salary" in society. She retreated from the city into nature to evoke a sacred and healing spirit that she contrasted against the meaning crisis of working in the finance sector. Ayahuasca, here, was not ambiguous but purely benevolent and largely beyond society and its focus on money. In the Chinese example, ayahuasca was depersonalized into an ambiguous tool in a nominally secular relationship that provided psychological development for Ting Ting. It also imparted a greater sense of mastery over her career goals. Ayahuasca and its visions were cryptic texts or imagery about a self that was seeking its own reinterpretation. Money was not deemed profane in this context. It was a tool that can create negative or positive consequences depending upon how the person uses it.

In Australia, most ayahuasca users would likely view the nominally secular visions in China as a departure from the brew's true spirit. Employing ayahuasca to improve business success is less a retreat into nature than an exaltation of capitalism and modernity. Conversely, the Shipibo approach of encountering sorcery attacks would, in turn, appear impossible or symbolic from the secular viewpoint of corporate Chinese ayahuasca users. Numerous other differences exist between these three contexts, including between what visions are actually seen in parallel to what ontological arrangements they appear within. To develop a theory of "common denominators" across ayahuasca experiences may be interesting but it could easily distort what actually makes the brew meaningful to those who drink it. Therefore, I take a different angle and use ethnography to triangulate different kinds of ayahuasca drinking, including how the brew is spoken about and lived with in different places, in order to better get at the visionary meaningfulness.

INNER AND OUTER WORLDS

Psychedelics can inspire profound euphoria, awe, and wonder in users (Voogelbreinder 2009:44), enhancing the meaningfulness of the experiences. Although it is possible to drink ayahuasca and have mundane sensations with no visions, along with boredom and even sleep, the brew is more likely to evoke an astonishing encounter with music and visual space; more so when consumed enough times, with the correct dosages, and in a safe setting sensitive to aesthetics. Afterwards, like other sources of awe, ayahuasca can be difficult to put into words. Reflecting on its great mystery, Luis Eduardo Luna wrote,

> Without a doubt, one of the questions that comes to mind when experiencing ayahuasca has to do with the origin of all this beauty, all these extraordinary patterns, cities, palaces, gardens, jewels and extraordinary beings. Where does it all come from? . . . Ayahuasca takes us to realms where normal rationality is irrelevant, and where we are submerged in worlds of wonder and awe. (2016:273)

Throughout Shanon's *The Antipodes of the Mind* (2002) the wonder and awe of ayahuasca experiences are recurring themes.

> The visions impress their viewers as marvellous, and when powerful they introduce drinkers to what seem to be enchanted realities that fill them

with wonder and awe (17). . . . It suddenly appears that everything is engulfed in great mystery. Consequently, the world is perceived as an object of great marvel and utmost wonder (61). . . . Akin to the aesthetical pleasure are several other reasons that entice people to go on and partake of Ayahuasca. My informants speak of the allure of magic and enchantment, the wonderment, the sense of perfect harmony, the all-embracing sentiment of love, as well as the thrill of adventure (324). . . . Thus, I can only say that Ayahuasca and the philosophical puzzles it raises mystify me now no less than when this brew first presented me with its wonders and struck me with its mysteries (402).

Among the ayahuasca narratives that I collected in Peru, Australia, and China, it was relatively common for the narrators to feel a deep sense of wonder towards the brew.

Wonder is a naturally elusive emotion. It unravels our understanding of things. From a psychological perspective, it includes a breakdown or opening in mental models (Shiota 2021; Candiotto 2019). These epistemic qualities make wonder highly relevant to knowledge and knowing. Psychedelic experiences can include a mysterious noetic quality, whereby simple truths suddenly make absolute sense and are accompanied by feelings of discovery (Shanon 2002; Richards 2016; Letheby 2021). Scholar of religion Wouter Hanegraaff (2012:409) noted how psychedelic varieties of "gnosis"—that is, the direct knowledge that comes from psychedelic experiences—have a vibrant history in twentieth-century Western spirituality, and that it "shows no sign of disappearing." During the decade or more since Hanegraaff pointed this out, psychedelic use has proliferated across the planet through a broad explosion of practices, raising the question of what kinds of knowledge are being revealed, reconstituted, and emboldened during ayahuasca and other psychedelic experiences. One currently widespread answer is therapeutic knowledge.

Psychologist Peter Hendricks (2018) suggested that psychedelic awe may be a core healing mechanism of psychedelic therapy. Considering how awe promotes a "small self," he argued that the vastness of psychedelic experience expands mental structures to promote healing. Ayahuasca experiences can be situated among other powerful sources of awe, beyond psychedelics.

Dacher Keltner and Yang Bai analyzed twenty-six hundred narratives of awe collected from across twenty-six countries (Keltner 2023:10–19). Exceptional virtues like courage, kindness, and strength, when perceived in other people, were the most common sources of awe. The researchers called this the capacity for "moral beauty." Ayahuasca is known globally for its therapeutic effects, awe-inspiring visions, and hedonic tones—including its beautiful and grotesque sensory worlds—but what is hardly acknowledged is its entanglement with moral life and moral knowledge.

Shipibo healers in the Peruvian Amazon who master psychedelic plants have embodied a special quality known as *quiqui*, which combines "correctness" and "beauty" (Gebhart-Sayer 2016:218). *Quiqui* can indicate good moral character, broadly speaking, and also refers to the beautiful "design medicine" that healers sing to shape the augmented senses of ayahuasca drinking. In this way, *quiqui* unifies the moral and the aesthetic with vision-inducing plants. In Amazonia, the brew has concerned normative aspects of life and assisted people in developing virtues, such as courage, kindness, tranquillity, and joy (Barbira Freedman 2016:194; Reichel-Dolmatoff 1997:234–235; Walker 2012:188), or those qualities deemed immoral and toxic and associated with sorcery and witchcraft (Whitehead and Wright 2004). Ayahuasca, like wonder and awe, can be morally ambiguous.

In contemporary English parlance, the notion of wonder tends to be stripped of its ambiguous moral tones and cast as a mood to enhance positive psychology. People usually only speak of wonder in a positive light. Yet wonder can occur during fearful encounters and with painful aspects. In Old English, wonder comes from *wundor*, which is possibly a cognate of the German *wunde* or "wound," as cut or gash (Parsons 1969:85). The philosopher Mary-Jane Rubenstein described how "wonder can function as a wound in the everyday . . . [and] opens an originary rift in thought, an unsuturable gash that both constitutes and deconstitutes thinking" (2008:31). Similarly, philosopher Howard Parsons wrote poetically in the 1960s that wonder "would thus suggest a breach in the membrane of awareness, a sudden opening in a man's system of established and expected meanings, a blow as if one were struck or stunned. To be wonderstruck is to be wounded by the sword of strange events, to be stabbed awake by the striking" (1969:85).

Experiences of awe and wonder may be uplifting, positive, and beautiful, but also grotesque, painful, and terrifying. A wide analysis of texts from across scholarly disciplines suggested the core experiential tones of awe are "threat, beauty, exceptional ability, virtue, and the supernatural" (Keltner and Haidt 2003:297). The connection between wonder and threat is interesting in the context of ayahuasca drinking. An internal psychological violence often occurs during the sessions, particularly among those who are new to the brew or suffering deeply. Pain and violence are common in Indigenous origin myths about ayahuasca (Calavia Sáez 2011). This points to how learning to navigate and sit in psychedelic states is not always easy. It can be challenging and has been widely described as "work" that requires courage in the face of suffering. Some Australians called this work "aligning" and "resonating" with the spirit of the brew, the music, the group energy, and the environment.

Ayahuasca may inspire wondrous visions, but this is not guaranteed. A sense of mystery clouds when a particularly meaningful experience will emerge. The same people drinking the same brew can each experience something very different on the second or third night together. Gerardo Reichel-Dolmatoff commented on the unpredictable side of ayahuasca among Desana men in the 1960s Upper Amazon, writing, "Some see colors and jumbled forms, some experience an entire mythological scenario, others vomit and see nothing at all. There is a sense of chance, an intense expectation that hangs over the men" (1972:101). The lack of gaining an epiphany on demand only adds to ayahuasca's mystery. When the epiphany does arrive, however, there is not always agreement over which visions should or can elicit profound wonder and which should be shrugged off or even downplayed and criticized. What appears as an eternal vision of utmost importance to one person may appear as a humorous and forgettable irony to another.

Experiences of wonder, generally speaking, can involve an ontological unraveling or crisis, particularly when intense (Scott 2016, 2014; Srinivas 2018). Such breakdowns and openings occur in the context of social and historical environments that lend political and moral valence to the experiences of wonder (Hughes-Warrington 2018; Vincent 2017; Scott 2017). But in the context of psychedelic use, wonder is simply one mood among many other possible ones. Whether a feeling of spiritual unity during an ayahuasca session is fleeting or abundant, or grotesque or beautiful, the hedonic register can amplify across the spectrum, including fear, disgust, joy, equanimity, and so on. Examples of moral beauty can appear in the visionary experiences—whether encountering powerful gods, spirit helpers, technological utopias, or social memories.

Context and social relations help constitute the wonder of ayahuasca experiences and the cosmological frameworks that house them. Much ethnographic research has demonstrated how Indigenous cosmologies were not bounded and separated from colonialism and capitalism but have spectacularly engaged conditions of modernity in sorcery, witchcraft, and possession (Stoller 1984; Whitehead and Wright 2004; Comaroff and Comaroff 2001; Taussig 1987). In their volume *Framing Cosmologies: The Anthropology of Worlds (2014)*, Allen Abramson and Martin Holdbraad described that in these anthropological approaches, "indigenous cosmologies [became] contingent, neutered and ultimately epiphenomenal to something else" such as market relations, government policies, and postcolonial conditions. They cautioned against approaching such cosmologies as simply preexisting "local" responses to "global" conditions of neoliberalism, liquid modernity, and postcolonialism. Cosmologies are also sites of novelty, plurality, and change (Palmer 2021; Abramson and Holdbraad 2014) that may include yet transcend any neat reduction to conditions of late modernity. They are not simply epiphenomenal but isomorphic and mixed or overlapping with social elements (Abramson and Holdbraad 2014). Cosmologies may provide visions of possible new worlds, however entangled with legacies of the old.

Talking about ayahuasca experiences has become a common way of consolidating cosmological shifts in perspective for many, but certainly not all, global approaches to the brew. Dramatic ayahuasca narratives can affirm the vitality of the person and strengthen their ontological commitment at the same time. Across non-Indigenous and psychonautic corners, stories of profound visions are now perhaps the main cliché of the brew. As scholar Des Tramacchi explained, psychedelics in "post-industrial societies are often used by loose-knit communities of vision seekers who construct new cosmologies to culturally codify their visionary experiences" (2009:7). There is an energetic grappling or creativity put to work on the mystery of the experiences. It summons metaphors, analogies, alternate somatic views, maybe memories or even different animal and human perspectives.

Ayahuasca drinking has spread across the planet during the previous forty years, taking root in different cosmologies. It nonetheless appears to have some dominant patterns of practice, religiosity, and attitude. Forests and organic life are often sacred, redemptive, and alive with more-than-human persons that become visible with the careful use of ayahuasca. This organicism includes whether the plant teachers or plant doctors are related symbolically or socially within the ayahuasca session. For many neoshamanic drinkers, Mother Nature—wounded, mysterious, and powerful—is a space of refuge, an agent of healing, and also the sister or mirror of Mother Ayahuasca. The return-to-nature ethic of global ayahuasca comes with an environmentalist charge or at least a spiritual appreciation for the suffering of ecological systems and the beauty and healing of nature. Plant spirits of special trees, shrubs, and vines feature widely in some Indigenous ayahuasca drinking (Luna 1986, 1984, 2011) which has resonated with global enthusiasts and even become a new stereotype of Amazonian shamanism.

The blue cover of *Global Ayahuasca* is an ayahuasca vision painted by the Amazonian healer Pablo Amaringo (1938–2009) that displays shamanic masters flying through the cosmos on magical trees. Titled *"Arbol Magico,"* the vision includes vegetal agencies in humanized shrubs and towering trees that silhouette an ayahuasca session. Plant persons exist among cloud spirits, colonial and alien vehicles, and celestial palaces in the sky. The tree magic is rooted in a wider cosmic dynamism that is bustling in many directions, across various elementals. Amaringo was a shaman and healer whose painted ayahuasca visions were made globally famous by an anthropologist and an ethnopharmacologist (Luna and Amaringo 1999; Charing, Cloudsley, and Amaringo 2011). He founded an art school near Pucallpa dedicated to shamanic visions. By doing so, he helped to spawn the New Amazonian Art movement and materialized his own plant-induced experiences across dozens of large paintings.

Today, ayahuasca experiences are increasingly influenced by global flows of people, techniques, environments, and capital that entangle together. Ayahuasca drinking is a potent example of what scholars have called worldmaking or worlding (Roy and Ong 2011; Abramson and Holbraad 2014; Tsing 2015). Silvia Mesturini Cappo (2017) examined how the agency of ayahuasca—including its visionary spirits and sensory turns—come together in a "relational dwelling" of international networks connected with colonial legacies, foreign desires, and interspecies relations. Ayahuasca has diverse world-making capacities that draw from the lives of those who consume it. For example, those I researched in Peru, Australia, and mainland China were unique in the ways they each involved different cultural legacies, plants, environments, and visions, including in overlapping ways at the intercultural sites.

It appears that ayahuasca drinking can help in dissolving or strengthening past views or new attitudes in people, whether towards nature, urban life, collective traumas, or utopian futures. It has an aqueous capacity to morph, embolden, and dissipate perspectives. Like other psychedelic substances, it comes with an inbuilt "cultural plasticity" (Langlitz et al. 2021) to adapt to different social and historical contexts. Depending upon the person and session, ayahuasca experiences may appear as very real and dynamic vectors of this world, or they may appear as awe-inspiring disclosures of otherwise invisible places underground, in the sky, or in outer space. But at the end of the session, the experiences fade and the person returns to sober reality. They also find themselves among their everyday "outer" habits, actions, and views, which wait to be cultivated by living with ayahuasca visions. Inner and outer worlds, defined as such, are less binary than interdependent. They may aim at balance, symmetry, and integration, bringing something ideal and good into calibration with the messy contingencies of everyday life. Or, sometimes, the everyday social world becomes overdetermined with cosmic and visionary ruptures dominating, antagonizing, and even testing survival. Balanced or asymmetrical, relations between inner and outer worlds or dimensions are paramount to the ways that healing has been pursued with ayahuasca.

The sense of other-worldliness intrinsic to many ayahuasca narratives lends the brew a cosmopolitan or socially expansive edge. This applies to Indigenous visions of foreign civilizations, towering cities, neon lights, and mechanical wonders (Harner 1973, Luna and Amaringo 1999; Taussig 1987:438; Townsley 1993; Brown 1988) as much as it applies to urban city-dwellers from the United States, Brazil, and Australia seeing nature spirits, Gaia, ancient shamans, or extraterrestrials in their visions (Shanon 2002; Gearin 2017; Gearin and Calavia Sáez 2021). Beat author William Burroughs was told in the 1970s Colombian Amazon that ayahuasca could accurately translocate vision to neighboring and distant cities, streets, and houses. Indigenous vision narratives have included cities, boat motors, hypodermic needles, helicopters, and spaceships (Townsley 1993; Brown 1988; Gearin and Sáez 2021). Luis Eduardo Luna noted that the ayahuasca visions painted by Amazonian healers, including Pablo Amaringo, included cities and a sense of global or even intergalactic connection: "Their architecture is either diffusely Eastern—Chinese, Arabic, Indian—or futuristic, or both. They may be located in the underwater world or on another planet" (Luna and Amaringo 1999:41).

But local animals and plants appear to have featured more than cities, machines, and devices in Amaringo's paintings and perhaps in Indigenous ayahuasca narratives more broadly (Luna and Amaringo 1999; Luna 1986; Gearin and Calavia Sáez 2021; Shanon 2002). Taking an expanded account of the diversity of ayahuasca experiences can reflect the brew's cosmopolitan, worldly, and otherworldly qualities. The life forces evoked by the visionary plants can give their worlding capacities a vitalizing and healing undergrowth of well-being within drinkers. But ayahuasca's capacity for assisting in sorcery and aggravating suffering should balance any romantic views of the healing challenges that the brew can inspire.

A short note on the concept of "ayahuasca visions" is needed. Ayahuasca can inspire a range of marvelous and odd experiences. The modulation of vision by the sonic breath of oral musical traditions can be wondrous. But there are many other aesthetic combinations of sensory merging and mixing. Melodies and rhythms can appear as visual forms that also touch the body as tactile forms. Hearing to seeing or seeing to touching synesthesia appear to be simply two combinations among a wide rainbow of sensory potencies. However, an interplay between seeing and hearing appears to operate more generally with the music's frequencies, styles, and affective landscapes, thus amplifying the auditory channel. In total darkness, or near total darkness, the sensorial porosity of ayahuasca experiences to music represents a key means by which specialists guide the experiences of others. Music as guide or vessel is widespread and has been noted across shamanic approaches in Amazonia where "songs and other auditory cues play an important role in managing the content of collective [plant-induced] trance" (Shepard 2004:257; see also Calavia Sáez 2014; Brabec de Mori 2012; Luna and Amaringo 1999;

Townsley 1993). These shamans embody various states of synesthesia while conducting sessions, such as singing "fragrant songs" or "patterned songs" (Reichel-Dolmatoff 1997; Gebhart-Sayer 1985; Townsley 1993; Brabec de Mori 2012). For some ayahuasca drinkers in Australia, the synesthetic qualities of the brew helped them purge and heal or indicated that it was a bigger and more cleansing release than usual.

Despite the regularity of altered states of seeing, hearing, feeling, smelling, proprioception, and mood with ayahuasca, the notion of "ayahuasca vision" or "visions" has often, cross-culturally, come to stand for what is truly a multisensory experience. In this book, I sometimes adopt the lay term ayahuasca "visions" because it is the main narrative trope of ayahuasca drinking stories that I gathered. For example, having a good "vision" in Australia was synonymous with having a good "journey" or good "ceremony." The brew may inspire a total sensory experience, involving super senses that enhance and remix visual, auditory, and olfactory dimensions into a feeling of mind-body wholeness. However, the dominance of vision as a narrative trope suggests that altered ocular perception carries a special significance to many ayahuasca drinkers.

Author Erik Davis noted how the idea of psychedelic visions can refer to psychonauts gazing at the "phenomenal visions" as simply observers of their experience, but that people also report deep encounters with worlds and entities that demand immersion and even interaction. "The transitive shift from observer to participant, from gaze to encounter, requires both active engagement and a passive willingness to allow the phenomenon to reveal itself in its own term" (Davis 2019:153). Many of the ayahuasca drinkers I spoke with employed the notion of "ayahuasca visions" to refer to observing sensory elements, like colorful patterns, but many also used it to refer to what they understood as multisensory encounters with plant spirits, deceased loved ones, and other non-ordinary persons.

There is a history of the senses waiting to learn how vision has become a key trope of global psychedelic networks (see also Gearin and Calavia Sáez 2021). Even if the neurological grooves of ayahuasca molecules favor the visual cortex for some people, other ayahuasca drinkers have lacked elaborate visual experiences, while still reporting deep wonder and awe at their more-than-visual experiences. The English author Aldous Huxley, who was once almost blind from cataracts, did not report hyperdominant visual experiences with mescaline, LSD, or other materials. Yet, by contrast, many of the visual artists I witnessed drinking ayahuasca tended to narrate more complex visionary scenes and forms.

People seem to bring their prior sensory and somatic education along for the ride with ayahuasca. These backgrounds can make the visions more personal or even truthful in their alignment with the shimmering social qualities of the brew.

It is difficult to define the influence of ayahuasca on those who cultivate ongoing relationships with it. But a salient influence would include the shaping of perceptions towards others, including human and more-than-human persons, strangers and affines, friends and foes.

The mirror sits at the border of consciousness as a popular metaphor to help make sense of ayahuasca. The visionary experiences have been termed a mirror of mind, person, and society. Benny Shanon described ayahuasca as the "mirror of the soul" and the antipode of the mind (2002:376). In 1970s southern Colombia, Tukano shamans described ayahuasca drinking as a metaphorical process of removing the mercury from the mirror, causing the illusion of the self to dissolve into the invisible world or *dey biri turi* (Reichel-Dolmatoff 1997). Anthropologist Michael Taussig entered a mirror world when personally drinking ayahuasca. "Then this second me, this objective and detached observer, succumbs too and I have to dissociate into a third and then a fourth [version of the self] as the relation between my-selves breaks, creating an almost infinite series of fluttering mirrors of watching selves and feeling others" (Taussig 1987:141).

Shanon relayed what he deemed some negative experiences of ayahuasca drinkers, which included a dosed user literally looking in a physical mirror and seeing themselves disappear (2002:85). There is something existential and revealing about the motif of the mirror in ayahuasca narratives. A dissolving self can find a high fidelity in the cosmic refractions of ayahuasca experiences. Provisionally stabilized aspects of the self can become recontextualized against something explicitly Other and beyond, or invisible and between in the relational sense.

Ayahuasca visions have included refractions of a "colonial mirror" of wildness and brutality among Indigenous and non-Indigenous laborers in the Colombian Amazon (Taussig 1987:134). In the 1970s, an elderly Ingano specialist described seeing visions of a golden army. Attempting to cure a woman suffering from a splitting headache, the healer embarked on a *yagé* session that inspired visions of birds, angels, and special spirits adorned with designs that mirrored the shaman's attire and face paint. A battalion of the army appeared. "They wear pants, and boots to the knee of pure gold, all in gold, everything," the healer explained, among a description of the battalion (Taussig 1993:61–62). The military, as an institution, is defined by its encounters with the Other, whether violent or not, and it helps to produce and maintain geographical, cognitive, and ethical borders between "us" and "them." Taussig suggested these military aspects of ayahuasca experiences represented psychic artefacts of the Colombian government's impact on Amazonian lifeworlds.

> Surely this battalion is an intercultural, spliced, image, using the magic of *yage* for the State, and the magic of the State for *yage*, referring in part to the *yage* spirits and healers, but primarily to the Colombian army itself, hastily recruited and sent to fight the frontier war with Peru—an army that many Indians, like Florencio, assisted as canoeists and porters. (1993:61–62).

Chapter three of *Global Ayahuasca* analyzes how military motifs in visions of Shipibo healers of ayahuasca tourism embody traces of the bloody period in Peru of civil unrest and guerrilla warfare in the 1980s and early 1990s. The argument made throughout this book is that the mirroring, memetic, or patterned qualities of ayahuasca experiences are social and cultural as much as they are psychological and personal.

The social dimension of ayahuasca visions is just as apparent when cultural worlds collide. What it means to be Indigenous Amazonian and drink ayahuasca is something very different for Shipibo healers and their families compared to what ayahuasca means for people in New York, Paris, or Beijing. Plus, to add diversity to these different perspectives, people can see very different kinds of ayahuasca visions depending upon their sociocultural background and context. Considering such differences, Anne-Marie Losonczy and Silvia Mesturini Cappo (2014) demonstrated how "successful misunderstanding dynamics" between healers and international visitors, at Amazonian ayahuasca tourism retreats, provided a special basis for intercultural healing. But at a more fundamental level, both visitors and locals tend to see in ayahuasca visions an opening to something deemed hidden and foundational to the fabric of everyday life.

Whatever the relevance of the sense of otherness intrinsic to many ayahuasca narratives, the experiential wonders of the brew have brought people together, including for seasonal festivities (Spruce and Wallace 1908); a family trying to heal a sick member (Dobkin de Rios 1972; Brown 1986:62); mourning loss and connecting with the dead (Gonzales et al. 2019); strategizing how to overcome a social issue or hunting problem (Beyer 2009; Shepard 2004; Brown 1986:62); and trading visions to strengthen a connection with foreigners (Langdon 1981; Virtanen 2014). These qualities of relatedness also refer to the dozens of Indigenous Amazonian healers who have traveled to perform ceremonies across the planet—during the previous few decades—to share their songs, ayahuasca, and visions with others.

This rapid rise in popularity of ayahuasca around the globe, however, did not happen in a vacuum. It shares the spirituality marketplace with parallel modalities of altering consciousness that ayahuasca drinkers may also frequent, such as holotropic breathing workshops, guided meditation seminars, channeling retreats, and Taoist tourism. The ayahuasca circles I studied in Australia, and to some extent for the international visitors at Indigenous healer centers in Peru, shared a critical poise with the neoshamanism of the 1960s and 1970s (Znamenski 2007:210) and New Age spirituality during the 1990s and beyond (Brown 2002:103; Hanegraaff 1996:515). These participants tend to find in ayahuasca an archaic and mysterious vitality that opposed the synthetic and human-centered stresses of modern life. Organic spiritual visions of nature, plant spirits, Gaia earth, and Mother Ayahuasca help to cure an urban restlessness and disenchantment.

Yet, by contrast, the use of ayahuasca by corporate leaders and urban professionals in China includes an instrumentalization of visionary navigation that shamelessly reproduces dominant values of capitalist society. With a penchant for competition, mixed with financial wealth and an entrepreneurial spirit, most of the young professionals I encountered drinking the brew in China hardly embodied any of the "countercultural" legacies found in Australia or North America. Not desiring to escape the spiritual decay of the city for a utopian nature, they embraced a pragmatic approach to help enhance the mastery of modern life with ayahuasca and other consciousness-altering techniques, seemingly generating more worldly or mundane visions.

As we will see, this pursuit of modernity through the brew overlaps some aspects of Indigenous approaches to ayahuasca tourism. In Chapter 3, Shipibo healers treating international guests seek unique kinds of modernization with ayahuasca, whereby the allure of accumulating financial capital meets the drive to heal large groups of wealthy visitors. The different ethnographic locales of ayahuasca drinking explored in this book triangulate modernity with sharp contrasts and attitudes towards capitalism—some contexts unashamedly entangle the brew with a capitalist drive for wealth accumulation, while others reject modernity wholesale as toxic and immoral. These differences can shape the raw sensory features of ayahuasca experiences, sometimes in striking ways.

Drinking ayahuasca is not necessarily easy. A major global proponent, the American ethnopharmacologist Dennis McKenna, famously explained that "ayahuasca does not require belief, but courage," alluding to its intense experiences that can occur regardless of metaphysical training. Global ayahuasca is an ethnopharmacological example of the democratization of ecstatic experience that rides the wave of popular global trends in religiosity (Hannerz 1996:8). People are attracted to it partly because of the direct, unmediated, and embodied experiences it offers.

As commercial spaces, the ayahuasca retreats I studied involved market exchange features that likely reflect other emerging kinds of psychedelic therapy. Contexts of ayahuasca drinking, like contemporary spirituality more broadly, have been influenced by capitalist dynamics. Sociologist Zygmunt Bauman (1997:70) argued that spirituality workshops and services that promote "peak experiences" and "self-improvement" are training "our consumerist potential" in self-indulgent ways. Such a cynical view falls short when considering ayahuasca healing tourism in Indigenous Amazonia or elsewhere. Most ayahuasca drinkers I met approach the "peak experiences" with a healthy dose of caution, or even fear, and often with a hope that it will relieve suffering. Ayahuasca drinking, with its intense visions and vomiting, is more like an ordeal therapy than an indulgence. It makes little sense to group ayahuasca with naive pleasure-seeking notions of drug use. However, the global emergence of ayahuasca has grown from the digital soil of Instagram and other commercial influences that can spike descriptions of ayahuasca with an unusually high dose of positivity, pleasure, and bliss.

Given the great diversity of approaches to drinking ayahuasca across Indigenous, non-Indigenous, neoshamanic, therapeutic, and religious milieus (Harner 1973; Luna and White 2016; Labate and Cavnar 2014), the attempt to explore something like "global ayahuasca" may appear futile. But this book focuses precisely on commercial ayahuasca services. Unlike at the Brazilian ayahuasca churches, or the family- and community-based Indigenous sessions, that embody different exchange norms to capitalist businesses, the ayahuasca drinking I examined exists among a wider sector of wellness services designed to heal and enlighten consumers. I refer to this loosely defined category as "global ayahuasca," given that it is characterized by transactional relations and an entrepreneurial approach of psychedelic wellness, alternative spirituality, and primitivist tourism.

The book does not employ the notion of the global to capture all approaches to drinking ayahuasca. Instead, I refer to the classic social theory sense of economic and cultural flows that span global assemblages (Hannerz 1996). Many ayahuasca roads lead to the global tourism boom in places like Iquitos and Pucallpa, Peru. Daniela Peluso explained in 2017 that ayahuasca globalization "developed in only a few decades from an obscure practice into a cosmopolitan capitalist endeavour" that now contributes to the larger ecotourism economy of Amazonia (203). By doing so, ayahuasca has taken on some generic commercial and exchange features of tourism—whether we call it shamanic tourism or wellness tourism—often representing a globalizing or rendering of the brew as archaic, exotic, and ecological.

ETHNOGRAPHIC FIELDWORK

Pushing against the perennial impulse to universalize ayahuasca experiences, this book provides ethnographic descriptions and analyses of practices and stories in three locales: shamanic tourism centers in Peru; New Age and neo-shamanic networks in Australia; and nominally secular retreats in mainland China. My focus is not primarily on ayahuasca experiences but on the contextual factors that help shape meaningful relationships with ayahuasca and its visionary worlds, while also considering the ideologies, perceptions, and efforts that actively deny, discourage, or distort such relations. Although the research parameter is global, the book's explanatory ambitions take root at the local level.

From 2011 to 2014, I conducted a large study on ayahuasca groups in Australia for my PhD research at the University of Queensland. This included twenty-four months of intermittent fieldwork at retreats and related social events on the east coast of Australia, particularly near Melbourne, Brisbane, and Byron Bay. Ayahuasca was almost always consumed outside cities in natural environments on private properties. I attended thirty retreat ceremonies, conducted forty semistructured interviews, and received 105 responses to a large Australia-wide email questionnaire completed by ayahuasca drinkers (mostly from one large network that spanned fifteen or more years across Melbourne, Brisbane and northern NSW, and Perth). The interview and survey questions included a focus on intention, healing, visions, sensory and bodily experience, integration challenges and benefits, biographical information, and everyday life. Research was conducted on five different Australian ayahuasca groups. Two isomorphic groups in particular were studied, one of which was the oldest and largest in the country. Research participants were dominantly of Anglo-Celtic and European descent. Average age was thirty-five to forty-five (range eighteen to seventy-six). Employment of participants varied. It attracted many therapists or healers or people working in health-related services. Also present in higher numbers were artists or musicians. There was a trend of self-employment. People drank ayahuasca, on average, once every three months. The retreats typically included two nights (two ceremonies) and cost $320 to $550 AUD. All informants' names and locations have been anonymized and coded. Ayahuasca possession and consumption was and still is criminalized in Australia.

The Peruvian ethnography draws on fieldwork done in the winter of 2019 at the Pachamama Temple center outside Pucallpa, Peru, and at several Shipibo organizations in Yarinacocha. Around four months of ethnographic fieldwork in the region, including four ayahuasca retreat packages, which included twenty-six ayahuasca drinking ceremonies with Shipibo healers. Semistructured interviews were undertaken with twelve Shipibo healers. Most were healers at the temple, all of whom are related as family members, a mother, one daughter, three sons, one son-in-law, and one nephew. Five Shipibo healers who worked elsewhere were also interviewed. The interview questions directed at Shipibo healers included a focus on healing techniques, sensory and bodily aspects of ayahuasca drinking, differences in healing locals compared to international visitors or outsiders, plant dieting and training, sorcery and disputes, personal biography, and Shipibo history. Spending months living on the temple grounds with the healers and facilitators and staff enabled many ethnographic perspectives.

Several healers could only speak Shipibo or some broken Spanish. Interviews were conducted with English-to-Spanish translation by Sonia Lunceford (a visitor who had lived with the healers at the Temple for twelve months). Jessica Bertram (a European with decades of experience living in the area) and Mateo Norzi (a filmmaker familiar with Shipibo culture) also supported interviews. Mama Maria's and other interviews were conducted in Shipibo with translation to Spanish provided by Sandro Marquez Sanchez (her grandson). In sum, all of these interview materials were carefully transcribed and translated into English from Spanish by Sven Perlberg, Maria Riega, Michael Stanley, and Jessica Bertram.

A qualitative online survey was conducted in English by forty-three previous participants of the temple. Presented in descending order from most popular, the surveyed and interviewed temple guests registered their country of origin as The Netherlands, France, United Kingdom, Germany, Poland, United States, Canada, Australia, South Africa, India, Mexico, Singapore, and Iran. The mean age was thirty-nine (range twenty-two to sixty-three). The mean annual income of the surveyed and interviewed center participants was $38,000 USD. Occupations varied, with a trend towards health care, mental health services, and alternative therapies, but also included marketing, banking, hospitality, academia, and the arts. Most of the participants were new to drinking ayahuasca and had consumed the brew fewer than ten times.

Finally, fieldwork and interviews were conducted on ayahuasca drinkers in mainland China in 2019 and 2020. Given the draconian drug policies and risks involved with conducting this research, methodological information is minimized. After some hesitation, I decided to attend one ayahuasca retreat in China to observe its approach and style, including the auxiliary social activities that surround it, such as sharing circles, ecstatic dance, meditation, and other activities. Interviews were conducted with eight Chinese ayahuasca drinkers in person or over video call, outside the weekend retreats. The interviews were conducted mainly in English with some Mandarin Chinese. Three interlocutors were interviewed twice, across a six-to-twelve-month period. Two non-Chinese individuals who drank ayahuasca with the same network in China were also interviewed. The organizer of the ayahuasca events was interviewed three times over a period of twelve months. All interview data was transcribed with names coded and files digitally encrypted to ensure the safety and privacy of the participants. Audio files of the interviews were deleted. Translation of Chinese terms was verified by Emily Zong. A research assistant, who requested to remain anonymous, helped to collect antidrug psychedelic propaganda from the Chinese social media platform Weibo in 2020. One evening of drinking ayahuasca cost 2,000 RMB ($300 USD). As explored in Chapter 6, some clients were undertaking a coaching program that cost 60,000 RMB ($9,000 USD) and included two or three group ayahuasca sessions across three months. Eight participants interviewed lived and worked in a first-tier city in China, three in second-tier cities. Given the high financial costs of attending the ayahuasca sessions, the participants tended to be wealthy. Many worked in corporate firms as managers.

During my fieldwork, I learned to cultivate wonder as an anthropological method. I first encountered ayahuasca in 2008, at twenty-four years of age, with a healthy dose of wonder. At the time, I had prior interest in the psychonautic underground of drug experimentation in Melbourne, including with people passionate about the psychopharmacology of new and rare substances. My initial fieldwork in Australia started in 2011, when I was a total outsider to ayahuasca networks. I had developed a deep curiosity towards the anthropology of Amazonian societies, knowing that I planned to also do ethnographic research there someday, but also because Brazilian and Colombian anthropology and other writing about Amazonian life were far more developed and complicated than humanistic studies on New Age spirituality and neoshamanism.

In retrospect, the sincere wonder and curiosity I felt towards psychedelic substances and their cultural worlds was acting as a method. This should come as no surprise to other anthropologists. Wonder should assist ethnographic research along, as Margaret Mead suggested. "Anthropology demands the open-mindedness with which one must look and listen, record in astonishment and wonder that which one would not have been able to guess" (1977:ix).

Studying a wonder vortex like ayahuasca only encouraged in me this wider affective tendency in my research discipline. While attending ayahuasca sessions—whether in Australia, Peru, or China—my ability to be astonished by another person's descriptions of drinking ayahuasca was sometimes necessary to deepen the conversation, disclose salient meaning, build rapport, and expand my analytical abilities. To diminish someone else's ayahuasca narratives was potentially rude and demoralizing. Ethnographic knowledge emerged from being open-minded to how others related to the mysteries of ayahuasca. Wonder was serving as an invisible method that eventually appeared and brought my data to life as an analytical device.

The empirical evidence in this book, and emerging from new ethnographic studies, suggests that it would be virtually impossible to create a global cartography of ayahuasca visions and organize and explain them in some meaningful totality. Such an enterprise would likely fall victim to the biases of the researcher and suffer in a way similar to when the English anthropologist Augustus Pitt-Rivers collected thousands of cultural artifacts from across the globe—including pottery, utensils, and weapons—and developed a flawed theory of cultural evolution based upon the varied designs. The enormousness of the experiential content that ayahuasca drinking has inspired at the planetary scale arguably defies meaningful quantification. Perhaps in some distant future when our brains are inseparable from digital networks such an approach might bear fruit. But even if that were possible, the qualitative universes of ayahuasca bring the brew squarely into humanities and social science research. Ethnographic descriptions can elucidate the messy influence of social context and everyday life on the visionary properties of the brew. Locating visions in the lives and places that they occur is important for considering the weight that many ayahuasca drinkers place on *not consuming* the brew too much in order to "integrate the experiences" sufficiently, that is, to live in a right and balanced relationship with ayahuasca. What is truly important to ayahuasca drinkers, and thus should concern researchers, is how ayahuasca is part of lived experience.

The core of *Global Ayahuasca* is built upon ethnographic engagements with ayahuasca drinkers across the three different locations of Peru, Australia, and China. Before exploring these sites, Chapter 1, "Colonial and Postcolonial Roots," introduces a brief and patchy history of ayahuasca visions during the colonial and postcolonial periods, particularly in Peru but also across wider Amazonia. Then, following its ethnographic chapters, the book finishes with a conclusion that zooms out to consider again the universalist impulse that has motivated researchers to find the perennial ayahuasca experiences.

Thinking a lot about ayahuasca in context has left me with the conviction that it is not possible to get a view of the visionary experiences from nowhere. Researchers studying the experiences are never simply objective observers of the universal. We are implicated in the social worlds of the visions we describe and analyze because, to bear witness to an ayahuasca vision, or even simply to learn about it, is to enter its world.

ONE

COLONIAL AND POSTCOLONIAL ROOTS

A brief survey of historical information about Indigenous ayahuasca use demonstrates that the contemporary global practices arrived on top of hundreds of years of proselytizing agendas, imperialistic racism, and commercial interests. Far from scenes of an idyllic healer living in isolation amidst the benevolent aura of the rainforest, the colonial histories indicate something else. Ayahuasca and other shamanistic plants, while demonized and ridiculed by colonists, helped Amazonians creatively deal with the atrocities of foreign incursions for centuries.

Today, the brew offers a vehicle for Indigenous masters to accumulate capital and seek modernization and global exchange. As described by Oscar Calavia Sáez, ayahuasca has become a "missionary enterprise that Indigenous Amazonians have directed toward the same societies that bombarded them with their own missionaries for centuries" (2014: xxiii). With this sudden reversal in mind, the first half of this chapter focuses on how missionary and colonial contexts shaped European perceptions of ayahuasca during the seventeenth century. The middle explores the neutral and wondrous depictions of ayahuasca written by nineteenth- and twentieth-century naturalists and explorers. Then, it ends by considering key twentieth-century Anglophone influences on popular global interest in the visions.

Overall, the chapter demonstrates that, for hundreds of years, different versions of the "primitive" and the "civilized" informed European and Indigenous views of ayahuasca and its visionary mysteries. Moral asymmetries of the primitive-civilized schema flipped and rearranged across these long and thick centuries, landing in the current period wherein global networks drink the Amazonian plant brew to heal from civilization itself.

FROM MISSIONARY DEMONS

While strong archaeological evidence is lacking on whether there was any ancient ayahuasca use (Torres 2018:239), psychedelic snuff use has been traced back four thousand years in both the Andes and the Amazon basin (Torres and Repke 2006:35, 61). The term "ayahuasca" is derived from Quechua, which was the dominant trade language in the Upper Amazon prior to the European colonization, which began around 1500. Quechua provided a means of communication for trade and exchange between peoples living in the lowlands and highlands. This suggests the brew was probably on the radar of networks that extended across and beyond the Amazon basin.

Before Europeans arrived, Amazonian Indigenous settlements were already familiar with possibilities of radical social change given that they "must have been confronted from time to time with new and powerful religious ideologies emanating from Andean polities to the west or from emerging Amazonian chiefdoms closer to home" (Brown 1991:391). Amazonian groups were not living in isolated settlements outside of history but were entwined in a vast and dynamic political landscape with widespread plant domestication and exchange (Clement et al. 2015). Ayahuasca plant species were cultivated across different parts of the Amazon basin (Luis and White 2016). Ethnobotanists in the twentieth century were puzzled by the uncanny abilities of Indigenous specialists to identify species of ayahuasca (Sheldrake 2020). Siona specialists described fifteen kinds of ayahuasca vines, based upon their physical characteristics and also the kinds of visions they produced (Langdon 1981). The most popular ayahuasca brew consumed today consists of boiling the vine *Banisteriopsis caapi* with the shrub *Psychotria viridis*. Indigenous practices of brewing, however, often included other plants too. These dozens of botanical additives or admixtures appear to modulate the brew's phenomenological and therapeutic effects (McKenna, Luna, and Towers 1995; Voogelbreinder 2009:58–59). Although contemporary researchers have suggested around

160 Indigenous groups have used ayahuasca (Tukano 2022; Luna and White 2016), the brew's potentially ancient origins may never be known due to a lack of archaeological evidence in a tropical climate of rotting and decomposition.

Many of the earliest written accounts of ayahuasca were made by European missionaries. For the most part, they demonize ayahuasca and Indigenous shamanism. During the late seventeenth century, Jesuit Father Juan Lorenzo Lucero traveled along the Parosa river and encountered "savage" Jivaroan groups drinking "evil . . . intoxicating herbs" that caused the drinker to lie on the ground in "service of the devil." He wrote in 1682,

> They put together these evil herbs [*Datura, Banisteriopsis*, and other narcotic plants] with *guañusa* and tobacco, also invented by the devil, and allow them to boil until a small remaining quantity of juice becomes the quintessence of evil, and the faith of those who drink it is rewarded with the fruit of malediction. (Patiño 1968:311)

It is difficult to imagine what exactly Father Lucero thought of the experiential qualities of drinking ayahuasca. The narcotic knowledge among early colonial figures of South America was quite limited. Lucero's closest reference to ayahuasca and San Pedro cactus (a psychedelic in the Andes) was likely reports of opium intoxication from Asia. Nonetheless, whatever he imagined, anything perceived as obstructing the Christian doctrine and the missionaries' proselytizing agenda was associated with the workings of the devil. Ayahuasca came to be described as "devil vine" or *diablo-huasca* by missionaries and was thus positioned as a counterforce to their divine task. In no small irony, the term "*lucero*" (bright star) was used during the late twentieth century and today by vegetalismo shamans in Iquitos, Peru—the mecca of global ayahuasca tourism—to refer to a species of the ayahuasca vine (see also Dobkin de Rios and Rumrrill 2008:101; Luna 1986:151). Approximately 350 years prior in the same region, Father Lucero was demonizing ayahuasca in his role as superior of the Maynas Jesuit missions.

The first decades of European evangelizing in Peru occurred in the mountainous Andes to the west of the Amazon basin. Some missionaries attempted to convert through persuasion but then resorted to coercion, given that they "came to think that Andean cultures could not sustain an understanding of Christianity which came from within those cultures" (Maccormack

1985:446). Early missionaries embodied a chivalric, masculine, Christian culture. They viewed the Indigenous Andean use of the San Pedro cactus with the same kind of demonization that was later directed at ayahuasca down the mountains. In 1653, a Spanish Jesuit priest described the cactus as "the plant [with] which the Devil deceived the Indians of Peru in their paganism . . . transported by this drink, the Indian dreams a thousand absurdities and believed them as if they were true" (Jay 2019:25).

Jesuit priests and Franciscan monks set up missions in the Maynas and Ucayali areas of Peru during the early seventeenth century. Their primary goal, as conferred by the Spanish viceroy, was to convert the native population to Christianity. Like other Jesuit approaches to evangelizing in the Americas, at Maynas they sought to make the original inhabitants accept "faith through fear" and employed a notion of "just war" to justify terror and enslavement (Loureiro Dias 2012:98). But some Indigenous voluntarily joined the missions for a range of reasons. Some wanted to acquire tools and political advantage over trade in the region. The Conibo—who eventually merged with the Shipibo and today include dozens of world-famous ayahuasca shamans—existed on the periphery of the early Jesuit missions. They dominated trade on the Ucayali River and had an exchange monopoly with the Jesuits to stop other groups gaining direct access (Golub 1982:171). Life was tough in the Ucayali and Maynas missions during the late seventeenth and early eighteenth centuries. Indigenous members died at alarming rates due to pestilence. They viewed the missionaries as people "who possessed the unusual ability to manipulate spiritual forces [to create] blessings as well as plagues and curses" (Carvalho cited in Puls 2017). Motivated by their relatively small numbers and lack of power to dominate, the missionaries contradicted their initial refusal to accept any "heathen belief" by allowing Indigenous shamanic ideas in the missions.

The first written description of an ayahuasca ritual, made by Jesuits somewhere between 1648 and 1698, is anything but ambivalent. Like Father Lucero's account, it portrays ayahuasca as the work of the devil. Here, the brew emerges as a kind of hyperreflector that brings into focus that which it opposes: the missionaries. The account was produced by Jesuit historian Jose Chantre y Herrera during the eighteenth century. It was based not upon firsthand experience in the Amazon region but rather on missionary diaries or

COLONIAL AND POSTCOLONIAL ROOTS   41

historical interviews with returned Jesuits. Jesuit historians of his period often transcribed missionary reports verbatim in their histories, but I was unable to find the original source. The document begins by explaining that "sorcerers and liars" exist in all Indigenous societies. Primitives, it continues, seek their clairvoyance when misfortune strikes. The seventeenth-century author then describes a social ayahuasca ceremony in a large house.

> Benches are placed on one side for the men and the rest of the space is left clear for the women. The diviner [shaman] hangs his hammock in the middle and makes his raised platform or small stage and, beside it, places an infernal beverage that they call *ayaguasca*, which is singularly efficient in depriving one of one's senses. They make this concoction of vines or bitter herbs, which, after a great deal of boiling, becomes very thick. . . . The sorcerer, each time he drinks, consumes very small amounts, and knows very well how many times he can drink the potion without losing his sanity in order to carry out the ceremony with due solemnity and direct chorus, since everyone responds to his invocation of the devil.
>
> With things in their place in this manner, the diviner sits down among the men and, in full view of everyone, pours a small amount of the prepared brew into a small glass and takes one or two sips in silence. In a short time, *ayaguasca* begins to take effect, making the diviner grow warm, and produces the usual chant with the following words . . . "Let the divination begin!" The whole chorus responds in the same way . . . and the same thing happens with the invocation: the people continually repeat all the words of the diviner . . . "Listen, listen . . . Listen well, listen well . . . Come soon, come soon . . . I won't do what you tell me, I won't do what you tell me."
>
> Everyone is then astonished and full of fear and panic when they hear these words, thinking that the devil is angry. But the diviner, who knows very well that there is no reason to be frightened, lifts his hand in a knowing way and drinks again, saying . . . "he doesn't want to hear, he doesn't want to hear." The people look at each other, frightened and trembling. The liar repeats the same words many times, and a murmuring rises from the people, who speak in low voices, afraid of what will happen. When the sorcerer sees the assembled people possessed and fixed in fear, he screams

and says . . . "You will hear, you will hear." And, with this, the people are consoled and filled with high hopes.

The author then described the "sorcerer" drinking more ayahuasca, screaming, and grimacing in a crazed and incoherent fury, and then falling asleep. When he awakens, people are curious to learn more from the "devil's art."

> Then he tells of the visions he has had and the things his soul has learned with great effort. The diviners say whatever they want or what they had been thinking, but with hesitation, confusion, and trickery, so that their predictions can always be verified, whatever happens. In this frightening task of divination, cleverness as a dominant technique is reduced to getting drunk and having the nerve to lie shamelessly and find the art to decipher enigmas in a particular way, something that is not exactly difficult among people who are so simple and stupid.

As a symbol of the metaphysical challenge confronting missionaries, ayahuasca absorbed a range of negative connotations. These were used to bolster a view of the missionaries as good, truthful, mature, divine, and civilized. As Luna and White pointed out, the "object of [Herrera's] history was to present the Jesuit mission in the most heroic light" (2016:142). The "devil's art" of ayahuasca drinking was not simply performed by a "stupid, trickster, liar" to the early Jesuits. It provided them with a potent negative charge to justify their gallant missionary struggles.

This kind of demonization made its way into the popular European imagination during the eighteenth century. The term "devil vine" appeared in the genre of travel compilations. In a work called *El Viagero Universal* (1798) penned by the Spanish writer and literary critic Father Pedro Estala (1757–1815), ayahuasca is strangely placed with exotic commercial products from Peru. Estala described ayahuasca in Maynas in an account inspired by missionary writings.

> The *devil-huasca* is a very esteemed vine of the Agorian Indians of the Lamas, Maynas, Jaen and other countries of Mission people, because they believe that the boiled water, that intoxicates, gives them the virtue of being clairvoyant to discover the subterranean treasures: this madness

according to the dose lasts twenty-four hours, and like the opium to the Asians, creates in the natives a delirium of happy ideas. (Estala 1798)

Three centuries since Father Lucero described ayahuasca as the work of the devil, the powerful Amazonian brew is still demonized by missionaries and local Christian priests in the region today. Contemporary Shipibo healers in Pucallpa described stories to me of local priests ridiculing ayahuasca and its global appeal. This is despite centuries of Christian symbolism being incorporated into Indigenous shamanic practices (Chaumeil 1992; Taussig 1987), including among many urban ayahuasca specialists more recently (Beyer 2009).

The encounter between Jesuits and Amazonian plant shamanism occurred during a tragic, turbulent, and dynamic period. Jesuit Father Franz Xavier Veigl (1723–1798) arrived in South America during the mid-eighteenth century to begin what would be approximately a decade of proselytizing and bioprospecting. On one expedition, in 1765, he traveled up the Ucayali River and encountered ayahuasca. Veigl briefly mentioned ayahuasca as something worth knowing about. This description differs considerably from the earlier moralizing and demonizing that colored Jesuit writings about ayahuasca. The observant Veigl wrote in 1768,

> Of plants worth mentioning, it is necessary to mention in the first place the ayahuasca, which means, "bitter rope," and used only for superstitious practices and witchcraft. . . . The Indians, taking the concoction prepared with I don't know what ritual, fall into a prolonged state of complete unconsciousness. (Veigl 1798:180)

Historian Justin Williams (2015) illustrated how the intellectual and economic preoccupations of European societies may have prevented Father Veigl and other colonial figures from developing a genuine interest in ayahuasca. Veigl would send reports and botanical specimens back to Europe for assessment, but ayahuasca was never a feature of his exploits. There are undoubtedly many unknowable reasons why ayahuasca appeared to have failed to penetrate the desire machine of Veigl's consciousness in enough depth to write more about it. Williams (2015:29–39) suggests the Jesuit scientist simply did not see commercial interest in it.

Explorers and naturalists outside the Jesuit tradition also encountered ayahuasca during the early to mid-colonial era. In 1743, the French naturalist and explorer Charles-Marie de La Condamine was the first European to travel the length of the Amazon River. He returned home to Paris with samples of rubber and tales of strange people, animals, and plants, which he published in accounts read across eighteenth-century Europe. During his travels to the interior of the continent, La Condamine stopped at the Maynas mission and learned from Father Magnin about Indigenous plant use. There is no mention of ayahuasca in his travel writings, but La Condamine does briefly describe Omagua groups using a psychoactive snuff that causes "extraordinary visions" (1808:226)—most likely the DMT-containing *Anadenanthera* seeds (Torres 2018). His writing on Amazonian shamanic plant use does not include references to the devil or evil, but aligns more with the descriptive neutrality of science.

La Condamine, however, was no angel and perpetuated the prevalent racism of his era. His widely read ethnographic descriptions were extremely condescending. He perceived Indigenous Amazonians as lazy, stupid, immature, and beastly, while stating that "the reasoning mind cannot but feel humiliation, contemplating how little man, in a state of nature, and destitute of instruction and society, is removed in condition from beasts" (222). Demonic or beastly, Indigenous Amazonians were approached by European explorers, missionaries, and traders of the early colonial period as sources of knowledge on plants and animals with commercial potential, and for those plants that could aid survival in alien environments—but the wondrous brew ayahuasca was largely overlooked.

In a remarkable oddity spotted by historian Emily Berquist, imagery of ayahuasca experiences may have covertly entered the European imagination in the eighteenth century in Spain. In the illustrations and writing of the Spanish bishop Martínez Compañón (1737–1797), the artist-writer avoided the trend of moralizing Indigenous plant use in Peru (such as coca) and instead described it through a kind of neutral naturalism. Volume six of Compañón's codex is made up of over a hundred illustrations of animals with a single striking anomaly. Berquist (2014:172–173) suggested that the inclusion of a supernatural double-headed snake wrapping around a tree in the watercolor painting *"Omeco Machacuai"* may be early evidence of ayahuasca use. It is the only time a supernatural creature appears in the otherwise naturalistic survey of plants. The image also foregrounds a large plant leaf and motifs of animal metamorphism.

As Berquist suggested, the bishop may have classified a supernatural ayahuasca in the naturalistic depiction of a two-headed snake to sneakily obscure a reference to a botanical shamanic practice. For the wide viewership of Compañón's work back in Spain, the bishop "may have hoped that the reader would not notice how strange the *omeco* snake was, or might simply believe that Peru was a strange and exotic land where two-headed snakes could be found deep in the Amazonian jungle" (2014:173). His work represents what might have been the first visual representation of ayahuasca experiences to penetrate, however covertly, the European imagination.

The first written descriptions of ayahuasca drinkers were penned in the nineteenth century by naturalists and explorers. One of the earliest is by the

FIGURE 1.1 Watercolor illustration by Spanish bishop Martínez Compañón (1782–1785) called *"Omeca Machacuai"*; possible depiction of ayahuasca.

46   GLOBAL AYAHUASCA

English botanist Richard Spruce (1817–1893). While collecting plant specimens from across vast stretches of the Amazon basin, he was invited one evening to a gathering in the village of Panure on the Vaupés river in the Brazilian Amazon. This area was later described by many ayahuasca masters of Colombia as containing the most powerful *yagé* healers (Chaumeil 1992:108; Taussig 1987:398), and anthropologists have argued it is possibly the historical origin of ayahuasca drinking (Brabec de Mori 2011). Spruce's personal account of drinking the brew is far removed from the phantasmagorical narratives of many twenty-first-century enthusiasts. But he did note the wondrous synesthetic effects of ayahuasca while paraphrasing descriptions made by other foreigners who had drunk the brew. He commented,

> White men who have partaken in caapi [ayahuasca] in the proper way concur in the account of their sensations under its influence. They feel alternations of cold and heat, fear and boldness. The sight is disturbed, and visions pass rapidly before the eyes, wherein everything gorgeous and magnificent they have heard or read seems combined; and presently the scene changes to things uncouth and horrible. (Spruce and Wallace 1908:420)

Spruce drank ayahuasca in 1853 among a social and celebratory atmosphere in which the Tukanoan "ruler of the feast" served him ayahuasca followed by beer, wine, and tobacco. He retreated to his hammock in a dizzy and nauseating spin. Spruce's account can be read in a posthumous volume published in 1908 with the evolutionist Alfred Wallace (1823–1913).

> I had gone with the full intention of experimenting the caapi on myself, but I had scarcely dispatched one cup of the nauseating beverage, which is but half a dose, when the ruler of the feast—desirous, apparently, that I should taste all his delicacies at once—came up with a woman carrying a large calabash of *caxiri* (*madnidocca* beer), of which I must needs take a copious drought, and as I knew the mode of its preparation, it was gulped down with secret loathing. Scarcely I had accomplished this feat when a large cigar, 2 feet long and as thick as the wrist, was lighted and put into my hand, and etiquette demanded that I should take a few whiffs of it—I, who

had never in my life smoked a cigar or pipe tobacco. Above all this, I must drink a large cup of palm wine, and it will be readily understood that the effect of such a complex dose was a strong inclination to vomit, which was only overcome by laying down in a hammock. (Spruce and Wallace 1908)

Some contemporary ayahuasca drinkers may assume the combination of beer, wine, and tobacco with ayahuasca was the reason why Spruce did not attain a visionary experience. But this would be too simple. After witnessing dozens of people drink ayahuasca for the first time, it appears to me quite normal for some people to report uneventful experiences during the first few times. In the late 1940s, it took the German trader Heinz Kusel three separate evenings of drinking ayahuasca with Campa in Peru before its visionary marvels opened to him (Kusel 1965). With virgin neurons that were underwhelmed by half a dose of ayahuasca, Spruce did not have a very compelling experience, but he nevertheless sent samples of the ayahuasca vine back to Kew Gardens in London and gave it the scientific name *Banisteriopsis caapi* (Schultes and Raffauf 1992).

Around the same time, the Ecuadorian geographer Manuel Villavicencio (1822–1871) too consumed the brew. But he described a wondrous event. In *Geography of the Republic of Ecuador* published in Spanish in 1858, Villavicencio called ayahuasca "the magic drink" and advocated for the brew's significance. "We will not pass in silence one of the things that draws our attention," he commented while introducing ayahuasca to his readers. Exploring the Rio Napo Basin in east Ecuador in the 1850s, Villavicencio encountered ayahuasca among Shuar and other settlements. His ethnographic accounts describe ayahuasca being used "to foresee and to answer accurately in difficult cases, be it to reply opportunely to ambassadors from other tribes in a question of war; to decipher plans of the enemy through the medium of this magic drink and take proper steps for attack and defense; to ascertain when a relative is sick, what sorcerer has put a carousel to carry out a friendly visit to other tribes; to welcome foreign travelers or, at last, to make sure of the love of their womenfolk."

Before describing his own personal experience drinking ayahuasca, he provided an ethnographic account of the brew's effects:

Its action appears to excite the nervous system; all the senses liven up and all faculties awaken; they feel vertigo and spinning in the head, then a sensation of being lifted into the air and beginning an aerial journey; the possessed begins in the first moments to see the most delicious apparitions, in conformity with his ideas and knowledge: the savages say that they see gorgeous lakes, forests covered with fruit, the prettiest birds who communicate to them the nicest and the most favourable things they want to hear, and other beautiful things relating to their savage life. When this instant passes they begin to see terrible horrors out to devour them, their first flight ceases and they descend to earth to combat the terrors who communicate to them all the adversities and misfortunes awaiting them. (Villavicencio 1858)

And for his own personal experience, he wrote,

When I have partaken of ayahuasca, my head has immediately begun to swim, then I have seemed to enter an aerial voyage, wherein I thought I saw the most charming landscapes, great cities, lofty towers, beautiful parks, and other delightful things. Then all at once I found myself deserted in a forest and attacked by beasts of prey, against which I tried to defend myself. Lastly, I began to come around, but with a feeling of excessive drowsiness, headache, and sometimes general malaise. (Villavicencio 1858)

The naturalists provided a new representation of ayahuasca in text, one that had shifted beyond the demonic missionary vision. The representations benefited from the detailed and somewhat dry analysis typical of scientific and commercial enquiry. Williams (2015:43) described how Villavicencio's education at University of Quito and his upbringing in an elite Ecuadorian family developed in him an ability to appeal to the European penchant for economic thinking, while simultaneously respecting Indigenous societies and knowledge. But this is just the surface. There is a much larger history of early European encounters with ayahuasca waiting to be researched.

WILD AND CIVILIZED MONTAGES

Colonial perceptions of the "civilized" and the "primitive" came to shape Amazonian shamanism in the nineteenth century. Tensions between demonization and desire, and civilization and savagery, came to infuse early European perceptions of ayahuasca with ambivalence. In a study of witchcraft trials in the 1700s at the margins of the Spanish empire, in what is now Ecuador and southern Colombia, Frank Salomon (1983) noted how colonial administrators failed to interpret Indigenous sorcery acts as politically significant and in doing so failed to see their importance to Indigenous governance.

Colonial authorities perceived natives accused of sorcery like they did European witches—as deviant, secret, poor, and low-status individuals—yet acts of shamanic attack were being employed by Indigenous political leaders and were sometimes combined into a "new mode of indigenous power wrapped in colonial legality" (Salomon 1983:425). In one particular case, judges were concerned about reports of Spaniards seeking the shamanic services of an Indigenous man locally accused of six accounts of sorcery. The reported Indigenous victims attempted to remedy their sickness with a Sibundoy curer who administered "a vision inducing drug . . . a potion of a forest vine," most likely ayahuasca, that enabled the victims to heal and to see who had attacked them (Saloman 1983:416). Their colonists' fear of Amazonian shamanism had the "paradoxical effect of accrediting [the] shamans' magical potency in European eyes and strengthening the conviction that peoples of the colonial periphery were ungovernable and dangerous" (413). This conviction enabled more space for autonomous modes of social transformation.

Michael Taussig produced one of the most innovative studies on ayahuasca in *Shamanism, Colonialism, and the Wild Man: A Study in Terror and Healing* (1987), which examines *yagé* use in the Putumayo region of southern Colombia, both historically and ethnographically. The book covers the brutality of the colonial rubber industries in the 1800s and 1900s, in combination with an ethnography of shamanism in the same region during the 1970s. When beginning fieldwork, Taussig was surprised to learn that white urban laborers and farm owners were seeking curing from Indigenous healers despite the pervasive racism among many urban Colombians (Taussig and Lamborn Wilson 2002). He undertook an analysis of the ambiguity of social

50   GLOBAL AYAHUASCA

relations between the region's peasant and wage societies to consider how colonial fantasies helped in the horrific and brutal exploitation of Indigenous Amazonians but also granted their healers and sorcerers magical powers. He examined how this "politics of epistemic murk" infused both "the myth and magic of colonial violence" and the possibility for its healing. Representing a kind of social talisman, the urban perceptions of the "wild Indian" were absorbed by Indigenous healers who manipulated the concept to subvert colonial powers. Taussig argued,

> So it has been through the sweep of colonial history where the colonizers provided the colonized with the left-handed gift of the image of the wild man—a gift whose powers the colonizers would be blind to, were it not for the reciprocation of the colonized, bringing together in the dialogical imagination of colonization an image that wrests from civilization its demonic power. (Taussig 1987:467)

A historical and colonial production of identities helped define the magic attributed to the "wild Indians," and this intercultural space, Taussig demonstrated, was essential to understanding the curative powers and visionary marvels of ayahuasca. He described an ayahuasca drinking event where laborers had come to seek curing from an Inga healer during an evening of songs, vomiting, and "fragments of memory pictures." At the beginning of the evening, the healer described what ayahuasca may entail:

> You take it as a cure, as something to improve your life, and for intelligence—so you can see danger and be more astute. You see beautiful things or horrible things according to the state of your heart. If it's clean, you see beauty. You can see what's happening in Barranquilla, Bogota, Cartagena, Cali . . . wherever. (1987:438)

Taussig demonstrated how the ayahuasca visions or *pintas* in the region were part of a wider economic sensorium in which Indigenous healers and urban subjects deal in perceptions of the civilized and the primitive. He examined how these stereotypes provided the psychic mirrors from which visions of terror and healing emerged.

Introducing a useful cinematic analogy, Taussig (1987:435–446) defined ayahuasca visions as special kinds of montage. Such an approach accommo-

COLONIAL AND POSTCOLONIAL ROOTS   51

dates a much more realistic phenomenological representation of ayahuasca experiences compared to the neat narrative plots of much anthropological writing on the topic. Ayahuasca visions are often unstable, switching, swerving, and transforming. Although talented healers seek to direct visions through songs, perfumes, performances, and special operations, it is not always possible for them to grasp and direct their own visions. Novice drinkers are often even less able to perform such intentional feats. They are passengers interacting with the visions but are also subject to the brew's visceral intensities, metamorphing scenes, and chaotic undulations. An evening of drinking ayahuasca can include a massive array of visual materials, even sometimes for just one person across a single session. Acknowledging these chaotic and montage qualities, Taussig described the session mentioned above.

> The power of this *yagé* night came only in part from what could be called "mysticism," and that mystery concerned the quite unconscious way in which whites like Elisio and his two companions from Boyacá attribute magical power to the "Indians." . . . In this most crucial sense, savagery has not been tamed—and therein lies the magic of colonial healing through the figure of the "Indian." The "mystical insights" given by the visions and tumbling fragments of memory pictures oscillating in a polyphonic discursive room full of leaping shadows and sensory pandemoniums are not insights granted by depths mysterious and other. Rather, they are made, not granted in the ability of montage to provoke sudden and infinite connections between dissimilars. (1987:441)

Cinematic theory lends itself to thinking about ayahuasca visions. In the late twentieth century, Amazonians described ayahuasca as the cinema of the rainforest or the forest TV (Calavia Sáez 2014; Narby 1998; Reichel-Dolmatoff 1997). After a Yaminahua shaman attended a cinema for the first time in the 1980s—where he watched a Bruce Lee martial arts film at a cinema in Ucayali, Peru—he returned to his forest village to drink ayahuasca and sing visionary "song paths" to make sense of the cinema (Townsley and Reid 1989). The following day, he exclaimed to his family that the cinema shows "sick" visions on the screen that are not as good as strong ayahuasca.

Some recent film techniques appear to mimic the evocative feeling and sensory effects of ayahuasca. The spectacular aesthetics of Ciro Guerra's

Embrace of the Serpent (2015) freely uses montage to bring a psychedelic aura to the story of two ethnographers who search, at different periods of the twentieth century, for a magical plant in the Colombian Amazon. The transtemporal strategy of the two stories mixes in montages that unsettle any ordinary sense of cinematic narrative. The litany of clichés about primitive peoples, lost worlds, and headhunters that have permeated film on Indigenous Amazonia (Nugent 2007) are absent or replaced in Guerra's portrayal of the terror and brutality of colonialism and the mystery and healing of plant medicines. Imagery of ordinary life, missionary perversions and brutalities, the harsh realities of disease, and psychedelic montages of mysterious plant medicines bring to the cinema an ayahuasca-feel that is rooted in place and history.

Describing the montage qualities of ayahuasca visions, Taussig wrote that "the manner of interruptedness; the sudden scene changing . . . breaks up an attempt at narrative ordering and which trips up sensationalism" (1987:441). His research on ayahuasca and colonialism intervenes in scholarly debates while also dabbling in a similar stylization to what was later employed in Guerra's artistic film. His ethnographic writing weaves narratives from different temporal periods, economic systems, epistemic worlds, and states of consciousness. Part trickster, part theorist, Taussig unsettles the pretense and narrative authority of anthropology through a kind of literary shamanism. His work shows how certain kinds of writing, like certain kinds of cinema, are perhaps spiritual cousins of ayahuasca.

The historical impacts of colonialism upon Indigenous ayahuasca drinking are widespread. In a speculative albeit sober analysis, Peter Gow (1994) suggested the source of much ayahuasca shamanism in western Amazonia is entangled firmly in colonial encounters. The assumption that today's styles ayahuasca shamanism reflect pre-Colombian traditions (Luna 1986; Naranjo 1986) appeared unlikely to him given the widespread use of ayahuasca by "mestizo" or "mixed race" specialists that descended from those working in the 1800s and early 1900s industries. He does not deny that ayahuasca may have been widely used in pre-Colombian times, but he suggested that many of

COLONIAL AND POSTCOLONIAL ROOTS   53

the ayahuasca practices reported by anthropologists during the 1900s probably have a more recent origin.

Bernd Brabec de Mori (2011) lent support to Gow's thesis through a linguistic analysis of ayahuasca curing songs. His study suggested that ayahuasca
drinking became widely distributed across Indigenous groups only during
the previous two centuries. Various Indigenous groups have openly explained
to anthropologists that they received ayahuasca relatively recently (Shepard
2014; Gearin and Calavia Sáez 2021). In his seminal paper on the source of
ayahuasca shamanism, Gow was struck by a lack of ayahuasca use by remote
Indigenous groups that managed to avoid the colonial industries, and by contradictory explanations from ayahuasca specialists about the source of shamanic authority. Vegetalismo and urban ayahuasca specialists in Peruvian
rainforest cities such as Pucallpa and Iquitos attributed "supreme authority
to forest Indian sources" while remote Indigenous specialists located "that
authority among urban practitioners" (1994:97). He argued that the reason
for this paradox is not simply because people like to locate greater shamanic
power beyond themselves or beyond their familiar worlds, but because of a
cultural and historical logic in the social category of "mestizo" and its mediating position between the city and the forest.

The forest is a regenerating source of commodities for capitalists—in the
form of extracting rubber, coca, timber, and so on—and a regenerative source
of healing powers for urban ayahuasca shamans—in the form of taming the
primordial forces of spiritual ecologies. Urban ayahuasca specialists have located shamanic authority and powers among the remote Indians and their
connection with the regenerative forest, while those in remote Indigenous
settlements have perceived in urban shaman's access to the primordial origins
of a colonial past from which they have been dominated (Gow 1994, 1993).
This paradox reveals how ayahuasca can be a portal or means of entangling
people from across very different social and historical contexts.

COSMOPOLITAN VISIONS

In the decades following Gow's study of ayahuasca's cultural economy, a new
engine of exchange rocked the landscape. An international tourist scene in
and around the Peruvian cities of Iquitos, Pucallpa, and elsewhere trans-

formed some of the region's ayahuasca practices. Prior to the 2019 coronavirus pandemic, there were approximately 70 ayahuasca retreat centers operating outside Iquitos, mainly owned and run by foreigners, Shipibo healer Mataeo Arvalo Maynas told me in disappointment. His calculations were likely accurate; in 2019, the popular retreat booking website Retreat Guru advertised 63 retreat organizations in the Iquitos region and 144 in total across Peru. The platform advertised 452 organizations operating ayahuasca retreats across the globe, with the most popular countries, listed in descending order, being Peru, Ecuador, Costa Rica, Mexico, United States, Netherlands, and Spain. None of the ayahuasca retreats in Australia were listed on Retreat Guru. It only included retreats conducted in legal or semilegal areas.

International interest in ayahuasca has brought new opportunities for capital that have redefined some aspects of Amazonian shamanism. In the early 1990s, Gow commented that he found "no cases where white people, in the sense of actual immigrants from outside Amazonia, are categorically attributed shamanic power . . . nobody in Amazonia attributes them with knowledge of ayahuasca shamanism" (1994:98). Today, there are many white people who have trained with Indigenous specialists and made a lucrative career conducting ayahuasca services in Peru and across the globe. During a retreat I attended in Melbourne, Australia, in 2013, the visiting mestizo *curandero* from Pucallpa made it very clear that he was not simply the host's shamanic teacher but also his student. He had just flown to Australia directly from delivering sessions in Russia and across Europe. The renowned healer told the seventy people in attendance that he had learned a great deal about ayahuasca from his host, a white Australian who helped to facilitate his tour in the country.

It took many decades or more for global ayahuasca to expand into what it was in 2019. The beginnings of ayahuasca tourism in the Amazon are difficult to pinpoint. Key precursors would include the global dissemination of texts in the mid-twentieth century by journalists, anthropologists, ethnobotanists, novelists, and others. This included earlier works such as William Safford's *Narcotic Plants and Stimulants of the Ancient Americas* (1917); Louis Lewin's *Phantastica: Narcotic and Stimulating Drugs, Their Use and Abuse* (1931); Robert De Ropp's *Drugs and the Mind* (1957:264–69); Peter Matthiessen's novel *At Play in the Fields of the Lord* (1965), then an increase during the 1970s

COLONIAL AND POSTCOLONIAL ROOTS   55

with Manuel Cordova-Rios's and Bruce Lamb's *Wizard of the Upper Amazon* (1974); Michael Harner's *Hallucinogens and Shamanism* (1973); Terence and Dennis McKenna's *The Invisible Landscape: Mind, Hallucinogens and the I Ching* (1975); Peter Furst's *Hallucinogens and Culture* (1976); Richard Evans-Schultes and Albert Hofmann's *Plants of the Gods: Origins of Hallucinogen Use* (1979); and Andrew Weil's *Yagé: The Vine That Speaks* (1979), Luis Eduardo Luna and Pablo Amaringo's *Ayahuasca Visions* (1991), and Jeremy Narby's *The Cosmic Serpent* (1998), among others.

The American novelist William Burroughs and the beat poet Allen Ginsberg helped popularize ayahuasca to the Euro-American and other imaginations with *The Yagé Letters*, published in 1963 (Burroughs and Ginsberg 2006). The brew had already been on Burroughs's mind for a decade. The end of his book *Junky*, originally published under the pen name Lee in 1953, finishes with a special hope attributed to ayahuasca. "*Yage* is supposed to increase telepathic sensitivity. . . . Maybe I will find in *yage* what I was looking for in junk and weed and coke. *Yage* may be the final fix," Burroughs wrote. He traveled to the Amazon in search of ayahuasca in 1953, the same year *Junky* was published. *The Yagé Letters* consists of creative rewritten letters from Burroughs to Ginsberg about their experiences with *yagé* during separate trips to Amazonia (Harris 2017). Burroughs's use of his pen name William Lee brings a fictional freedom and personal disclosure to the writing.

Burroughs was a bona fide drug aficionado who had tried many substances before ayahuasca. What Graham St John called his "brazen willingness to trek the pharmaceutical frontier" (2015:21) took Burroughs to drink the Amazonian elixir. He had learned about the brew directly from the Harvard University ethnobotanist Richard Evans Schultes. *The Yagé Letters* describes Burroughs's somewhat underwhelming experience drinking ayahuasca. But as St John noted, Burroughs "did have a breakthrough with yage" (25), which he shared in an initially unpublished letter to Ginsberg. Describing drinking ayahuasca in Pucallpa, Peru, Burroughs wrote, "What follows was indescribable. It was like possession by a blue spirit. . . . Blue purple. And definitely South Pacific, like Easter Island or Maori design, a blue substance throughout my body, and an archaic grinning face" (1994:171–180).

He explained in later letters that ayahuasca was "the most powerful drug I have ever experienced. . . . Yage is it. . . . It is like nothing else" (St John

2015:25). Melanie Keomany (2016) interpreted *The Yagé Letters* through a post-colonial lens. After detailing the colonial attitudes in Burroughs's depictions of white men in the Colombian Amazon, Keomany examined Burroughs's final ayahuasca vision. She interpreted it as the disintegration of racial hierarchies and a psychological confrontation with the neo-imperial United States. Burroughs's pen name Lee describes undergoing "space time travel" wherein the room "seemed to shake and vibrate with motion." Then, a "Composite City" or kind of cosmopolitan realm passed through his body in which "many races" including "Negro, Polynesian, Mountain Mongol, Desert Nomad," along with "all human potential." The experience reached towards a universalism through something like the cut-up technique Burroughs introduced to literature. By mashing and mixing parts of stories, his work hints at how ayahuasca experiences are full of composites and are ripe for analogy in the service of ontology. Ayahuasca later featured in several of Burroughs's texts, including the popular novel *Naked Lunch* published in 1959, wherein *yagé* is sometimes made ordinary and used as a symbol of daily alcohol, opium, and other drug use.

The other voice in *The Yagé Letters*, beat poet Ginsberg, described drinking ayahuasca and undergoing a colorful shamanic flight through the universe, encountering "ministering angels," vomiting embodied visionary snakes, and then dissolving into "the Great Being." His narrative of merging with an omnipotent entity represents a precursor to the cosmology of ego dissolution and mystical-type experiences popular in global ayahuasca and clinical psychedelic use. Similarly, the "Composite City" of Burroughs's visionary experience could represent but another version of the cosmopolitan qualities of ayahuasca (Peluso 2017) that have, paradoxically, come to define the Indigenous brew of the remote rainforest.

Published around the same period, *Wizard of the Upper Amazon* (Córdova-Rios and Lamb 1974) chronicles a biography of a Peruvian rubber tapper during the early-to-mid 1900s who was "abducted" in the Upper Amazon and shown the secret arts of ayahuasca. The text, a collaboration between healer Manuel Córdova-Rios and author Frank Bruce Lamb, was widely read, but it has been heavily criticized by anthropologists, including Robert L. Carneiro who claimed that it "consists of fragmentary ethnographic titbits gleaned indiscriminately from many tribes and encased in a matrix of personal fantasy"

(Carneiro 1980:95). Despite or even because of these fantastical qualities, the ayahuasca narratives in *Wizard* would sound familiar to many contemporary global enthusiasts. Describing drinking the brew with Huni Kuin shamans in the Brazilian Amazon, the text reads in wonder,

> With the chant of the boa, a giant constrictor appeared slowly gliding through the forest. Blue lights intensified an intricate design of scroll configurations that seemed to float along the boa's spine. Light flashed from his eyes and tongue. The bold patterns on the snake's skin glowed with intestines and varied colors. (Córdova-Rios and Lamb 1974, 38)

Recasting the text as a shamanistic enterprise, Luna and White (2016:25) explained, somewhat apologetically, that *Wizard* was partly a myth-making project around the authors. They suggested it was a "construction intended to establish the charismatic aura around [Córdova-Rios's] person," which they added may create a therapeutic effect similar to how shamans locate power in animals. The seminal text reads with the suspense and fascination of an adventure novel. But it would be unfair to dismiss the work as pure fantasy. Compared to *The Yagé Letters*, it incorporates a vast amount of Indigenous perspective and does not revert to the naturalistic detachment of the earlier US writings about ayahuasca.

Yet despite their differences, both works, *The Yagé Letters* and *Wizard of the Upper Amazon*, embody early images of what became global renditions of ayahuasca shamanism. Both emphasized the brew's visionary qualities and its ability to provide access to shamanic worlds that transcend modern life.

It is difficult to estimate how much ayahuasca is currently drunk across the planet. Many drinkers in Europe, North America, Asia, and elsewhere have good reason to keep their practice private to avoid getting arrested and detained. However, the nonprofit organization International Center for Ethnobotanical Education, Research, and Service (ICEERS), based in Spain, recently published a report suggesting that about four million people worldwide have consumed ayahuasca (Suárez Álvarez 2023). They also estimated that during 2019 about 820,000 people consumed, indicating a recent uptake in usage. In parallel, the Global Ayahuasca Project, directed by Australian researcher Daniel Perkins, surveyed approximately 12,000 ayahuasca drinkers. Examining the data from across the globe, spanning religious groups, neoshamanic networks, and therapeutic groups, the results suggest that there are high rates of "adverse reactions" to drinking ayahuasca (Bouso et al. 2022). Around 55 percent of respondents acknowledged experiencing adverse mental health effects in the weeks or months after consumption. However, 88 percent considered "such mental health effects as part of a positive process of growth or integration" (Bouso et al. 2022). The high rate of adverse physical and challenging psychological effects was "generally not severe" and most people continued to drink ayahuasca.

In Girona, Spain, in 2019, the World Ayahuasca Conference attracted thirteen hundred people to learn and connect. The event covered the latest studies about the brew's therapeutic potential. Dozens of Indigenous healers and social scientists discussed topics including sustainability, tourism, and healing, accompanied by an art and multimedia exhibition with live painting by Indigenous and non-Indigenous artists, a virtual reality experience of ayahuasca in the Peruvian Amazon called "Ayahuasca: Kosmic Journey" produced by French filmmaker Jan Kounen. In addition, a multidimension artwork was on display, through a collaboration between Belgian artist Naziha Mestaoui and the voice of Huni Kuin shaman Ibã Huni Kuin. In *Sounds of Light*, the shaman's wondrous songs vibrate water into synesthetic and cymatic patterns.

Organized by ICEERS, it was the third time the World Ayahuasca Conference had been held. The first was in Ibiza, Spain, in 2014 and the second in 2016 in Rio Branco, Brazil. In late 2018, representatives of Shipibo ayahuasca traditions were featured at the Parliament of the World's Religions (Gearin 2019). It was the first time Indigenous Amazonians were formally hosted by the organization since its inception 120 years prior.

Indigenous ayahuasca has been increasingly finding its way into global popular culture. In early 2019, models in Paris marched a visionary fashion runway silhouetted by a massive installation of Peruvian ayahuasca art painted by the late Pablo Amaringo (1938–2009). Ayahuasca visions have given inspiration to pottery, textiles, jewelry, sand art, wall art, and now, fashion runways. The Paris Kenzo show highlights a new era of ayahuasca design.

It is a striking example of the brew being distilled by wealthy alchemists of fashion capitalism. The models walked the runway each wearing around $2,500 worth of shoes, designer pants, and other dazzling attire. Like the machinery of inequality itself, the indifferent and mechanical expressions on the models' faces, as they walk the runway, fade into the background. Colorful ayahuasca art and hip fashion converge to seduce and boost consumption.

Five years prior, the world's largest fashion magazine, *Elle*, published a feature article about ayahuasca. The article describes the brew as a beauty and glamor tonic that can enhance how you look. The opening paragraph reads,

> My friend was glowing. Not post-sex glowing or good-makeup glowing or beach-vacation glowing. This was different. . . . Her body language seemed remade, lighter yet more deliberate. "Oh!" she laughed. "I'm just back from Peru. It's probably the ayahuasca."

With a monthly audience of sixty-nine million fashion-interested users, *Elle* described ayahuasca in the language that its readers apparently wanted to hear and with an image of glowing women dressed in high-fashion attire.

FIGURE 1.2 Image in American fashion magazine *Elle* in 2014, part of a seven-page article celebrating ayahuasca as a spiritual, healing, and beauty tonic.

Ayahuasca was incorporated into the fashion and lifestyle industry in the same way as other Indigenous products. It arrived under the banner of the exotic and strange.

In his book *The Post-Colonial Exotic: Marketing the Margins*, Graham Huggan (2001) suggested that exotic products are created by making strange things of other cultures more familiar but never fully like "us." It is the sense of an eternal otherness that gives the exotic its price. At the Kenzo fashion event, a kind of essence of ayahuasca had become extracted from the wider Amazonian lifeworlds depicted in Amaringo's paintings and reduced to an exotic backdrop. The show was a natural progression of Kenzo's earlier show titled "Kenzotopia," which the company described on its website as "equal parts opulent and psychedelic . . . attire for new ceremonies of the future." It is not clear what these new ceremonies are, and that is precisely the point. Exotic high fashion strips Indigenous culture of its histories and ceremonies and repackages it for the consumer to design themselves however they wish. This purging the essence out of culture is part of what cultural theorist Stanley Fish (1997) called boutique multiculturalism, or when cultural differences are celebrated but reduced to superficialities. A simple example would be if a person looked at a Pablo Amaringo artwork and exclaimed, "I love traditional ayahuasca culture!" but they had virtually no knowledge of Indigenous ayahuasca use. The Kenzo show shaped and capitalized on the boutique multiculturalism of ayahuasca in global fashion.

But, as Gayle Highpine (2018) describes, the sacred Amazonian brew is no stranger to the flow of the economy and has been commercialized by Indigenous peoples for centuries. In 2019, popular ayahuasca healing services in Iquitos, Peru, charged international visitors $3,000 for a ten-day retreat— roughly the same cost of a total Kenzo outfit. The question of whether ayahuasca commercialization is actually wrong took some Amazonian healers by surprise. "The assumptions behind the question [of commercializing ayahuasca] were completely foreign to them" (Highpine 2018). The issue is clearly not *if* ayahuasca can be commercialized, but *how* and to whose benefit it is marketed and sold. A genuine respect for difference and diversity, an honest curiosity for learning about other cultures, and therapeutic perspectives driven by Indigenous experts—these are areas that welcome ethical and creative attention.

Daniela Peluso (2017) pointed out that foreign investment dominates the "entrepreneurial ecosystem" of ayahuasca tourism in Peru. The result of this, she suggested, is that Indigenous people are disadvantaged and the benefits of the foreigner are privileged. This can be observed by considering the ambient poverty of many Shipibo living in Pucallpa and the wider Ucayali region. They are the most internationally renowned group to use ayahuasca, but Bernd Brabec de Mori observed in 2014 that as little as a few dozen of fifty thousand Shipibo earned enough to live well on the ayahuasca tourism economy. Issues of water sanitization, food security, and poor health are rampant in areas of Pucallpa and Iquitos. Meanwhile, ayahuasca visions have become a trendy fashion accessory for the wealthy in Paris. This is the globally polarized world of ayahuasca we currently inhabit.

TWO

GLOBAL SHAMANIC TOURISM IN PERU

Upon arriving at the remote Peruvian city of Pucallpa in winter 2019, I had a few days to spare before heading to the outskirts of town for fieldwork at Pachamama Temple, an ayahuasca healing center led by Shipibo healers catering to international visitors. While appreciating the edges of the beautiful Yarinacocha lagoon, among slums scattered with dilapidated wooden dwellings raised off the ground in anticipation of the annual flood season, I befriended a young Shipibo motor-taxi driver named Pedro. He offered to show me around for a small fee. The dwellings accommodated Shipibo and other Indigenous groups along the dry and bumpy dirt roads near the lagoon. This impoverished urban landscape showed a genuine side of Shipibo life that was hardly visible on the websites and advertisements of "authentic" ayahuasca retreats. The retreat websites typically depicted lush forests with beautiful ceremonial halls, comfortable and clean accommodation, and Shipibo healers dressed in beautiful *cushma* gowns and other colorful tribal signifiers.

As we cruised through clouds of exhaust fumes in his gasoline-fueled tricycle, Pedro showed me many of the psychedelic murals that adorn the walls of Yarinacocha with shamanic imagery of jaguars, river dolphins, and plant medicines. The urban landscape of Pucallpa and neighboring Yarinacocha is subject to economic precarity and ambient poverty, particularly among the informal settlements where many Shipibo and recent rural migrants live. Around 2014, there was approximately 20 percent unemployment in Pucallpa, which likely reached 50 percent when adding the informal settlements (Padoch, Steward, Pinedo-Vasquez, Putzel, and Miranda Ruiz 2014:330). Employment, if it was available, was mostly in the timber, logging, and wood industries. For Pedro, such a challenging economic environment was compounded by racism and prejudice. Shipibo have long been regarded as subhuman and cannibals by members of urban Peruvian society (Hern 1992:3).

Shipibo-Conibo are part of the Pano linguistic family. They represent one of the largest ethnic minorities in Peru with between thirty-five thousand and fifty thousand members, many of whom live near Pucallpa in the Ucayali region. Contemporary Shipibo youths find themselves in an ambivalent position in which they may express embarrassment about their culture and are reluctant to wear traditional clothing or speak Shipibo in public (Hilario 2010:79, 88). Oscar Espinosa (2012) described how many Shipibo feel their culture is undergoing a crisis in hostile urban environments where they are subject to discrimination and different values, expectations, and opportunities. Pedro, my motor-taxi driver, appeared to be moving rapidly beyond his Shipibo identity, or at least his actions showed a lack of concern for the cultural crisis that others perceive. When I asked if he participates in Shipibo cultural events, he replied that his dream is to become a mechanic and own a house with a pool for his children and wife. He told me he had no interest in drinking ayahuasca, adding he was healthy and that ayahuasca is for sorcerers (*brujos*) and tourists. However, many Shipibo have expressed concern about the future of their culture (Espinosa 2012; Hilario 2010; Oyarce-Cruz, Medina Paredes, and Maier 2019) and are actively working to promote Shipibo activities, values, and ways of life. At the intersection of cultural crisis, change, and continuity reside the reasons why Shipibo have become incredibly successful international ayahuasca healers.

Operating on the outskirts of Pucallpa, Pachamama Temple is a globally famous ayahuasca retreat that is centered upon a family of Shipibo healers, and in particular, Mama Maria, matriarch, seventy-six years of age at the time of my fieldwork, who inspired her children to train in ayahuasca, plant dieting, and the craft of healing tourists. It is one of the dozens of ayahuasca healing retreats—also called lodges, temples, or centers—that are active outside remote cities of Peru and provide shamanic services to global markets.

Featuring at the top of internet search engines and booking websites, it accommodated hundreds of international guests annually. Given its global popularity, it was also the target of sorcery attacks by local *curanderos*. Unbeknownst to the international guests at the retreat, sorcery has long been an inevitable dimension of healing for Shipibo ayahuasca specialists. When curing locals, Shipibo healers would drink ayahuasca to engage tensions of the patient's social world (Illius 1992; Brabec de Mori 2012). This involved juggling morally ambiguous fields of *brujeria* (sorcery) populated by human or nonhuman persons, such as other healers, kin, animals, plants, and nonmaterial beings.

The fact that sorcery and occult practices have become emboldened by modernization, capitalism, and development has become something of an anthropological truism (Taussig 1987; Comaroff and Comaroff 2001). As the so-called dark side of shamanism, sorcery can unfold into social subjugation, scapegoating, and domination. But it can also represent routes of justice, virtue, and autonomy by attempting to tip the social and cosmological balance of power in favor of certain persons, values, and moral projects. The often morally ambiguous terrain of shamanism (Whitehead and Wright 2004) can help explain its prevalence as a mode of social change (Zelenietz 1981) and social control (Brown 1986:104), given its capacity to mediate social contradictions, inequalities, and tensions. This can partially explain the prevalence of sorcery in the ayahuasca tourism economy.

But sorcery, in the context of ayahuasca tourism, engenders a unique problem and opportunity for healers. The international clients of the global market arrive from foreign social and cosmological worlds that make them typically uninterested in the morally ambiguous practice of sorcery-healing. Tourists tend to disregard sorcery as backwards, irrational, and impossible and seek a different therapeutic model that idealizes unambiguously benevolent healers. In the context of ayahuasca tourism, the moral economy of sorcery has become largely covert and insulated within networks of local healers and their concerns for wealth, power, and international clients. To appreciate the new economic and shamanic dynamics of ayahuasca tourism on Shipibo healing practices, first we need to outline some key aspects of Shipibo cosmovision and its sensory and psychedelic conceptions.

Nihue is a complex Shipibo term at the core of healing and sorcery. It has several meanings, including (1) wind, air, breath, and song, and (2) smell, aura, and atmosphere (Brabec de Mori 2012; Illius 1992). A healer's song embodies *nihue*, which may cure, protect, or bewitch against another *nihue* that was generated by a different healer, or a nonhuman person. During the ayahuasca sessions, the healers breathe in power and whistle, sing, and blow away to manipulate the negative, smelly, and pathogenic *nihue* embodied in the patient. To help with this, they may use tobacco smoke and fragrant perfumes. Ayahuasca (*oni* in Shipibo) can assist in handling *nihue* by enhancing multisensory perception and disclosing what Fernando Santos-Granero termed noncorporeal vitalities of perception (2006:61). An important way healing may be pursued is through the healer taking on the perspective of another being. The idea of perspective shifting between species and lifeforms is widespread in Amazonian metaphysics.

When a Shipibo healer becomes a jaguar to converse with the spirit house of the big cat, the healer may perceive and interact with the jaguar *ibo* (spirit double) in the form of its inner human. From the perspective of human onlookers, the transformed healer would appear as a jaguar, but his now embodied jaguar-perspective, and the jaguar persons he interacts with, appear to him in human form. Importantly, switching these kinds of perspectives is dangerous, whether it happens voluntarily or involuntarily. As Eduardo Viveiros de Castro explained, to switch perspectives could mean seeing family and friends as prey or predators (1998:470). Illness, disease, and immoral behavior can emerge from a person unwittingly becoming an animal, plant, or other nonhuman person (Londono Sulkin 2005; Vivieros de Castro 1998). But to intentionally switch perspectives and communicate within a multispecies "ecology of selves" is part of the social and ethical skill-set of healers and sorcerers (Kohn 2013). Body paint, clothing, adornments, performance, and psychedelic plants have supported practitioners in undertaking

GLOBAL AYAHUASCA

a visual or "somatic perspectivism" shift (Viveiros de Castro 1996). Studying Shipibo healing practices, Bernd Brabec de Mori demonstrated how breath, song, and bodily experience combine into a "sonic perspectivism" that actually enables healers to switch views. He argued that the visual elements of ayahuasca drinking and body adornment are more descriptive and metaphorical, whereas the audible and sonic vibrations of song are the primary "tools for achieving mimesis, transformation, and the construction of worlds" (Brabec de Mori 2012:96). Other Indigenous approaches to ayahuasca have emphasized the auditory and musical elements of the experiences more than the visual elements (Walker 2012:190; Townsley 1993; Gearin and Calavia Sáez 2021). Like other Amazonians, Shipibo may refer to themselves as "The Real people" or *noa jonikon*. Brabec de Mori illustrated how the distinction between who and what is deemed "Real people," and not just "people," differentiated which plants and animals have human consciousness (2013:76). *Ibo* spirit mothers or spirit masters, whether jaguar, anaconda, or parrot, can provide perspectives for knowing and acting on the world in different ways.

Plant life has a special agency across some, but certainly not all, Amazonian uses of ayahuasca (Luna 1984; Århem 1996; Shepard 2017; Dev 2018; Lopez Sanchez 2023). Plant persons feature widely in Shipibo healing and sorcery. Deliberately welcoming a *bobinsana* plant person, *noya rao* plant person, or *yashingo* plant person into an ayahuasca session can lend power and knowledge to the healer for diagnosis and treatment. The healer-sorcerers undertake training with plants to develop ongoing relations with their spirit masters. The training is called "dieting" and may occur for days, weeks, or even years for one plant. It can involve social isolation, dream analysis, and food and behavior taboos, while regularly consuming a special plant until a clear relation with its master is established. Sometimes a special song is learned from the ally. The songs, commonly termed *icaros* from Inkan, help to cure, protect, bewitch, and restore harmony to a person. To diet a plant is to open a relationship with its *ibo* which in turn constitutes part of the identity of the healer. Maestra Mama Maria from Pachamama Temple explained her early dieting and training:

> I said to myself, now that I know more about the plants [from my mother's herbalism practice] I have to start a diet. . . . First I started with *niwe rao*

medicine. When I finished that I did a diet with *yoxte rao* medicine and then with a lot of other plant medicine. Thanks to those diets, I am who I am today.

She explained how ayahuasca, as a wise teacher plant, can be diagnostic of health through the visions it displays to the person.

When the person has their body clean, they can see what they want to see. But if they are not, they can suffer great consequences with ayahuasca because as it is known, ayahuasca is a wise plant. It knows if a person is well. It can make them see visions. But if they are not well, they will see negative things. For that reason, healthy people who take ayahuasca do so simply to learn or experiment with it. It was always this way.

Ayahuasca as teacher, therefore, suggests the brew has an educational and pedagogical side. This has prompted scholar Kenneth Tupper to suggest that psychedelics can teach through the wonder and meaningfulness they impart: "The educational value of entheogens and psychedelics may be their capacity to reliably evoke experiences of wonder and awe, to stimulate transcendental or mystical experience, and to catalyse a sense of life meaning or purpose" (2014:16).

The "school" of ayahuasca involves a sometimes arduous curriculum. Amazonian plant dieting can be dangerous. It may include training with psychoactive plants, such as ayahuasca, Brugmansia, Datura species, and *Nicotiana rustica*, and also with many non-psychoactive plants, such as *Calliandra angustifolia* or *bobinsana*. Some Shipibo healers explained to me that the risks of entering a psychic relationship with a plant too fast or too strongly, or exiting a diet too quickly and without adequate care, can result in any manner of afflictions. Drinking ayahuasca during a diet for another plant was sometimes used to enhance the other plant, that is, to improve its communication and strengthen its potency. Diets are central to a Shipibo ayahuasca healer's ability, identity, and strength.

Dieting is a kind of medicine, but the term *"medicina"* as used by Shipibo healers (borrowed from Spanish) requires clarification. *Medicina*, here, is not simply a curative substance but can refer to special powers, relationships, and skills accumulated in the body of the healer. Sometimes healers I spoke with described *medicina* as a special phlegm in the throat or upper stomach. These hidden *medicina* objects, or what I term "transbodied medicines" given their capacities to move between persons, are part of Shipibo healers' *shinan* or power. Transbodied medicines exist in psychoactive trees, such as ayahuasca, datura, and tobacco, and thus encompass pharmacological kinds of medicine, but they transcend naturalist medicine in a myriad of ways. Undertaking diets enables the healers to know plants, including their properties, temperaments, and energies, and also to embody and direct their power and presence. *Medicina* can be increased through undertaking more dieting to sustain and improve the relationships with the *ibo* in visions, dreams, and plant-consumption practices, or through receiving direct transmission from another practitioner, such as a father or uncle. This transbodied medicine can become depleted through various channels, including by treating sick and particularly difficult patients; receiving dramatic sorcery attacks by malevolent healers and nonhuman persons; and failing to undertake sufficient dietary training. Transbodied medicines may be directly transferred from healers to patients through song and ayahuasca. Maestro Juan articulated how *icaro* songs and *medicina* can heal others by removing and clearing pathological spirit essence.

> The *ícaros* come spontaneously, but each master has their own tone. The *ícaros* help each master see where to go. His own medicine comes and says "do it with this," then, ah very well, he knows how to heal. And the singing, the *ícaros* are the transmission of the medicine. And with each medicine, each type, what it does is release and cleanse. It moves the sickness away.

With its capacity to redirect spirit essence, this transbodied medicine is inherently ambiguous. It can cleanse and bewitch, empower and disempower, cure and harm. Yet all the healers at Pachamama Temple vowed to never retaliate against sorcery. They should only protect each other and themselves, while they wash away the bad *nihue* in the visiting guests' bodies. This marks an important difference in the Shipibo craft of healing visitors compared to healing locals, which is addressed below.

The Shipibo healers at Pachamama Temple are part of the largest union of Shipibo healers called ASOMASHK (*Asociación de Onanyabo Médicos Ancestrales Shipibo Konibo*). The key members of ASOMASHK emerged from the wider Shipibo political organization Coshicox. Some of those were part of the health organization AMETRA (Follér 1989) and the wider Madre de Dios health and environment group AMETRA-2001 (Peluso 2022; Alexiades and Lacaze 1996). AMETRA began in 1982 and sought cooperation between Indigenous and biomedical practice to promote "the application of medicinal plants in primary health among Shipibo Conibo." It occurred at the Hospital Amazonica and in Shipibo villages. It also included the promotion of medicine gardens in Shipibo villages, making plant remedies more available (Follér 1989:815). In the 1980s and beyond, many Shipibo were afflicted by what Paul Farmer termed "diseases of poverty." The most common were "gastro-intestinal ones, caused by parasites, microbes or malnutrition, and respiratory infections including tuberculosis and whooping-cough" (Follér 1989:812). The Shipibo healing practices of vomiting with ayahuasca and other emetic herbal substances have been part of local efforts to try to cure these gastro-intestinal issues. The Indigenous-led organization AMETRA-2001, operating from 1987 to 1991, also promoted cooperation between Indigenous plant medicine and biomedicine and was "influential in the emergence and re-emergence of ayahuasca in Madre de Dios" (Peluso 2022:33). ASOMASHK grew from these Shipibo health organizational roots to emerge decades later at the heights of ayahuasca tourism, just prior to the Covid-19 pandemic, which halted the flow of foreign clients in early 2020. With over one hundred Shipibo-Conibo healers, ASOMASHK was created in 2018 in response to the murder of Maestra Olivia Arevalo Lomas by a Canadian ayahuasca visitor. In the association's Yarinacocha Declaration (shipiboconibo. org), they stated,

1. Given their history, practice, and methodology, Shipibo-Konibo-Xetebo healing and expertise in medicinal plants are anti-colonialist forms of practice and knowledge, able to resist, transform and reconfigure with every difficulty and threat. Thus healers, teachers, practitioners must remain aware and proud to cultivate the anti-colonialist nature of their practices.

2. The work of healing and the struggle towards self-determination are not separable. They must move forward on the same path.

Like for other Amazonian shamanistic practices, social welfare has been a major goal of Shipibo ayahuasca use, with examples of mediating social conflicts, engaging community disputes, and asymmetries of political power have been widely documented in Amazonia (Brabec de Mori 2012, 2011; Illius 1992; Luna 1986; Taussig 1987; Beyer 2009). The shadowy world of sorcery has not decreased following the boom in ayahuasca tourism. Instead, it has morphed, often in secret to minimize disrupting the ontological expectations of the visiting wealthy clients.

The ayahuasca economy was growing rapidly in Peru before the pandemic. Examining the Peruvian city of Iquitos—the most popular location for ayahuasca tourism—Carlos Suárez Álvarez (2019) verified that seventy ayahuasca retreat centers were serving international clients in 2019 (whereas only thirty centers were operating in 2016). He estimated that between fifteen thousand and twenty thousand international clients were drinking ayahuasca in the retreats annually, representing around $17.5 million USD in retreat booking sales. In addition, there were clusters of ayahuasca centers in other parts of Peru, such as Cusco and Pucallpa, and in other South American countries.

On the basis of decades of organization-building by local and global stakeholders, Shipibo healers have come to represent the cultural heart of the ayahuasca tourism economy in Peru (Brabec de Mori 2014, Peluso 2014, Fotiou 2014, Homan 2017) and signify a dominant archetype of indigenous ayahuasca use in the bourgeoning internationalization of the brew (Tupper 2009; Fotiou 2016; Labate, Cavnar, and Gearin 2017). For many people across the globe, Shipibo healers are the most renowned and powerful of all. They are popularly presented in internet media as timeless spiritual figures living in harmony with nature and constituted by a condition of nature that exceedingly transcends society and history. Such an image gives strength to their shamanic powers among the international guests. But this image of a pristine tribe historically detached from global or outside forces is very inaccurate.

Shipibo have had a tentative and complicated relationship with Jesuit missionaries and Franciscan monks during the last four hundred years, with a long resumé of "contact" with descendants of European societies (Myers 1974; Golub 1982). They were also heavily acculturated with colonists in the late nineteenth- and early twentieth-century rubber industries. During this period, the Shipibo, Conibo, and Setebo populations were reduced to only a few thousand people in total, and most if not all Shipibo worked in the rubber industries with "individual family groups . . . under the total domination of particular patrones" (Lathrap 1970:180). With the emergence of lucrative rubber farms in Malaysia, the Amazonian rubber boom came to an end in 1912. Shipibo left the rubber and many assembled in communities often around schools, missions (Roe 1982), and later, government reserves such as San Francisco de Yarinacocha (Putsche 2000), which has been an international tourist destination for buying Shipibo art, and more recently, for training with healers in shamanic dieting and ayahuasca.

Part of the broader revitalization of Amazonian shamanism, Anne-Marie Colpron (2013:372) argued, is due to how the openness and plasticity of Indigenous ontologies allowed shamanic practices to incorporate foreign ideas and technologies into preexisting cosmologies. Researchers acknowledged how ayahuasca tourism represents an extension of the classic shamanic view that emphasizes intercultural exchange, political mediation, and the building of inter-ethnic alliances (Davidov 2010:404–405; Virtanen 2014:67; Fotiou 2020:377). Indigenous visions have long been colored with motifs of visiting guests, strangers, or enemies (Calavia Sáez 2011), and the knowledge from visions can gain more power the further along visionary rivers and terrains that it is sourced (Barbira Freedman 2014:135; Calavia Sáez 2011:140). The shape-shifting and cosmopolitical abilities of shamans (Viveiros de Castro 1998) can help explain why Amazonian shamanism has not decreased but sometimes flourished during periods of exchange and confrontation with powerful alien societies, but it cannot tell us why Indigenous ayahuasca use was declining during the mid-twentieth century (Luna 1986:163; Dobkin de Rios 1972) or why specifically Shipibo healers have become perhaps the most successful shamans in the global revival of ayahuasca.

Part of the global popularity of Shipibo healers can seemingly be traced to gender. Among neoshamanic networks, ayahuasca is generally a female plant spirit and has become domesticated to ancient European narrative worlds. The femininity of ayahuasca parallels genres of a Western narrative complex

FIGURE 2.1 Shipibo family of healers at Pachamama Temple, posing for social media photos during winter 2019: Maestro Genaro Marquez Pinedo in front, then left to right Maestra Rosa Pinedo Vasquez, Maestra Adelina Marquez Lopez, Maestro Feliciano Marquez Pinedo, and Maestro Gilberto Picota Lopez. (Photo: Alex Gearin)

in which nature is female, such as Demeter and Gaia in Ancient Greek myth; Natura in medieval Europe; or Mother Nature in twentieth-century popular culture. Whether to be dominated, subjugated, or liberated, the feminine has long been associated with powers of nature in Western history (Ortner 1972). In Amazonia, by contrast, the division between nature and culture, or humans and nonhumans, has been spliced in veritably different ways (Viveiros de Castro 1996). The use of the psychoactive plants and brew have generally been a male occupation and, according to some research, its probable rise in popularity during the late nineteenth and early twentieth centuries in Northwest Amazonia (Gow 1994; Brabec de Mori 2011) may have minimized the role of female healers (Boschemeier and Carew 2018; Shepard 2014). Examining the Peruvian city of Iquitos around the year 2010, Barbira

Freedman (2010:139) counted only seven female shamans using ayahuasca in comparison to over one hundred male ayahuasca shamans. However, with the rise of international tourism, female healers have become increasingly desired and trained, resulting in what Evgenia Fotiou termed the "feminization of ayahuasca" (2014:171). Visitors have been traveling from the metropolis to the rainforest to experience nature's healing powers and their inner feminine. A touristic marriage between ayahuasca and the feminine is consistent with broader commercial trends given that tourism jobs across the globe are serviced primarily by women (UNWTO 2010).

When the Global North started to open its mind and stomach to ayahuasca and shamanic revitalization got started, Shipibo women increasingly became ayahuasca specialists. Shipibo descent and kinship historically have revolved around the matrilineal extended family, with "women playing a much greater public and economic role than they do in other Amazonian tribes," wrote Peter Roe (1982:36). There are examples of women gaining increased social, economic, and political authority in the ayahuasca tourism context, such as at the "female-only shaman" retreats, and the Shipibo shamanic union ASOMASHK, whose vice president is Elisa Vargas Fernández. This contrasts with urban Shipibo politics more generally, which, since the mobilization of Shipibo organizations and federations from the 1970s, has increasingly followed a "mestizo" model and been dominated by men (Hilario 2010:118–122), despite the ongoing efforts of Shipibo women.

Shipibo textiles and pottery have become a supplementary income for families working the tourist lodges. These exquisite objects are illuminated with psychedelic *kené* designs that materialize the visitors' visionary yearnings and memories. While ayahuasca tourists, and some anthropologists (Gebhart-Sayer 1985), perceive the Shipibo *kené* designs as representing a psychedelic aesthetic that is copied from the objective visionary states of drinking ayahuasca, Bernd Brabec de Mori and Laida Mori Silvano de Brabec (2009) suggested that these designs have long preceded the historical use of the psychedelic ayahuasca recipe among Shipibo.

Many Indigenous groups appear to have adopted the psychedelic version of the brew during the previous 150 years (Brabec de Mori 2011; Gearin and Calavia Sáez 2021; Gow 1994; Shepard 2014). Despite this research, ayahuasca is regularly marketed by ayahuasca tourist centers and websites—and described by scientists and influencers (Grob 2013; McKenna 2005)—as a pan-Amazonian practice that dates back thousands of years. The tendency for foreigners to manufacture a primordial story of ayahuasca aligns the brew with the long and wide tradition of primitivism.

Primitivist imaginaries permeate Indigenous tourist development across the globe in the form of exotic desires, objects, and performances (Salazar and Graburn 2014). According to Theodossopoulos (2014:60) and others, such imaginaries include two salient elements. Indigenous people are characterized by foreign consumers as, on the one hand, exotic, backwards, and lacking civilization, and on the other, noble savages living in harmony with nature. Ayahuasca tourism tends to emphasize the latter by situating Indigenous healers as uncorrupted by civilization and living simple lives in spiritual union with nature, in particular, with plant spirits. Many visitors arrive having felt disconnected from nature in their everyday lives. They come to drink ayahuasca to heal a personal malaise or affliction often ascribed to society's vicissitudes or a scarcity of authentic natural spirit.

Ayahuasca tourism can be situated among other examples of primitivist tourism (Stasch 2014, 2015; Desmond 1999) that aim to counteract modern life with an indigenous transcendence made utopic, fascinating, or sublime that is often charged with equal parts of fear and desire. Considering the boom in ethnic and tribal tourism that has emerged over the last few decades, Rupert Stasch (2014; 2016) suggested that, at its core, the "primitive" is an ideological formation that shapes extrasocial and intrasocial relations between visitors and the people being visited. With a problematic past in modern art and anthropology, the concept of the "primitive" nonetheless lives on in popular discourse, taking on new masks that still capture how tourists figure Indigenous peoples as an original, timeless, and primordial Other. Stasch defines "primitivist tourism" as a phenomenon wherein "leisure travelers from dominantly urban, industrialized countries seek meetings with people they understand to embody an archaic condition outside global consumer culture, marketized social relations, and the rule of states and proselytizing religions" (2015:433). It presents an opportunity to momentarily exit the strictures of modernity and encounter a way of life that is technologically and economically inferior but "superior in some aspects of spirit, social ethos, bodily aesthetics, or relations with nature" (Stasch 2014:195). Focusing on the globally-famous Korowai "tree house" or "Stone Age" peoples of West Papua, Stasch illustrated how a reflexive ambivalence was projected onto the Korowai as "monstrous inversions or utopian fulfillments" of the tourist's value commitments (193). The irony here, which Stasch unpacks, is that the objects of primitivist tourism—the Indigenous peoples—enact primitivism for the visitors as an opportunity to increase capital and enter modernity and the global economy.

Ayahuasca tourists arrive at the Amazon rainforest with similar ambivalent mores, but they differ from other types of primitivist tourists given they are seeking not leisure but healing and spiritual experiences. The challenging ceremonies of drinking ayahuasca—which may include terrifying visions and other sensory changes, along with violent acts of vomiting or purging—are hardly a leisure activity. Given this, the notion of tourism requires a critical unpacking to be adequately applied to analyses of intercultural ayahuasca centers in Amazonia.

Global visitors view their travels to Amazonia for ayahuasca as something more profound than tourism. Some researchers have taken a cynical angle and perceived the ayahuasca visitor as simply a "drug tourist . . . desperate to find the vanishing primitive" among "staged dramas" designed to "turn him on and extract his cash" (Dobkin de Rios 1994:17), yet the visitors typically reject the idea that they are "tourists" searching for "drugs" (Fotiou 2014:160, 2010; Winkelman 2005). During the late 1980s and early 1990s, researcher Jonathan Ott lamented the emergence of ayahuasca tourism. Concerned about how it was leading "inexorably to additional ecological and cultural disruption," Ott hoped that non-Indigenous ayahuasca drinkers would "stay home" and not travel to Amazonia, but rather should consume analogues or chemical equivalents of ayahuasca available from other plant sources (1996:254). Although concerns about the impact of tourism are legitimate, advocating firmly to "curtail ayahuasca tourism" (Ott 1996:254) ignores the many Indigenous voices cultivating the craft of treating the visitors. Also, it reproduces the perception that Indigenous societies are ahistorical and should be kept culturally "pristine" and outside of time and global relations (Fabian

2014). By contrast, anthropologist Laura Dev noted how "the performance of Shipibo healing rituals for outsiders can be seen as a way of reproducing the Shipibo lifeworld" (2019:159). Some international seekers of ayahuasca in Amazonia appear to play down the ways in which their presence is changing parts of Indigenous shamanism. This appears to be partly due to the positive powers many of them attribute to a vision of life beyond modernity.

The idealizations of the "primitive other," as expressed in the history of the Euro-American humanities (Lovejoy and Boas 1935; Torgovnick 1990) and in the everyday experience of ethnic tourism today (Stasch 2014), appears with new twists in ayahuasca neoshamanism. Ayahuasca signifies the consumption of primitivism as a medicine, which is remarkably novel in itself. By imbibing ayahuasca with Indigenous healers and entering an inner world of visions, enhanced meaning, and visceral intensity, the visitors embody a transcendental authenticity. Their existentially and psychologically vulnerable aspects become entangled in a therapeutic encounter that can foreground the power of Indigenous specialists. This allows for a certain reversal of power roles that is uncommon in other forms of ethnic tourism. The ayahuasca drinking ceremonies are described as resulting in life-changing healing for tourists—something that drug tourism and ordinary tourism generally do not entail.

During an ayahuasca retreat at Pachamama Temple, a fifty-eight-year-old male participant from the United States shared with the group, "I have suffered my whole life from anxiety, obsessive-compulsive disorder (OCD), and depression. I didn't come here for tourism or to blow my mind. I'm here for healing from the shamans." Ayahuasca retreats in Peru are generally more aligned with religious pilgrimage than recreational drug tourism given their emphasis on healing, self-transformation, and distant travels to sacred environments (Fotiou 2020:380). The profound and existential meaning of ayahuasca experiences are at odds with the banality of most tourism activities. Nonetheless, in this chapter, I cautiously employ the terms ayahuasca "tourist," "client," "visitor," "guest," or "participant" interchangeably and none of them in a pejorative or negative sense, but mainly to refer to mobility and the transient socialities of the clients in Peru. Similarly, local healers working at ayahuasca tourist centers commonly refer to clients as *pasajeros* (passengers), pointing to the visitors' tourist-like and transient behavior.

The hundreds of thousands of dollars needed to create and build a retreat in Peru, and the technical and cultural capabilities to run websites and market to international guests, have made it difficult for Indigenous experts to own their own successful ayahuasca business. Following the broader pattern of foreign-ownership dominating tourist enterprises in Latin America (Baud and Ypeij 2009:3), most ayahuasca tourist businesses in Peru are owned by entrepreneurs from North America and Europe. This brings ayahuasca tourism into the critical realms of what Martin Mowforth and Ian Munt termed a "new imperialism" (2003:51), with foreign investment driving novel dynamics of wealth and power.

Considering the boom in ayahuasca drinking in Peru, Daniela Peluso argued that the "emerging forms of entrepreneurism and cosmopolitanism of the ayahuasca industry participate in the historically ongoing economic and neo-colonization of South America in ways that privilege nonlocal profits and benefits" (2017:215). Some Shipibo healers in Pucallpa expressed frustration to me about the photos that visitors take of them. They believed the tourists take the photos home to the North and sell them for large amounts of money (see also Brabec de Mori 2014). When it was considering whether or not to collaborate with the popular ayahuasca information website Kahpi.net, a famous retreat center near Iquitos that is owned by a European entrepreneur suggested that their contracted Shipibo healers should be paid much less than what authors from North America and Europe are given for the same article type. If the Shipibo healers are paid too high, they suggested, it might create jealousy among the other healers.

Such asymmetries and inequalities of ayahuasca tourism are nothing new in Amazonia. However, the Pachamama Temple retreat center was somewhat unique in the ayahuasca tourism economy. It was co-owned by Shipibo healers in collaboration with a business partner from Poland. Most of the healers at Pachamama Temple had previously worked as ceremony contractors in foreign-owned ayahuasca healing centers in Iquitos and other remote Peruvian cities. They described how in these centers they were underpaid and needed to protect themselves from envious sorcery attacks committed by the other contracted healers.

Pachamama Temple was also different in the way it boasted a "more authentic" cultural experience for guests by including a range of interactions with healers beyond the ayahuasca ceremonies, such as brewing workshops,

Shipibo cultural lessons, multiple one-on-one conversations with healers, nature and boat adventures, and encounters with Shipibo youths from surrounding neighborhoods who visited a small school on the temple grounds each Sunday to learn Shipibo language and culture from healer Luis Marquez Pinedo. The healing center was also different given its positioning. Not located in a dense rainforest ecology but on the edges of Yarinacocha and surrounded by poor neighborhoods that have no running drinking water and limited electricity, Pachamama Temple brought guests closer to the reality of urban Shipibo life. Its retreat format was certainly crafted to inspire an enchanted encounter with otherworldly plant medicine, but the exotic otherness and mystique of the healers here were arguably less pronounced when compared to other popular retreats that are located in lush forest environments and that lack healer-guest interactions outside of the ayahuasca ceremonies.

HEALERS AND PASSENGERS

In the early darkness of the night at Pachamama Temple, the guests arrived and made themselves comfortable on their mattresses in anticipation of the evening ceremony. Before the Shipibo healers arrived, a facilitator from California conducted a forty-minute guided meditation session. We all relaxed into the soothing meditation, which began by directing us to follow our breath and slow our minds. The meditation built towards complex mental imagery and narrative scenes aimed at appreciating the virtues of acceptance, emancipation, and compassion. The guide finished by spraying sweet aromatic mist over each person.

Shortly after, the five Shipibo healers entered the *maloca* walking slow enough to navigate the darkness. Some whispered to each other. Others jovially laughed. And some healers quietly hummed or whistled ceremonial songs. They had their own mattresses circling the very middle of the *maloca* and were each equipped with stacks of *machapo* local cigars, four types of aromatic liquids, and a vomit bucket. After everyone had individually drunk the brew, including each healer, there was a period of thirty or forty-five minutes of silence as the thick syrup started to make its way through the gut. Some healers began to yawn, sometimes with a slight vibrato at the end of the yawn, calling in the spirits of different plant allies. Once the spirits arrived, the singing began. The healers each approached a guest and performed loud curative *icaros* or songs, generating a space in which a polyphonic soundscape of multiple songs occurred at the same time, each directed towards an individual guest. They sang, whistled, and blew over the guests to augment the visions and sensations of themselves and the guests.

At the end of each song, the healer would typically spray perfumed liquids over the guest from their mouth (this was before the Covid-19 pandemic). The guests were recommended to sit up and directly face the healer when receiving a song. But for many, the strength of the ayahuasca, or the combination of ayahuasca and the song, was so potent that they chose to lie down. The guests later described experiencing specific healing and special visions while receiving certain songs from particular healers. After around six or eight hours of songs, visions, and some occasional purging or vomiting, the ceremony finished in the early hours of the morning with a Shipibo healer striking a Tibetan prayer bowl three times. Over the months, as participants came and went through the center, they tended to identify the same two or three favorite healers. These healers were singing the most powerful and curative *icaros*, which appeared to have a greater ability to shape the guests' visionary journeys or produce more visionary narratives from them.

Many ayahuasca retreats in Peru appeared to minimize interactions between guests and Indigenous healers. This is most likely because healers are steeped in practices that push against key marketing efforts that target international clients. The notions of sorcery that underpin sickness etiologies, misfortune, and the phenomenology of ayahuasca experiences among Shipibo healers can elicit unwanted fear and confusion among visitors. The visitors come to dissolve their egos and embark upon visionary experiences deemed individual to the person having the vision. Nonetheless, these two worlds—Shipibo and global neoshamanic—overlap and interconnect. During each ayahuasca drinking ceremony at Pachamama Temple, with or without international guests, one healer always stayed in the middle of the *maloca* singing protective *icaros* or songs to fortify the ceremonial space. This allowed the other healers to sit in front of individual guests and transmit healing songs to them without needing to defend themselves against sorcery attacks launched by competitor shamans outside the retreat.

Although most psychedelic and ayahuasca information websites promoted users to surrender and dissolve into psychedelic visions, whether blissful or terrifying, the healers at Pachamama Temple proposed the opposite. If encountering negativity in visions—such as scary snakes, spiders, or monsters—then the ayahuasca drinker should "dominate" (*dominar*) the scary visions and will the negativity away. The goal is to banish the bad energies and promote positivity and joyful, fragrant, and luminous visions. According to the Shipibo healers, the ayahuasca drinker's bad or challenging visions are not merely reflections of his or her pathological mind or unresolved personal trauma but also are potentially signs of attack from powerful sorcerers or are negative energies from one person in the ceremony space unwittingly spilling over into another. As in other modes of Amazonian shamanism, the healers at Pachamama Temple encountered a visionary realm that is not otherworldly or confined to an individual's mind, but bustling with dangerous powers, intentions, and anxieties of ordinary social reality.

Conceptions of sorcery reside in a founding story of Pachamama Temple. All the healers working at the center are children of Mama Maria or are her

FIGURE 2.2 Ceremony *maloca*. Pachamama Temple, Peru, winter 2019. (Photo: Alex Gearin)

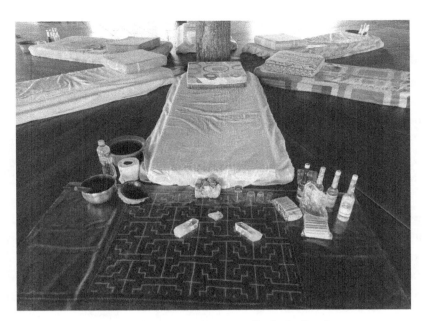

FIGURE 2.3 Shipibo *chaman*'s healing utensils, including four different-sized cups for administering ayahuasca to guests, thick raw "*mapacho*" tobacco, aromatic perfumes, quartz crystals, Tibetan prayer bowl, and bucket and tissue. (Photo: Alex Gearin)

FIGURE 2.4 Inside the ceremony *maloca* where visitors drink ayahuasca at Pachamama Temple, Peru, winter 2019. (Photo: Alex Gearin)

sons-in-law or nephew. She began her shamanic training in her late forties in the wake of her husband's death. She started drinking the brew in the hope of discovering the sorcerer who killed him. During her initiation periods and diets, she decided it was not right to revenge. Her daughter and sons described the tragedy of their father's death in ways that highlight increasing envy as a core issue of urban life. When they were young, their parents decided to leave the forest community and move to the edge of Pucallpa seeking to provide better education opportunities for them. The father was a great hunter, and while working as a groundskeeper for a wealthy man, he would go catch game at the end of the day to feed his family. He was allegedly murdered by urban sorcerers who were jealous of his hunting abilities. There is more envy in the cities than in the forest communities, the healers explained. Urban life thus is marked by an increased perception and ability to deal with envy. Several of her children found their calling to become a healer (*onanya*) and train with powerful plants after being attacked by sorcerers, experiencing sudden health problems, and desiring to heal and defend themselves and their family.

Four of the healers at Pachamama Temple were working on farms for low wages before joining the ayahuasca tourism economy. Two healers were language teachers who had undergone training in Spanish at local universities. In 2014, Bernd Brabec de Mori suggested that only a few dozen Shipibo lived well on the ayahuasca tourism economy. In 2019, the figure was likely larger given the increased number of tourist lodges. However, according to many Shipibo, becoming a shaman is not an ordinary or even respected path. When I asked the healers at Pachamama Temple if they want their children to become healers, they each told me "no" or looked somewhat confused by the question. The desire to become a shaman is typically not determined by personal choice, they told me. It is often the result of a crisis, such as being magically attacked by a shaman and then needing to learn how to cure and defend oneself—something most parents would not want for their child. Instead, all the healers at the temple hoped their children would study at university and become "professionals." Today, as in the past, many Shipibo strive to become *onanya joni*, or a wise person (Espinosa 2012). Shamans are called *onanya*, and thus the notion of a wise person finds its roots in shamanism. But, whereas *onanya* have typically drawn their supreme knowledge from relations with plant spirits and other shamanic sources mediated by ayahuasca and similar concoctions (Roe 1982, Luna 1986, Brabec de Mori 2012), this was not the only way to become *onanya joni*. In essence, the ideal of being a Shipibo wise person constitutes an ability to guarantee "food, safety, and wellbeing" for children while also being generous and caring to extended family and outsiders (Espinosa 2012:458). Thus anyone can become such a wise person, not only shamans, and Espinosa (2012) notes how these values are being maintained through new processes for Shipibo living in urban settings that require new strategies for assuring the safety and wellbeing of children and caring for family members and outsiders. To become *onanya joni* today also means accumulating large amounts of financial capital.

The healers at Pachamama Temple pursued the ideal of *onanya joni* by each drinking strong doses of ayahuasca approximately 130 nights of the year while performing healing *icaro* songs for tourists who were generally seeking to cure mental health issues or life crises. The healers told me they do this work because they wanted to heal people, and also because they wanted to afford good lives for their families. As explored further on, this key value of maximizing capital provides a stark contrast to the visiting guests' primitivist perception of the shamanic ceremonies.

Ayahuasca tourist centers in Peru are hubs of interculturality and social change steeped in contradiction and mutual misunderstandings (Losonczy and Cappo 2014). As Peluso and Alexiades (2006) have described, ayahuasca tourism includes a "hyper-traditionalism" forged by a double dislocation: Indigenous healers are dislocated from the place, context, and moral order of their existing local shamanic practices, and ayahuasca tourists are dislocated from their homelands and ordinary cultural realities when embarking on pilgrimages to the Amazon rainforest.

International ayahuasca drinkers in Peru are unique tourists. While many types of primitivist tourism draw abundantly upon fascination, ayahuasca tourism tends to embody a more pressing drive associated with illness, disease, and healing. For visitors, drinking ayahuasca with Shipibo shamans is numinous and lends itself to what religious scholar Rudolf Otto (1958) described as the *mysterium tremendum et fascinans*. Yet fascination, awe, and wonder were not enough to satisfy the "personal intentions" that each participant was asked to cultivate and bring to the retreats. In dedicated activities at the beginning of each retreat, the participants talked about their intentions with each other, which commonly included to overcome family-related trauma, drug addictions or alcoholism, or to bring insight to healing the sources of anxiety, depression, OCD, or other problems. Some participants' intentions were more spiritual and posthumanist and included a desire to find their spirit-animal guide, reconnect with their "higher-self," or become a shaman. But more often than not, they hoped the mysterious and tremendous experience would bring relief from specific maladies and suffering, and this positioned shamans as more like psychic technicians than religious icons or saints. Such pragmatism was emphasized in the metaphors the participants used to describe the healers. Shipibo shamans were "psychic plumbers" who unblocked trauma by helping the participants purge, "spiritual artists" who sang healing patterns into spiritually fractured bodies, and "ancient guides" who uncovered the truth of the self and its "ancestral programming." Psychoactive substances like ayahuasca appear to enhance sensations of meaningfulness in consumers (Hartogsohn 2018), and when visitors perceive in their own ayahuasca visions the iconic *kené* Shipibo designs or witness Shipibo "ancient guides" healing "broken DNA" in their family ancestry, what might have begun as a vague view of archaic and primordial shamans suddenly becomes an embodied healing reality infused with noetic significance.

The tourists arrive with heterogeneous problems and illnesses they hope to cure, and this hope can rest upon a homogeneous primitivism. Their suffering and affliction are experienced as planetary problems in which there is a pathological absence of natural energies in modern societies and urban lifestyles. Searching for healing among a simpler way of life, the ayahuasca visitors value acts of behavioral, psychological, and social negation and purging. They remove themselves from their metropolitan lives of work and family and enter into a minimalist habitation, including a reduced diet and little-to-no time spent on phones, laptops, and social media. They undergo a simplification of everyday behavior to try come into better alignment with nature. They experience a routine of flower baths, drinking daily "plant medications" for "opening the heart and mind," embarking on "jungle tours" while listening to supernatural stories of animals and plants, and, ultimately, drinking ayahuasca in ceremonies with Indigenous healers. In dramatic visionary and bodily acts, they purge traumas associated with family, work, society, and "the system." The symbolic gravity of negating, reducing, releasing, and purifying that permeates these activities represents a semiotic complex that builds upon existing primitivist imaginaries of relinquishing modern life for something more basic and primordial.

As participants progress through the retreat programs—which were seven or twelve days in duration—they tended to become quieter, more reserved, and more introspective. A sense of greater calm, peace, and general exhaustion was commonly expressed, often accompanied by feelings of gratitude to ayahuasca and the healers. When not engaging in the scheduled group activities, the participants meandered the retreat space, relaxing in hammocks and reading spiritual books, meditating in the gardens, writing personal journals, sharing stories with each other about the struggles and joys of their lives, or playing games with Shipibo children.

During a "flower bath" activity, when healers pour cold water infused with essential oils and fresh herbs over the guests, I was sitting in the hot sun with bare feet on the sandy ground next to Michael, a twenty-eight-year-old white New Zealander and electrician. He shared with me that he admired how the healers live such a simple life, adding, "We strive for so much wealth, but it doesn't bring us what we want. They are so happy and laughing, being together all the time. That's all they need." Like the other guests, Michael imagined a utopic primitivism, or a good life made from, to quote him, "removing all the unnecessary shit until the basics are left." Michael came to the retreat, he told the group, on a mission to accept himself, to "loosen the grip" of his ego, and to heal family trauma. One morning after drinking the brew, he enthusiastically shared with the other guests a powerful vision he had the night before. It included seeing a totem pole covered in beautiful naked human bodies, entwined, dancing slowly, their skin calmly breathing and glowing at the same pulse as his skin. During the vision, he felt forgiveness for the only person who had ever really hurt him and then love for his family members and friends back in New Zealand. He was also guided by a hummingbird covered in Shipibo patterns to see "forgotten images" of his youth, which made him vomit ferociously. All these visions, he concluded, made him realize how he had neglected his family through "striving to be a real man." The simple and joyful service of the family of healers at Pachamama Temple provided Michael with a primitivist encounter within a visionary environment that reinvigorated a positive attitude towards his own family. Ayahuasca, he shared with the group, strengthened his desire to support his depressed brother.

The Indigenous healers arrive at ceremonies and retreat activities embodying shamanic qualities that the tourists covet. As Oscar Calavia Sáez pointed out, ayahuasca has become "the motor of a missionary enterprise that Indigenous Amazonians have directed towards the same societies that bombarded them with their own missionaries for centuries" (2014: xxiii). Ayahuasca is a missionary motor in the sense of being shamanic, spiritual, or religious. But it is also a potent therapeutic mixture, and the health distinction adds a critical participatory edge in which primitivism is tied to the bodily and existential through sickness and healing. For ayahuasca tourists, a core value of the minimal—or a spiritual minimalism—is pursued through therapeutic agencies of the archaic, primitive, and natural. The pain of capital accumulation and materialism, the hallmarks of Michael's drive to "becoming a real man," is healed by a medicine and way of life that ideally is void of such things.

The tourists' positive perception of the lower economic standards of Indigenous healers represents a special kind of negative value regime. Several retreat participants expressed a preference for Pachamama Temple over more expensive and luxurious ayahuasca retreat centers in Costa Rica or European societies, stating that it is more authentic drinking ayahuasca with a Shipibo family in the "actual settings that they live." Here, ayahuasca is made authentic by its associations with relative poverty and "basic" material living conditions. In this sense, ayahuasca tourists are not ignoring the ambient poverty and economic scarcity of the healers but using it to reassure themselves of the authenticity of ayahuasca practice in a positive manner.

Desires for material wealth and capital, including for luxurious services such as hot water, electricity, personal bathrooms, and wifi, are complicated by the ayahuasca tourist market and its therapeutic primitivism. Such complication has placed the healers in a paradox that will be familiar to tourism scholars (Minca and Oakes 2006), wherein tourism objects—such as secluded beaches, "traditional" culture, national parks—are eroded or challenged by tourism activities. As we will now see, such a paradox has structured novel cosmological dimensions of Shipibo shamanistic practice.

CHANGING SHIPIBO THERAPIES

Ayahuasca tourism has introduced changes to Shipibo shamanistic practices in recent decades. Amazonian shamanism often involved social egalitarianisms (Hugh-Jones 1996; Viveiros de Castro 2014; Taylor 2018). Kaj Århem (1996) introduced the notion of "cosmonomics" to describe how shamanism works as a powerful means of limiting food accumulation through fears of retribution from nature spirits. Describing Jivaroan individuation practices of drinking ayahuasca and encountering the terrifying *arutam* spirit, Anne Christine Taylor (2018) explained how social competition "can never solidify into fixed positions of dominance" and that "achieved eminence automatically breeds challenge, and thus carries with it the seeds of its erosion" (44, 50). A resistance towards fixed social hierarchies can also be observed in pervasive understandings of health and healing in the horizontal-type of Amazonian shamanism.

In what has been termed a moral ambiguity complex, the magical arts that healers employ to cure can also be used for harm, and indeed, the act of healing sometimes required an act of magical harm (Whitehead and Wright 2004). Sorcery occurs at the opposite end of tranquillity, a key value across Amazonian societies. The magical arts involve currents of intention, and visionary performances and songs, that channel that which risks upsetting a peaceful, good life. As others have noted, this intrinsically ambiguous side of Indigenous ayahuasca use has hardly been embraced by ayahuasca tourists in Amazonia (Fausto 2004:172; Peluso and Alexiades 2006:74; Dobkin de Rios and Rumrrill 2008:12), nor has it been mentioned, in any widespread social significance, operating across non-Indigenous ayahuasca drinkers across the planet.

To unpack some new configurations of moral cosmology among Shipibo healers working at tourist centers, it helps to consider what preceded them. In the early 1970s, before ayahuasca tourists, Bruno Illius (1992) conducted an extensive study of Shipibo shamanism among rainforest communities near Pucallpa and recorded that healers virtually always associated disease and misfortune with sorcery from jealous and envious human or nonhuman persons. He described a closed cosmological system wherein the pathogenic substances that ayahuasca shamans see in patients' bodies cannot be destroyed but must circulate across the social body politic. He explained,

> [T]he shaman is able to remove *nihue* (or spirit essence) from a sick body but he cannot destroy it. If he doesn't want the *nihue* to stay in his immediate environment or on himself, he has to recast it on another living being who doesn't possess enough *shinan* (power) to repulse it. Thus, in curing one, he is always bewitching another. . . . The shaman, as manipulator of energies, sees his world with respect to the sum total of *nihue* and *shinan* as a closed system. (1992:71)

A different image of retributive shamanism has emerged in the ayahuasca tourist contexts. The healers at Pachamama Temple all told me that they would rather heal visitors than locals, not simply because visitors pay around ten times more money for their service, but also because visitors are easier to heal than locals. The *nihue* affecting the bodies of the international visitors, they explained, is weaker and different from that affecting Shipibo.

In contrast to Illius's description of a closed cosmological system in which spirit essence must circulate, the healers at Pachamama Temple employ a novel shamanic technology that enables them to vaporize and completely obliterate the bad energies of the visitors. One healer described it as, when he drinks ayahuasca and sings over a patient, he can see the bad *nihue* in their body appear like a dark cloud. His magical song blasts the dark cloud until the bad energy starts raining down and drains away from the body. When I asked, "But where does it go?", it is weak *nihue*, so it just disappears. Another healer described the difference, saying,

> [W]hen I sing over a *pasajero* [ayahuasca visitor], my medicine penetrates their body. I can see their body and energy. We remove the bad energies, leave him healed, and open his visions. But working with Shipibo patients can be different. There is a lot of black magic here, and people come with a lot of harm. Also, many people learn bad spells. The *pasajeros* don't arrive with witchcraft harms. They are just sick with mental disorders

and delusions, such as alcohol and drug addictions. Those cases are easy to heal. Being a *chaman* is easy; it's not tiring work, but *curanderismo* is very hard.

The healers make a distinction between *chamans* and *curanderos*. The first heals foreigners, the second Shipibo and local clients. In the new cosmological environment of international tourism, healers are not dealing with powerful sorcery substances in tourist patients' bodies, nor are they required to cure illness by generating harm elsewhere. The guests have introduced a lucrative-sounding opportunity for healers to drink ayahuasca and provide therapeutic services to persons not concerned with local moral economies of envy, jealousy, and other social afflictions.

As objects of primitivist fantasies, Shipibo healers are positioned outside the complicated moral space of *curanderismo* as a timeless, archaic Other. From this position, they can neutralize the bad energies of the visitors and make them evaporate into nothingness. Reckoning with the source of the visitors' illness is largely avoided from the perspective of the healers. They are tasked with magically cleansing the visitor's sickness with songs and plant spirit helpers. They are not embedded in a closed moral system of the foreign client's meaningful social universe. They operate a transient and detached moral service. The presence of wealthy international visitors with spiritual problems that are *not* ascribed to sorcery has thus opened a novel market in which foreign individualized illness and affliction are extinguished by new, generic song-healing techniques.

But the monetary value of working at the international retreats brings new shamanic problems for the healers, specifically jealousy from rival healers. When guests from abroad pay thousands of dollars to travel to remote Peru to undergo an ayahuasca retreat, they observe, on the way from airports to the retreat centers in Iquitos and Pucallpa, the slums, poverty, and general scarcity that many locals experience in the region. Likewise, locals observe the inverse and perceive the arrival of ayahuasca tourists as embodiments of wealth and the opposite of scarcity. This economic divide can easily promote envy towards the visitors and towards the locals who charge them for healing services. Not considering ayahuasca tourism but a similar Indigenous con-

GLOBAL AYAHUASCA

text of urbanization, Carolina Izquierdo and Allen Johnson suggested that envy and sorcery among Machiguenga have increased in urban contexts due to "greater inequality, more competition for resources, and increased societal and personal stress" (2007:421; see also Izquierdo, Johnson, and Shepard 2008). The association of rising envy and sorcery with urban living conditions represents an example of what George Foster termed "deprivation society" (1972:168), when scarcity and envy are mutually enforced in contexts of overt inequality. In the context of ayahuasca tourism, the international guests' bodies may arrive "clean" from sorcery "harms," but the ceremonies in which they receive healing mark a challenging space for healers, who need to protect each other against magical attacks from powerful enemies and rivals.

Accusations of envy and sorcery circulate the moral economy of healers and provide a negative discourse to illustrate and define ideals of being good, virtuous, and respectable. A key issue for the healers I talked with was the risk of unprofessional Shipibo serving ayahuasca without proper training and skills. One healer, working outside Pachamama Temple, explained that the untrained are robbing ayahuasca tourists with fake ceremonies that do not heal, but, also, that he is "not envious or hateful" towards the charlatans, and that he "doesn't feel those things." The drive to deflect accusations of envy is occurring within a lucrative economy of serving ayahuasca to wealthy international clients, in which, to quote another Shipibo healer, "fake" healers are "trying to overcome poverty by robbing our culture of its beauty." The minimalist material conditions of most Shipibo may represent a tonic for the ills of modern life for the ayahuasca visitors. However, they reflect a troubling issue of economic precarity and ambient poverty for healers that intersects with accusations of charlatans and narratives of sorcery and visionary defense.

The dramatic difference in economic standards and material conditions of existence between ayahuasca tourists and most Shipibo healers structure parallel streams of sorcery and healing. On the one hand, economic competition shapes sorcery acts that are observed in Shipibo descriptions of illness, disease, and misfortune and the healer's visions of snakes, spiders, and storms. On the other hand, the international visitors gain healing by momentarily renouncing the trappings of their own wealthy lives—to shake off modern life—and enter a therapeutic primitivism. In ayahuasca tourism, asymmetrical economic relations between healer and patient are fused into a cosmic

GLOBAL SHAMANIC TOURISM IN PERU   91

service. Such relations structure the intensification of sorcery, given the allure of large capital that wealthy international visitors bring.

CAPITALIST TENSIONS

Shipibo shamanism is no longer a means of dealing with the uncertainty and dangers of the natural environment, the missionary plagues of the seventeenth and eighteenth centuries, or the patrones of the extractive rubber tapping industries. Today, in places like Pachamama Temple, shamanism has come to represent a visionary confrontation with the conditions of urban life, economic precarity, and competitive individualism. Now Indigenous shamans must deal with entities attuned to the messy flow of capital, merchandise, and urban politics. The many songs for cleansing and protection in tourist ceremonies are a prophylactic against disease and illness and the envious energies of antagonistic competitors who are testing the healers' powers and trying to weaken or destroy them. In parallel, the drive to increase clients and expand the healing center meets the danger of increased attacks by municipal politicians and police trying to extort money. While capitalism situates competition as foundational to its ideal of incentivizing the production of valuable labor, shamanic competition, from the healers' perspective, was framed as an antagonistic, poisonous, and potentially lethal motivation that risks destroying them and their families.

The healers ideally draw their motivations from sources other than competing. When asked about the time a British guest seemingly had an ayahuasca-induced psychotic episode that lasted for several days, Maestro Juan explained that he becomes energized by the challenge to treat such a person. Such cases can require the shaman to drink extra ayahuasca to "dominate" the visions of the rowdy guest and to bring tranquillity and more calm back to the room. The healer's motivation ideally comes from testing his abilities to cure against the guest's illness or condition, and motivational sources derived from competing with other shamans are feared pathological in their association with envy and sorcery. During a Shipibo education session with one healer and a group of ayahuasca tourists, a Canadian guest asked about sorcery, enquiring "Why do people attack you?" Juan, the healer, replied,

We ask ourselves the same question. Think of it like this: all the countries want to be the best. It is the same with shamanism. There is much envy and problems. Now there are no shamanic wars, so things are better. But, instead, all the Shipibo are battling for modern things, merchandise, technology. But why the battle? We don't understand it.

The healers, here, explain to the guests that they have never learned how to retribute against the attackers, but only to cleanse. One story circulated among healers that a previous healer was always very curious about who was sending magical attacks and would engage them in an effort to learn. This, they said, invited more attacks, and eventually she was asked to leave.

The healers' ideal state was to be without envy, however attacks by envious *curanderos* can increase when a healer or center receives greater international recognition and customers. The simultaneous negation and escalation of sorcery that international tourists bring to Shipibo healers—by not arriving with sorcery harms in their bodies, but with significant capital that invokes envy among competitor healers—can co-occur during the same ceremonial situation. The ethnographic vignette described at the beginning of the Introduction illustrates this. Maestro Juan remained in the center of the ceremonial hall, singing protective songs to fortify the space, and began struggling with sorcery attacks while the guests gained personal healing by being taken in and out of their own suffering—related to personal family trauma—while following Juan's musical journey.

Juan was allegedly being attacked by jealous rival shamans at other retreats. "Pachamama is surrounded by sorcery because it is globally recognized," Maestro Ricardo told me. Reflecting on the vulnerabilities of the temple, Juan described how these particular sorcerers were attempting to "screw our passengers [clients], to make them think we are not masters and we know nothing and can't manage anything . . . that was their intention. But we said, *We're a family, the union gives us strength.* No one is going to make us fall, and no matter what, Pachamama will keep going forward."

The challenges of ayahuasca tourism appear in the healers' visionary encounters, such as when Juan had to deal with sorcery thieves across several ceremonies. Sorcery in ayahuasca tourism, therefore, differs from the global phenomenon of occult economies in which capital accumulation is gained from "commercial enchantments" like Tarot reading services, "dial-a-diviner," or "witchcraft summits" (Comaroff and Comaroff 2001:19–22). Sorcery in ayahuasca tourism does not serve clients but is manifest among service providers who are operating in environments of ambient poverty while trying to capitalize on the client's cosmic rejections of modern life. It is less an occult economy than a response to the socially disruptive force of capital and its inequalities.

Sorcery ideas and practices at ayahuasca tourist lodges are relatively hidden from international guests, and this indicates a social division in the occult economy. The main reason, it seems, is that sorcery does not sell well among the visitors. The emphasis on turning ayahuasca into medicine for the global market may help avoid the negative stereotyping of shamanism by sanitizing it as purely curative (Calavia Sáez 2011:135; Davidov 2010:392). But such sanitizing is a potent means of ignorance too. The denial of the reality of Shipibo sorcery by the international clients can be seen as a kind of secular enchantment that provides them with an ethical immunity against conceptualizing the dramatic inequalities that exist between them and the healers. By approaching negative, challenging, or "bad" ayahuasca visions as an individual and purely psychological phenomenon, and not an immediate social affliction like sorcery, the international guests are relatively blind to the capitalist anxieties of the healers' ayahuasca work and to their own implication in helping produce such anxieties.

The logic of capital, which now mediates the key Shipibo ideal of becoming an *onanya joni* in urban contexts characterized by financial expenses (such as education for children and the ownership of property or land), is changing moral-cosmological configurations of ayahuasca curing practices. In the retreats, capital appears to have changed the closed system circulation of *nihue* or spirit essence in a way that articulates with ideals of progress and a repetitive system of accumulation wherein tourist *nihue* can simply be annihilated. Freed from the social and moral issues of the tourists' lives, the healers somewhat transcend an egalitarian or relational shamanism aimed at flattening hierarchy and can scale their business without clients directly expecting them to enter the murky space of sorcery and its social tensions. This enables healers to expand their market by providing large group ceremonies and singing generic healing songs that are oceans away from the real-world tensions of the client's meaningful social reality.

Ayahuasca ceremonies have paradoxically become a source of progress and capital accumulation for Indigenous healers who are providing what visitors experience as an ahistorical space of mystical relief from the anxieties of modern life. The visitors often claim that drinking ayahuasca has generated life-changing healing for them, but as Jeremy Narby (2019) pointed out, "The Amazonian people who attend to them [typically get] some form of payment, but probably nothing so life-changing." By making ayahuasca an archaic and primordial antidote for sicknesses ascribed to the lifeworlds of people mainly from the wealthiest countries, the commercial agency of Indigenous healers, and their drive for social change along the lines of capital accumulation, becomes stunted by new paradoxes of primitivist tourism.

In tourist ceremonies, Shipibo acts of defense against sorcery represent tensions between the rapid social change that touristic capital brings and the social control inherent in discourses of *brujeria*. But these historical shamanic means of dealing with inequity and power through sorcery do not penetrate the tourist's imagination which, rather, requires new techniques of healing that synthesize primitivism into a pharmacological and ceremonial therapy. Considering such a paradox of ayahuasca tourism, filmmaker Jerónimo Mazarrasa (2019) called for more symmetry in the exchange of value between tourists and healers, while concluding that "we are both sick, from different things, and we have no choice but to help each other heal." If, how, and to what extent reciprocal healing can be achieved in the awkward challenge of commercializing therapeutic primitivism is a good topic for future studies.

What is anthropology to make of the influence of primitivist markets on the changing lives of Indigenous healers and their families and communities? Before the 1980s, anthropology tended to view Indigenous healing through the notion of "primitive medicine." It placed Indigenous medicine on the inferior side of binaries such as magic and science, traditional and modern, stasis and progress (Greene 1998:635). While anthropology is undergoing a reflexive period to heavily deconstruct such analytical othering as politically and theoretically problematic, ayahuasca tourism and its healing practices build upon an intercultural cosmology that reifies (and contests) such distinctions. For many ayahuasca tourists, the ahistorical stasis of Indigenous shamanism is therapeutic, relieving, and a retreat outside of modern life's pathological progress.

In a classic primitivist style, a popular scientific review article that synthesizes medical research on ayahuasca echoed these binaries with the title "The Therapeutic Potentials of Ayahuasca: Possible Effects Against Various Diseases of Civilization" (Frecska, Bokor, and Winkelman 2016). The ayahuasca economy has boomed in recent decades partly because the intercultural ceremonies help improve mental health for many people from the "civilized" wealthy countries of the North. Yet untangling why ayahuasca primitivism can be so healing from an anthropological perspective could require a reflexive interpretive stance that risks dismantling the very binaries which enable it to exist.

Anthropologists are trained to view binaries such as "traditional" and "modern" and "primitive" and "civilized" with discontent or irony, and this throws the therapeutic activities of Amazonian ayahuasca retreats into an awkward space. Anthropological deconstruction can become oddly imposing and even antithetical to ayahuasca healers and those they treat.

THREE

WONDER AND HEALING ON RETREAT

Ayahuasca is a wondrous thing. It is remarkable that a brew of plants can temporarily turn sounds into visions, give aromatic fumes the power to intoxicate the whole body, and open visionary worlds that illuminate with a vividness more pronounced than ordinary sight. Psychologist Benny Shanon underscored these qualities, describing ayahuasca visions as "marvelous, and when powerful they introduce drinkers to what seem to be enchanted realities that fill them with wonder and awe" (2002:17). The brew is so enigmatic that if it does not express some kind of amazement or shock in drinkers, this lack of reaction is itself something to consider. Why ayahuasca was rendered unworthy of astonishment by missionary priests, colonial technocrats, and foreign explorers for many centuries is a curious thing. Although the freedom and propensity to marvel openly at ayahuasca has not been distributed evenly, this chapter primarily explores the mysterious appeal rather than the unusual indifference or aversion the brew has evoked in people.

Wonder and awe are states of mind characterized by a diminishing sense of self (Stellar 2021) and a greater sense of absorption and fluidity between mind and world and imagination and perception (Lifshitz, van Elk, and Luhrmann 2019). Tanya Luhrmann and colleagues demonstrated the cultural variability of states of absorption among spiritual practices across the globe. They explored how socialization into the practices not only shaped how spiritual experiences were interpreted by practitioners, but that it collectively directed attention in ways that changed the cognitive nature of the experiences: "When people pay attention differently, certain patterns of experience become more habituated and more fluent for members of that social group" (Luhrmann 2020:153), which the author described as the cultural kindling of spiritual experiences.

In ayahuasca tourism, guests have a notably limited amount of interaction with Shipibo healers, a factor that plays into the kinds of ayahuasca experiences they have. This chapter demonstrates how this minimal immersion into Shipibo lifeworlds enhances the awe-inspiring nature of the guests' ayahuasca experiences. The participants' journey into mesmerizing visionary realms is precipitated by an abrupt exposure to the unfamiliarity of cultural otherness. The fluency of the ecstatic experience appears partly generated by the rawness of social difference and a lack of habituation between guests and healers.

This chapter explores the relational dynamics of wonder among retreats at Pachamama Temple in Peru, drawing inspiration from anthropologists who have treated wonder as a mood, experience, or discourse that challenges ontological foundations (Scott 2016; Srinivas 2018). Delving into Michael Scott's proposition that "wherever there is a strong or intensified mood of wonder . . . this may be a clue that received ontological assumptions are in crisis and undergoing transformation" (2014:44), I investigate the relationship between wonder and healing at these global ayahuasca retreats. Guests in Peru hoped for different transformations, ranging from the alleviation of distress to the attainment of peace, the restoration of health, or the transition from a state of malaise to one of meaning. While certain forms of wonder at Pachamama Temple seemed integral to these goals, other latent possibilities of wonder were overlooked, deemed trivial, fanciful, even pathological. This chapter does not focus on what I think is wondrous but on what inspired wonder among the ayahuasca visitors and healers I studied. Wonder ranges in intensity, and I am *not* referring to mundane acts, such as when someone wonders what time the bus will arrive or what they will have for dinner, but to deeper responses to what is deemed extraordinary. Wonder has been defined as an epistemic emotion (Paulson, Sideris, Steller, and Valdesolo 2021; Candiotto 2019). The contextual shaping of deep wonder is related to its ambiguous nature as both thought and emotion. Compared to shock or surprise, we wonder when our understandings become insufficient. Wonder is "intentional, in the sense that it is directed *at* something, like fear and other such responses, and it is cognitive in that it presupposes certain perceptions or beliefs, especially evaluations of what is perceived" (Sherry 2013:349). The violation of expectations that comes with experiencing wonder can shine brightly by eroding our mental models of the world.

Historians and anthropologists have examined wonder beyond its therapeutic, poetic, and aesthetic associations and recast it as an ethical and political mood (Hughes-Warrington 2018; Vincent 2017). Eve Vincent argued that "wonder is a sentiment that arises from the shock of the new but that shock needs to be grounded in the broader political and historical processes that are at play" (Vincent 2017; Scott 2017). Wonder can emerge from a sense of ontological instability that undoes the bolts of ordinary values, political tendencies, and moral horizons. Wonder can also impute and strengthen preexisting values and moral perspectives by blasting them with a hitherto level of astonishment and mystery.

In this chapter, the guests' seek healing with ayahuasca while experiencing various kinds of wonder, including when directed at the powers of the healer, the intensity of the visions, the mystery of purging, and the enigma of plant spirits. Wonder is an openness towards the non-ordinary, the space of mystery, but there are limits. Only particular ideas and experiences tended to evoke wonder in the guests.

MERCHANTS OF WONDER

Psychedelic substances like ayahuasca generate wonder at various levels of self and society. Referring to the stigmatization and negative propaganda surrounding psychedelic substances in the late 1960s, the American countercultural icon Timothy Leary is said to have brazenly suggested that LSD can inspire delusions among people who have never taken it. The outsider perspective on psychedelics can arouse a range of reactions, including fear and concern, but also a mysterious attraction. A sense of profound curiosity sometimes emerges among people who have never consumed the substances.

A good example is the story of a historian of classical Greek who spent ten years writing a fascinating book about a hidden psychedelic religion in European history. Brian Muraresku wrote *The Immortality Key* (2020) and sustained a zealous fascination towards psychedelic substances while allegedly remaining personally naive to the dazzling experiences he had investigated in vivid detail. His psychedelic sobriety, he explained, was motivated by the desire for his scholarly work to be taken seriously in academic circles.

The book guides readers with a sense of unfolding mystery that resembles an Indiana Jones blockbuster. Psychedelic substances often inspire a deep sense of wonderment in those who consume them, and in some cases, among those who have not consumed them. Part of their strange appeal appears to emerge from a series of paradoxes. LSD, psilocybin mushrooms, mescaline cactus, and ayahuasca historically have been demonized, criminalized, and pathologized by many social institutions and individuals, yet also sacralized, legitimated, and medicalized by others. Walking the sober line between such morally charged poles is ripe for evoking wonder.

For Mama Maria and her family of Shipibo healers in remote Peru, ayahuasca elicited a range of sensations that embodied a dynamic different from the paradoxes described above. They found special kinds of inspiration in their private ayahuasca drinking together, but they were also merchants of wonder who cultivated the mysterious art of curing foreigners. By appreciating how the foreigners they treated were typically unfamiliar with ayahuasca and arrived with a desire to transcend the stress and malaise of their modern lifestyles, the healers actively tried to evoke wonder by singing shamanic songs, sharing marvelous stories, and embodying a passion towards sociocultural differences. Ayahuasca also presented the healers with the opportunity of generating enough capital to secure a better future against the ambient poverty and harsh living conditions of the area. Ayahuasca was both mundane and wondrous to the healers in its ubiquity and its promise of helping them overcome precarity.

The healers often brought a level of playfulness to ceremonies that is somewhat unique (or refreshing) in the global context. Some neoshamanic ayahuasca drinkers in Australia, by contrast, arrived at the retreats in Australia with a very serious attitude. For these adepts, healing was approached

GLOBAL AYAHUASCA

like an important exam or a somber visit to the doctor. They were usually quiet, focused, contemplative, maybe pensive, and had come to "do the hard work" of healing, which involved a courageous dignity towards the seriousness of drinking ayahuasca. They contributed to generating an atmosphere that reflects the ceremonial order and gravity of Indigenous rituals depicted in some popular films, such as the final scene in *The Lost City of Z* (2016) when the English explorer Percy Fawcett drinks a deadly potion in a remote area of the Amazon Rainforest. In the scene, drums beat in a predictable and slow rhythm while Indigenous characters are spread across a landscape, holding candles, chanting in unison. There is a soberness to the ceremony that is expressed through a strict orchestration.

By contrast, many Shipibo healers today embody an almost diametrically opposed attitude. Joy, humor, and spontaneity are esteemed qualities when drinking ayahuasca. Such an approach is more Dionysian than Apollonian. As Michael Taussig (1987:443) pointed out, Indigenous ayahuasca drinking has often been far more chaotic and exuberant than anthropologists have liked to acknowledge. Shipibo healer Pedro Tango Lopez explained to me that he interpreted the foreigner's desire for ceremonial order as reflecting an unhealthy way of relating socially. Maestro Pedro said that many foreigners who came to drink ayahuasca with him arrived with a "cold and suspicious" attitude, whereas Shipibo typically "have a warm life when it comes to human relationships . . . we're very friendly, very happy, very warm, very talkative." This warmth, he added, is a "really big fortune. It's really valuable."

> We don't have much land or wealth, no airplanes, no cars, no mansions, but we have what a latest model car can't give you. We feel a great internal happiness. Our interior is filled with happiness and joy . . . ayahuasca helps us strengthen this value. The real masters of ayahuasca are the ones that start to feel this kind of energy inside and then what they do is help, help, help with it. That's our mission. That's our job. That's our responsibility. . . . The big benefit foreigners receive when they visit us in our communities in the Amazon rainforest is they return home with a new type of warm happiness.

A kind of warm happiness was on full display during the ayahuasca ceremonies at Pachamama Temple. When the healers arrived at the quiet and dark *maloca* at around 7:00 p.m., the guests had already completed a guided meditation for one hour and then remained in a private and introspective state for another hour. The healers got comfortable in the space, whispering to each other, giggling and joking, whistling tunes, sustaining a warm sociality. Maestro Jose opened the glass bottle and the pressure created a gas-release sound indicating the ayahuasca had accidentally fermented. Some healers giggled getting ready to drink and serve a brew that would likely upset the stomach more than usual.

Sometimes when Maestro Juan finished singing a healing *icaro* to a guest, with both parties dosed on ayahuasca, he erupted into a joyous and full-body laughter for a few seconds before moving on to the next guest. When I asked during the sober hours of daylight what was so funny, he responded, "Many things. Some *pasajeros* [visitors] try to block my *icaros* from entering their bodies. I don't know why they do this. It's funny." Bernd Brabec de Mori explained that provocative humor and playfulness have an important value among "Shipibo people [who] often share a fairly burlesque air among themselves" (2014:223). During ayahuasca sessions, the healers may draw upon a genre of "funny songs" or "laughing songs" called *osanti*, which come from the mouths of special animals sung through the healer, including the howler monkey, the dog, and the parrot. The ludic quality of the songs, which include "singing errors," are directed at various people and circumstances and also used to cheer up sick patients (Brabec de Mori 2012:83; 2014). Luis Eduardo Luna remarked about ayahuasca that "there is sometimes great humor in these inner realms" (2016:270). Maestro Juan's joy and larger-than-life attitude appeared part of the reason he was often praised by the hundreds of international guests that visited the retreat annually.

To put this in global context, many antidrug perspectives today might perceive ayahuasca as a psychoactive drug among other substances that promote hedonistic and addictive propensities. But it would be particularly unfair to term Juan's playful approach to ayahuasca as "recreational drug use" and bring it into the orbit of all that. Jonathan Ott (1996:16) pointed out how terms like "recreational" and "intoxication" prejudice and cheapen our understanding of psychedelic use by wrongly conflating it with alcohol consumption, video games, and pinball machines, including when substances like ayahuasca help inspire ludic, pleasurable, and playful experiences. He provided the neutral adjective "ludible," or that which is joyful and playful (16) to refer to the fun and humorous experiences of consuming psychedelics. For ayahuasca drinkers like those Australians noted earlier who approach ayahuasca largely without humor, playfulness, or other so-called "recreational" qualities, the ludible side of Juan's ayahuasca expertise could appear extra wondrous and otherworldly in its affective resonance. Wonder and joy can be registers of sociocultural differences in attitudes towards the affective norms of ayahuasca practices.

Shipibo ayahuasca healers working in the tourist economy are merchants of wonder. The humor and happiness they express during the ceremonies sometimes comes as a positive surprise to the visitors. Many guests described in amazement how the healers seemed so happy living without the expensive lifestyles of the modern world. This primitivist projection did not go unnoticed. The healers were well aware that happiness such as theirs is a "big fortune." Perhaps most impactfully, they actively worked to generate joy and wonder in the guests through the sensory artistry of ceremonial performance, namely, through song.

Maestro Juan had five main *icaros* that he typically sang. While he continued to learn new songs from the spirits of plants and animals during long *dietas*—and he had over a dozen songs in his full repertoire—he mainly sang just five *icaros* to the guests when I was there. They were "Cleaning" (*benxoaki*), "Visions" (*nete kepeni*), "Arcana" (*arcana*), "Protection" (*panati*), and "Happiness" (*shinan raroti*). Each song has around fifteen to twenty unique sentences that repeat. Each singing of the songs also ventured out into spontaneous lyrics, depending upon his visionary experience and the state of the person he was singing for.

Although the guests did not understand Shipibo and rarely learned any lyrics of the *icaros* they personally received, the healers actively tried to evoke wonder in the guests through singing wondrous lyrics. This was made crystal clear by the *icaro* titled "Visions." Sung in almost darkness, while he sat on the ground directly in front of the guest, Juan's performances were a loud and

WONDER AND HEALING ON RETREAT 103

compelling embodied experience. His arms gesticulated and helped to forge his vision-song and transmit it to the altered experience of the guests. He sang to each guest:

Visions (*nete kepeni*)

I

mia kanomatanan axonbobanon
jakon akinshamankin nete kepenxonboi
nokon jakon netebo kepenxonboban
nete kepenira bewa bewashamani

Properly forecasting your body
I will open the world of visions
Showing the wonders of visions
Singing, singing will open your visions

II

mia jainshamankin pikobobano
piko pikoshamani mia pikobobano
oinmabokin meskokeska netebo
oinmabokin meskokeska netebo

I will free you to that world
Free, liberate, free, liberate
Showing the wonderful world
Showing the wonderful world

III

nokon pene netebo biri birimabokin
jainshaman kanoyontana

104 GLOBAL AYAHUASCA

rao nete mia keponxonbobano
oni netebo kepoxonbonki
jejejejjejejejeeeeeee

Opening my wonderful world
Shining brilliantly
Guiding you to the world of visions
The wonderful world of ayahuasca
Heheheheheeeee

Juan and the other healers attempted to inspire the sensorium of the guests with the patterns and qualities of their own vision-songs. "Opening my wonderful world. Shining brilliantly. Guiding you to the world of visions," Juan sang. The healers intentionally evoked a wondrous world to inspire wonder in the guests. In doing so, they intentionally become the wonder of others. There was also one healer who, during every ceremony, remained in the middle of the *maloca* singing protective *icaros* to fortify the space from outside sorcery attacks. While he tried to dominate (*dominar*) and master his own visions in acts of psychic defense for the safety of everyone in the ceremony, Juan's song called "Vision" aimed not at mastery but at encouraging a mystifying and spontaneous mood of wonder.

The healers' will to be a wonder reflects what Michael Scott called the wonder of identity (2014:42). During the marvelous encounter between healer and guest, wonder permeates who the healers are as persons and what they are as shamans connected to visionary worlds and spirit allies. This is achieved relationally by the expectations and attitudes of the guests in tandem with the desires and creativity of the healers.

In contrast to the international guests, many Indigenous patients or clients have approached ayahuasca healers less with wonder than with pragmatic demands to reverse witchcraft, heal a malady, or solve a crime (Brown 1988; Luna 1986; Dobkin de Rios 1972). This indicates a theoretical limit to any hope that wonder and awe are universal explanations for ayahuasca or psychedelic use. For example, Michael Brown's (1988:103) description of an Aguaruna ayahuasca healing session included a shaman entering into a heated dialogue with a patient's family while concomitantly negotiating with spirits and singing a curative song. Concerned that the healer might himself be a sorcerer, the Aguaruna family demanded he indicate his legitimacy. The healer defended his powers while describing the weakness and ill intentions of other healers. His techniques of healing, and the image he helped to generate in the patient's mind, could not have been more different from those employed by Amazonian shamans towards clients in the ayahuasca tourism networks that I researched.

The will to be a wonder that Juan embodied was made possible by a long and convoluted history of Western stereotyping and primitivist imagining, in addition to the contemporary differences in material conditions and economic lifestyles between healer and guest.

Wonder is built into the international guests' expectations before they come to the ayahuasca retreat, largely through internet media. In an online survey I did of forty-three guests who had attended Pachamama Temple, many described learning about ayahuasca through YouTube videos of ordinary people discussing their own experience drinking ayahuasca. There is a large genre of social media videos of individuals sharing amazing and miraculous ayahuasca visions and healing experiences. Other sources of inspiration included popular books about ayahuasca, such as Jeremy Narby's *The Cosmic Serpent*, Rick Strassman's *DMT: The Spirit Molecule*, and Graham Hancock's *Supernatural*, in addition to podcasts. All these media include potent kinds of wonder discourse that attracted guests to ayahuasca retreats and helped to define their expectations and perhaps even their visions.

The ayahuasca businesses in Peru and elsewhere typically had social media channels on YouTube, Instagram, and Facebook. The most popular video on Pachamama Temple's YouTube channel is of a middle-aged man from India. He shared,

> I came a long way to find some answers. . . . I came here to improve my relationship with myself, my loved ones, my life's work, all of that. I'm really glad that I got, kind of, three tick-marks across those three dimensions thanks to Pachamama Temple. I really appreciate the work

106 GLOBAL AYAHUASCA

> the maestros did during the ceremonies. It was extremely magical . . . one of the facilitators here mentioned that each ceremony is equal to fifteen years of counseling. I think that's true, hands down, and I totally experienced a sense of that. The amount of work that happened in me through these ceremonies is just remarkable. It was a very deep cleansing type of experience. I experienced a lot of clarity of thought, positive emotions, and it definitely felt like the part of myself that was not serving me was shedding away.

The guests sometimes described being motivated to drink ayahuasca by a lack of wonder, a lack of purpose, and a feeling of dullness and flatness. Another popular video on the temple's channel is of a middle-aged woman from The Netherlands describing her ayahuasca experience in less dramatic terms.

> I want to tell you something about my time at the Pachamama Temple in Peru, where I had my first ayahuasca experience. . . . To be honest, I was pretty skeptical about the whole ayahuasca thing. I watched a lot of video reports on YouTube before I came to Peru and they were all full of praise and life-changing stories. But since I have been suffering from depression for many years now, and I tried a lot of things to make my life more pleasant, I thought, why not try this so-called miracle medicine. And so I did. The videos I watched on YouTube also made me have expectations which I want to warn people who are considering ayahuasca, because I believe that different people have different experiences and also different ways of putting them in words. For me, it took several ceremonies, but in the end, certain things I can't explain did happen. But it all went the hard way, because I went through a lot of pain, mentally and physically, and I pretty much got ill during every ceremony. It took me some discipline to finish the retreat. In the end, I'm glad I did, because it gave me some valuable insights about myself and my behavior of which I can say it was worth it. . . . Then, of course, I have to mention the maestros and maestras who are such lovely, caring people who make me smile all the time, and together with their family they introduced me to their Shipibo culture. The program of the retreat is set around that. . . . Yeah, just see for yourself. Go there. You won't regret it.

International visitors who wonder about ayahuasca and the spiritual wisdom of Indigenous healers deeply enough to travel to Peru are often stimulated by a restlessness. Some guests arrived with a calling and described their journey to ayahuasca as a long string of strange synchronicities, or what one European guest called "nudges from the universe" directing him to the temple. In some of the most wondrous examples, the guests arrived convinced they had already seen the healers' faces in dreams before meeting them or seeing any website images of them before.

Anthropologist Michael Jackson described how synchronicities arrest our attention by channeling the intensity of subjective life into the concrete tapestry of objective reality. The "search for outward signs that register one's inchoate feelings," he explained, "is the way those feelings become thinkable, manageable, narratable, and shareable" (2021:6). Synchronicities, including during psychedelic experiences, can help people navigate the vicissitudes and possibilities of life.

English neurologist Andrew Lees—someone partial to ayahuasca—once had a dream of the molecular structure of an obscure drug called apomorphine, triggering a series of synchronicities. First, he decided to try the drug on himself and on his Parkinson's disease patients, which ultimately translated into a widely popular new medicine, sold under the brand name Apokyn (Lees 2017). During his discovery period, Lees was reading William Burrough's book *Naked Lunch*, wherein the American author celebrates apomorphine as "junk vaccine." Lees took his own strange dream of the molecule seriously as something that was possibly more than just a random impression. Being open to synchronicities can involve ontological rupture, inspiring intrigue by attaching the person to an intuitive perception.

When a North American encounters an Indigenous shaman in a dream before meeting them in ordinary reality, the older experience becomes an image of the present and unfolding future. Dreams and intuition can compel people towards ayahuasca. At the same time, drinking the brew can enhance the vividness of dreams and intuitive feelings through a wondrous looping state in which issues from ordinary life entangle visionary encounters that then inspire intuitive perceptions within ordinary life.

In the mild tropical winter of 2019, I and a dozen others left the urban district of Yarinacocha in remote Peru on the back of motorized tricycles that for twenty minutes weaved on bumpy roads towards Pachamama Temple. The constant dust from the road created a hazy glow that made it hard to see. Poor wooden dwellings and fields of corn appeared through the orange plumes of dust. The other guests covered their faces with shirts or a scarf as the drivers navigated the fast traffic. On the way, we passed *Discoteque Pescadoras*, or Fisherman's Bar, a dilapidated wooden structure that was the source of electronic music heard in the distance during some of the evening ayahuasca sessions. While many ayahuasca retreats in Peru boast the sanctity of being immersed in deep rainforests and surrounded only by throbbing ecological soundscapes, Pachamama Temple was on the edges of a rural area. Jordan, the main foreign stakeholder, wanted visitors to experience what "Shipibo culture is actually about." Stepping off the tricycle, I wiped the dust off my face and entered the retreat grounds with lingering vibrations from the ride.

Meeting Indigenous Amazonian healers for the first time is a wondrous event for many if not all of the guests. As we entered, the healers were dressed in full-body *cushma* robes, bare feet on the dusty ground, and smiling. Most guests cannot speak Spanish, and the healers cannot speak English. The two groups faced each other, sharing nonverbal gestures, nodding, smiling, sometimes giggling. Later in the day, the guests came together to introduce themselves to each other in a meeting without the healers, where they also learned about the retreat's format and rules.

Then, after a few hours of relaxing, the first evening's ayahuasca ceremony started, which was called a "traditional ceremony" given that only the healers drank the brew. As usual, guests lay in designated places around the large *maloca*'s perimeter with the healers in the middle. After the healers drank the brew, it was silent in the ceremony space for about forty minutes. Music, laughter, and socializing from Fisherman's Bar and elsewhere nearby could be faintly heard in the distance. We could also hear a natural symphony of frogs, cicadas, birds, and other forest life emanating from around the *maloca*, but the pounding bass coming from the distant bars was constant and clashing. We were all aware of being on the edge of an urban environment. A guard armed with torches and access to a megaphone walked around the temple grounds, contained within eight-foot-high wooden walls, to monitor the space at night.

The healers began to sing their individual songs, generating a polyphonic soundscape. The singing lasted for several hours. All the participants later described falling asleep during the traditional ceremony. They had not taken any ayahuasca. Thea, a staff member who oversees the retreats program and facilitates relations with the healers, told me that the ceremony helped guests feel safe and it gives them a clearer expectation of the format ahead. It enables them to experience the process with a sober mind and to imagine what it will be like the following evening when they drink too. Some guests were anxious during the traditional ceremony, in anticipation of drinking the brew, they later told me. The traditional ceremony therefore both generates and dissipates wonder among the guests; the mystery of drinking ayahuasca with Indigenous healers on the edge of Yarinacocha was slightly demystified. It points to a tension or balance in which too much wonder was unwanted and possibly unhelpful to the intercultural healing space.

GROUNDED ASTONISHMENT

The mysteries of ayahuasca visions have an inbuilt excess that applies to scholarly understandings as well as to the views of the ayahuasca drinkers I studied, whether they used the brew for gaining healing, cultivating virtues, or resolving everyday dilemmas. The types of wonder that occurred during the Pachamama Temple guests' visionary experiences were made possible by the intercultural relations between guests and Indigenous healers. These relations, however, tended to prescribed certain limits of wonder. It was possible for wonder to extend beyond healing into what the retreat organizers and some guests described as fancifulness, sickness, or meaninglessness.

But before demonstrating these ethnographic divergences of wonder, first we will explore a more general framework for approaching ayahuasca visions, meaning making, and its relationship to cultural context. This should help to clarify the affective dimensions of ayahuasca tourism—in particular, the feelings of astonishment and wonder that guests experience when drinking the brew. Let's explores how cultural meaning can provide the grounds upon which psychedelic wonder and awe are embodied and pursued.

As the previous chapters have illustrated in different ways, the brew frequently evokes awe, wonder, and astonishment in drinkers, particularly if they are new to the brew, but also these moods and experiences can become an enduring quality across long-term practice. Ayahuasca visions can resemble the idea of synchronicity as described by Michael Jackson (2021), given their special relationship between inner and outer worlds or between altered and ordinary perceptions. Ayahuasca can inspire a sense of meaningfulness given its ability to amplify epistemic moods. The world can emanate with a curious aura of significance under its influence (Hartogsohn 2018). Gestures, ideas, and thoughts may take on special qualities. Ayahuasca has been described as an "existential amplifier" within Shuar lifeworlds (Taylor 1993:666). Benny Shanon emphasized these qualities while describing ayahuasca and meaning.

> Under the Ayahuasca inebriation, things seem to be ingrained with meaning . . . it dawns upon one that there is a sense and reason to it all. With this appreciation, insights are gained and new understandings are reached. . . . [I]t is very common for drinkers to feel that they suddenly understand why things are the way they are, to find deep, heretofore hidden, meanings in verbal expressions and in texts, to discover the true sense of their own lives. (2002:60, 243)

Psychologists from The Netherlands and Spain tested the capacity for ayahuasca sessions to augment creative thinking. They recruited twenty-six male and female white participants, each of whom had previously drunk ayahuasca approximately thirty times. The participants' were motivated to drink the brew to "enhance introspection, self-knowledge, and personal growth" (Kuypers et al. 2016). They underwent creativity tests before and during the ayahuasca drinking sessions. One test involved images of seemingly random objects, such as an apple, an umbrella, and a computer, with an instruction to find any meaningful associations. The participants' capacity to make ordinary or "convergent" associations between the objects decreased on ayahuasca compared to when sober. The brew seemed to increase the capacity for divergent thinking. People who think divergently tend to be more creative, and the researchers considered whether this enhanced ability could be a factor in the mental health benefits of ayahuasca retreats.

This creativity study corroborates neuroscience research about how different parts of the brain communicate with much more intensity and in divergent neural pathways on psychedelics compared to sober (Carhart-Harris 2018; Brouwer and Carhart-Harris 2021). This entropic theory of the psychedelic brain brings a neurological twist to an idea previously proposed in the 1950s by the English writer Aldous Huxley. In a long essay titled *The Doors of Perception* (1954), Huxley philosophically described his first time consuming mescaline in the hills of Hollywood. He explored an expansion of the mind beyond the cognitive convergence of language, symbolism, and ordinary reality.

> To make biological survival possible, Mind at Large has to be funneled through the reducing valve of the brain and nervous system. What comes out at the other end is a measly trickle of the kind of consciousness which will help us to stay alive on the surface of this particular planet. To formulate and express the contents of this reduced awareness, man has invented and endlessly elaborated those symbol-systems and implicit philosophies which we call languages. . . . Most people, most of the time, know only what comes through the reducing valve and is consecrated as genuinely real by the local language. Certain persons, however, seem to be born with a kind of by-pass that circumvents the reducing valve. In others temporary bypasses may be acquired either spontaneously, or as the result of deliberate "spiritual exercises," or through hypnosis, or by means of drugs.

Huxley attempted to demonstrate how religiosity and spirituality are vectors of a perennial experience, which the "Mind at Large" theory and the brain's "reducing valve" reflected. In this approach, psychedelic substances temporarily suspended the mental associations and cognitive "filters" built by biological evolution, socialization, and language to reveal what Huxley called "the infinite value and meaningfulness of naked existence." The theory finds itself at home with many of the universalist claims in the current pop psychology of ayahuasca, but it also exposes a sharp paradox due to its relationship with what Ido Hartogsohn (2020) described as the most enduring concept in psychedelic therapy. The notion of "set" and "setting," originally proposed by psychologists in the United States in the 1960s, suggested that the social and environmental setting of psychedelic use can play a big role in shaping the experiences people have. This grounded model problematizes the perennialist

112 **GLOBAL AYAHUASCA**

project by situating plant-induced visions firmly in the world, even when they evoke wondrous, otherworldly, and ineffable dimensions.

Set and setting theory suggests that the encultured reducing valve of the brain is not fully transcended during psychedelic experiences. Commenting on Huxley's theorization, Jeffrey Kripal (2007:115) noted how the "filters" of consciousness always return eventually, given that the substances wear off and the person returns to the social needs and moral concerns of everyday life. There is also a sense—suggested by set and setting—in which the filters were never simply obstacles that are left behind. After all, the perennial philosophy espoused by Huxley was an "anthological potpourri" defined by his attraction to particular religious traditions and not others (Langlitz 2013:247). Reframing Huxley's perennialism in the ancient tradition of eclecticism, Nicolas Langlitz suggested that quests of finding universality and perennial truths—whether spiritual, biological, or otherwise—should not always be dismissed as simply misguided reductionism. He wondered, rather, whether perennialisms, in the plural, were unstable historical projects that constantly required renewal, whereby "Life in all its iridescent universality" is an enduring source of wonder (251). These revolving historical views of grasping at the heavens would include when an ayahuasca vision reverberates with a feeling of universal qualities that nonetheless include features of social context and the life experience of the user.

Psychedelic experiences, like ordinary life, can be mercurial. They can come with ambiguities and uncertainties that produce an interpretive demand, which represents another way that social contexts shape visionary meaning. For Shipibo healers, ayahuasca helps them direct *nihue* or spirit essence, but the visions are not always clear and may require decoding. Maestro Juan explained that a vision is potentially pathological or medicinal, and that understanding its properties requires discernment and sometimes skepticism. While telling a group of international visitors about the importance of approaching ayahuasca with an intention to avoid getting lost in the visions, he shared,

> What ayahuasca shows you is how you are thinking. That's why I was telling you that ayahuasca never tells you anything in concrete. It's like a parable. Sometimes you see something and think, "What is that? What is

that?" Sometimes the ayahuasca confuses you. . . . If you see something that's not what you want, well, but if ayahuasca shows you, then that's how you are. If it confuses you, it means that in your life, your regular life, you have those things too. Maybe sometimes you get lost a little. Sometimes you think, "What is it that I want in life?" "What is it that I want to do?" "What can I do?" So, then, ayahuasca, through that, shows you, "This is how your mind is confused." That's why the ayahuasca is never going to tell you, "Hey, you're confused." But it's going to show you what confusion looks like for you.

By showing and not telling, ayahuasca teaches through a relational pedagogy that requires active participation by the student. During a session, voluntary and involuntary mental and emotional activity can expand outwards and inwards to be deeply resonant with the visionary worlds.

The mind is laid bare in a social space often populated by "telepathic" spirits, agents, and others. When chemical isolates from the ayahuasca vine were first purified by the Colombian chemist Guillermo Fischer Cárdenas in 1923, he termed them "telepathine," seemingly to pay respect to Indigenous reports of ayahuasca's effects (Beyer 2007). Soon after it was learned that the molecules had already been discovered in *Pegnaum harmala*, a plant growing across Eurasia, "telepathine" was displaced by the dry nomenclature of "harmine." In Australia, ayahuasca drinkers frequently referred to telepathic mental states. They commented that when drinking the brew "it's not possible to hide from ayahuasca," "running away is futile," and "resistance is persistence." During this strange merging of the inner and outer, the subject and object, meaning making is not simply a reflective act of disengaged reasoning—like a scientist observing an amethyst stone and contemplating its photon charge—but meaning becomes a deeply immersive experience. Mental life, in this altered state, is not necessarily a reflection made against some other realm outside the mind but an action within an expanded mindscape that may feel oddly public and exposed to a theater of plant spirits and others.

The visionary environment may ebb and flow to the musical tune of thoughts, feelings, and sensations of meaningfulness—whether beautiful or grotesque, attractive or repulsive, foreign or familiar. It is difficult but certainly possible to "will away" some visionary experiences and to invite in others. When a Canadian visitor in Peru described a terrifying vision in which he saw purple and black clouds hovering above him, filled with swarming snakes, insects, and animated faces flicking their tongues like Maori *haka* dancers, Maestro Juan told him that he should "dominate the visions . . . take a deep breath . . . make a protection pose with your arms and generate positive light to dispel them," adding, "the next day, you should think about the vision to understand its origins, its meaning." Thus the wondrous qualities of the visions can guard the experiences from complete epistemological capture. Spectacular experiences can be hard to understand, and when reflecting upon them afterwards, they may slide through the mind like shimmering water through fingers.

The visitor, in this occasion, was a bit confused by Juan's advice, because while Shipibo healers encouraged him and the other visitors to dominate and banish their difficult visions, he was receiving a different message on the internet. Psychedelic science and psychotherapy have promoted "letting go" into the perennial mystical experience, whereas the Shipibo healers that treat international visitors sing *icaros* to generate joyful, wondrous, and courageous moods, but also sometimes to provide protection, rather than surrender, towards afflictive experiences. The healers sometimes encountered local tensions and injustices in their own ayahuasca experiences during these ceremonies, dealing with sorcery and personal struggles, not universal vectors of Oneness or cosmic unity of the mystic.

The capacity for ayahuasca to evoke wonder during Shipibo tourism retreats is inspired but also tempered by the historical and intercultural differences between the healers and the guests. Wonder can reflect a magic generated by the epistemic space that emerges between healer and client. However, this magic has limits and asymmetries wherein some realities are blurred and banished while others are amplified beyond their original forms. Allow me to demonstrate.

As part of the formal retreat program at Pachamama Temple, one morning eight guests and I walked for twenty minutes to attend a boat ride across Yarinococha lagoon with a Shipibo friend of the healers. Carlos, our guide, was a funny and entertaining raconteur with a wealth of knowledge about local plants and animals. We arrived at the small canal about one kilometer from the temple and got in his skinny wooden boat. Carlos paddled us downstream telling stories about the white clay from the bottom of the canal that is used for making Shipibo ceramics. Decades before ayahuasca tourism, Shipibo ceramics were sold locally to tourists and purchased by iconic museums and galleries across the globe. Filled with intrigue, the *pasajeros* handled the fine, silky clay and asked Carlos about the traditional technique of making pots.

As he slowly paddled us down the canal, between towering walls of soil and vegetation on each side, he spoke about how in the 1980s and early 1990s, the *Sendero Luminoso* (Shining Path) and other Túpac Amaru Revolutionary Movement (MRTA) militias had come through this area attempting to rally support from Indigenous communities and violently slaughtered "all of the Shipibo in this area. . . . Many dead bodies were thrown into these canals."

FIGURE 3.1 Carlos, a friend of the Pachamama Temple healers, leading a boat tour into the Yarinacocha lagoon, Pucallpa, Peru, winter 2019. (Photo: Alex Gearin)

FIGURE 3.2 Pachamama Temple attendees on boat tour, Peru, winter 2019. (Photo: Alex Gearin)

The guests went silent. Carlos described the difficulties the Shipibo and other Indigenous groups faced during this period. He narrated these tragic stories with an energetic tone while smiling; a protective emotional cloak that enabled him to remember and recount the horrors. The guests never probed or asked him about these histories, nor did I hear any of them speak about it later. This was consistent among most of the other retreats I participated in at Pachamama Temple.

Among those executed by Shining Path in the 1980s were members of Mama Maria's own and her late husband's families. The militia group was created by a Peruvian philosophy professor in the late 1960s after he had traveled to China and gained inspiration from Mao Zedong's ideologies. After returning, he led a communist uprising in Southern Peru that turned increasingly violent from the early 1980s and was at the heart of the turbulent war period during the mid-1990s (Stern 1998). The organization included the militia *Ejército Guerrillero Popular* (The People's Guerrilla Army) that aggressively fought against both state-funded forces and competing leftist organizations. While terrorizing rural and metropolitan communities, they attempted to mobilize support and raise income for the Shining Path.

Mama Maria described to me how her own upbringing as a child in the 1940s and 1950s was a golden period with the rivers full of fish. Back then, she explained, it was safe to travel at night and even to sleep in random places along the river bank without fear of violence. She recounted the prophetic words her mother told to her when she was a child: "My mother explained to me and my sister that one day the *mestizos* would arrive on our land. If they didn't kill us, we would live with them; instead of being in our land, they would take us with them. And our children, when we one day have them, will have a hard life."

Reflecting on the violent tragedies of the 1980s, Mama Maria's eldest son, Jose, later lamented to me, "We've been through a lot. How many shamans, non-shamans, women, young women, teenagers, that have been killed. Sometimes they would go to a community and grab people, accuse them of being a liar, tie them up, pull their tongues out and smash them." When I asked Maestro Ricardo whether Shipibo healers were busy curing communities of trauma during this period, he said they were too focused on defending themselves and their families. He also, however, narrated a story about how Shipibo healers helped to end the militias. In the 1990s, a group of Shipibo healers drank ayahuasca and magically visited the Peruvian president Alberto Fujimori in their visions and "convinced him to send the army to destroy" the Shining Path and MRTA. "Many healers rose up," he added. "The thoughts they had, bad thoughts, all that got transformed with love in each of their senses and they sent this to the ones at the top [of the Peruvian government]. Then, the two [militia groups] were captured."

Several Shipibo healers I interviewed described military motifs in the visionary ordeals they experienced when training to become a healer. When under the effects of an initiatory ayahuasca brew, Maestro Manuel, a nephew of Mama Maria, swallowed tobacco smoke to transform his body into an airplane to escape from a vision of a military helicopter. "The sound of the blades was very loud. It was just like in the film *Rambo*," he explained. When the rampant violence and instability of the war period ended in the early 1990s, Peru was again placed back on the international tourist map (Peluso 2017:208). By the mid-to-late 1990s, the seeds of ayahuasca tourism were beginning to germinate with small centers and trickles of international visitors emerging.

118   GLOBAL AYAHUASCA

This violent recent history typically remained unknown to the visiting guests at ayahuasca retreats in Peru. When Carlos told us about the Shining Path militia murdering Shipibo and dumping their bodies in the canal we were floating down, the guests remained silent. Ayahuasca tourism is aimed at personal healing, and while it emphasizes intercultural sharing and exchange, it is categorically different from "dark tourism," a niche for travelers looking for historical atrocities and systemic violence (Robb 2009). The *pasajeros* of ayahuasca tourism usually described their motivations as a mix between healing, awakening their inner spirituality, and connecting with authentic Indigenous culture. Generally, they appeared focused on healing themselves, which may explain why they tended towards positive kinds of wonder in their perceptions of Shipibo life and history.

Guests were particularly vulnerable during evenings of drinking ayahuasca, and they probably wanted to avoid the potential risk of dark, violent, and terrorizing qualia overtaking their visionary experiences. During an ayahuasca ceremony I attended elsewhere, moments before we drank the brew, I was conversing with a Japanese tattoo artist about the macabre dance style Butoh and the way it expresses a tortured aesthetics of nuclear war. At one stage during the ceremony, I had vivid visions of nuclear Armageddon and perceived cities exploding with bombs. While certainly not always the case, ayahuasca visions can absorb ideas and conversations from the immediate social environment of the session in which it is consumed.

Learning about traumatic aspects of Shipibo history is generally avoided by the ayahuasca visitors, probably given the risk that such knowledge could derail their primary goals of spiritually healing and purifying and enlightening themselves. Although wonder is an inherently ambivalent mood, which in European antiquity encompassed "an uncanny opening, rift, or wound in the everyday," along with its more positive attributes that characterize modern usage (Rubenstein 2008:10), the unsettling side of wonder reaches a threshold among ayahuasca guests in Peru and their desire to connect with the authenticity of Shipibo lifeworlds. The atrocities in recent living memory, which haunt the local area, are relegated and hidden behind positive types of *pasajero* wonder associated with plant spirits, marvelous visions, forest ecologies, and simple living conditions.

As we continued down the canal, soon to arrive at the open expanse of Yarinacocha lagoon, Carlos warned us jokingly, "Be careful not to rest your feet in the water too long. Some piranhas will bite your toes. Others will bite your wallet." During the boat ride, we saw a sloth and its baby, freshwater dolphins, huge spiders, and a range of medicine plants. The guests' imaginations and interests were activated as they vibrantly chatted about the rainforest and spotted animals. Carlos told us stories about when he helped the television channel National Geographic film the capture and release of a giant anaconda deep in the rainforest. He said he would take us to "lovers island" to see the "Avatar tree," which the guests expressed excitement about. The tree appeared like one giant weaving root system, without a trunk, but instead with many roots weaving up to the beautiful green foliage. With participants coming from temperate climates, and mainly Western societies, the tour was an excursion into alien bio- and cultural diversity. The guests were engaged and excited about the animals and plants and the stories of large anacondas in the deep rainforest.

The next evening, the *pasajeros* attended their next ayahuasca ceremony. We entered with our embodied minds having absorbed impressions from the rainforest and exotic animals of Carlos's boat tour. Nature is central to ayahuasca tourism. The visitors were seeking curing from healers whose special abilities are borne from alliances with the spirits of the rainforest. However, ambient poverty and harsh social conditions also shaped each healer's relationships, struggles, and achievements in drinking ayahuasca and singing powerful curing songs. The guests attuned to the emotional and visionary currents of shamanic songs that united them not only with the healers' plant and animal spirit allies, but with a strength forged out of the terrible kinds of social suffering that tend to inflict people at the exploited fringes of modernity.

Maestro Ricardo told me that when you drink ayahuasca as much as they do, you learn all the spirits' tricks and they cannot dominate you anymore. Shipibo healers resist the attacks of malevolent agents by generating the musical power to dominate and counteract the negative visions. The ayahuasca practice of resisting "domination," I argue, is a shamanic response to wider social realities of oppression that were familiar to the Shipibo family, including stories of the colonial rubber barons who brutalized their ancestors, the militias that committed genocide in recent decades, and the urban mestizos and Peruvians who taunt and racially discriminate against their children today.

There is a great irony in the popular Western mythology that depicts Indigenous ayahuasca healers as stewards of an archaic way of life uncorrupted by the ills of civilization. I do not mean to disregard the personal suffering of international guests but to highlight how the Indigenous maestros who heal them tend to come from much more challenging social environments. This positions Indigenous ayahuasca centers, and the suffering and strength of life in the developing world, as a spiritual resource for curing the maladies of people from the developed world.

The experiences of wonder that ayahuasca inspires, or fails to inspire, can expose all sorts of moral fault lines. Jordan, the European co-owner of Pachamama Temple, expressed to me the ethical concerns he had as an ayahuasca service provider. He recognized that some people received profound healing, insight, and inspiration at the retreat center, but emphasized that "many people don't have a massive breakthrough and some people can become worse." He described a series of "the worst" things that happened at Pachamama Temple. In one dramatic example, a young man from England, seemingly dealing with psychosis, drank ayahuasca and realized he was a messiah sent to save humanity. He was loud, running around and shouting throughout the ceremony, and continued to disrupt the program during the next day. Thea, the retreat facilitator, unsure what to do, called the police after other guests voiced their concerns. The problematic guest explained that he was Romeo and that Thea was Juliet, and that he had to sacrifice himself to save her and the world. When the police arrived, the guest ran to a water tower and climbed 25 meters to the top while screaming about his divine mission.

The police filmed parts of the episode and the footage was released on local news media. They asked Pachamama Temple for 2,000 soles ($500 USD) to avoid creating any excess trouble, and returned days later demanding 3,000 ($800 USD) more while threatening to undertake a three-month investigation during which the retreat would be closed. The money was paid and the police left. The Englishman continued creating disturbance and visited the retreat while staying at a local hotel. The temple shamans visited him each day trying to keep him from doing anything reckless.

Most ayahuasca retreats ask all their clients whether they had ever been diagnosed with psychosis, schizophrenia, or bipolar disorder, and they refuse those who acknowledge such diagnoses. Jordan noted that "because the man thought he was healthy and sane, he filled out the application form saying he was sane and okay." Lamenting these difficulties, Jordan wished ayahuasca was legal and integrated into Western societies with requirements for full medical checks for all clients. He shared concerns about his own responsibility in cases such as the psychotic episode above. "Out of every 150 guests who visit Pachamama Temple," he believed "one or two leave full of awe, transformed in a positive way" and "open up and soar like an Amazonian bird in full plumage." They leave "with a remarkable energy and vision to make a good impact in the world." But, he said, "the amount of shit we have to go through for that is insane." He spoke about another case of a guest who thought he was a messiah. During a ceremony, a young American was allegedly "channeling dark primeval energy, mumbling and burping like a beastly goblin." He continued, "The maestros tried to calm him down. His loud explosions of roaring and monstrous noises were disturbing the group." Jordan described him to me privately as an ugly and sick caged animal that was trying to escape from itself. Almost all the guests were troubled by the man's loud outbursts, and several complained to the organizers, expressing concerns for their safety. However, one guest, a woman from the United Kingdom, perceived "the beast as the messiah" and the next day overtly encouraged his behavior. She claimed that the man was enlightened and should be helping the Shipibo maestros heal the guests, and that the maestros could learn from him. The pair ended up falling in love. After the ayahuasca retreat, she divorced her husband, he split from his girlfriend, and they moved to the United States together. Jordan shared these "worst stories" with a sense of guilt and confusion around the ethics of his business. In a sincere yet comic tone, he stated his concern that he is "breeding loonies."

These two incidents represent examples of anti-wonder at ayahuasca retreats. They were both described by Jordan, and most guests, using medicalized language that included descriptors that deflate a sense of authentic wonder. "Psychosis," "loonies," "sick beast" are all signs that the wonder of ayahuasca has become misguided, misplaced, and even something else entirely. The ontological instability of the "loonies" and their disturbing behaviors and speech were too unstable for the others. Healing at Pachamama Temple was partly based on regulating what were deemed appropriate types of wonder, awe, and other moods, especially when a person's expressive behavior disturbs the other clients' ayahuasca experiences. Despite these challenging cases, Jordan felt that his ayahuasca business provided an overall positive healing service. While only a handful out of a few hundred might have a dramatically positive transformation from one single retreat, many people described gaining some benefits, he shared.

CONTRADICTORY MARVELS

Jordan's belief that ayahuasca ceremonies are a positive healing service to the world was echoed throughout an online survey I conducted of previous Pachamama Temple guests. Out of the forty-three participants surveyed, forty-one answered "yes" to the question, "Has ayahuasca healed or has ayahuasca been healing anything in your life?" Most of the participants, mainly European or North American, indicated they would prefer to drink ayahuasca in ceremonies conducted by Indigenous specialists rather than non-Indigenous specialists. The main reason for this preference was based on viewing Indigenous settings to be more authentic given their perceived long historical uses of the brew. Presented in order of most popular, the Pachamama Temple guests who completed the survey were from The Netherlands, France, United Kingdom, Germany, Poland, United States, Canada, Australia, South Africa, India, Mexico, Singapore, and Iran. Thirty-nine years was the mean age. Twenty-four participants were male, nineteen were female. The mean income was $38,000 USD. Occupations varied, with a trend towards health care, mental health services, and alternative therapies, but also included marketing, banking, hospitality, academia, and the arts.

The Shipibo songs were often described as crucial to participants' healing and spiritual experiences. Explaining why they preferred drinking with Indigenous specialists, some participants commented, "[Ayahuasca] is in their DNA. It's a natural thing for them"; "*Icaros* in Shipibo are part of the power of the medicine"; "I already knew from meditation that altered states of consciousness are rather bizarre and unusual and I wanted to have people who are knowledgeable and experienced with the brew"; "They are Maestros of plant medicine and plant healing. I would never go to a mechanic if I have a broken leg, if you know what I mean"; "Shamans are the anchors and safety for my voyage. But most importantly, they provide vibrations and telepathic teachings during ceremony"; "They have ancient knowledge buried in the depths of their skin. I feel like Westerners are clueless and are just bred to make money. I wouldn't trust them with my soul"; and finally, "Shamans act as a bridge between the different dimensions and realities. They have an intimate relationship with the medicine and ideally are able to guide, protect, and heal you." The belief that the Indigenous healers are able to shape other peoples' inner visionary experiences represents a common theme in the reasons why the guests prefer Indigenous ayahuasca specialists.

There was significant variability in the psychoactive responses that guests at the retreat had. When people fell asleep shortly after drinking a strong dose, the brew did not necessarily sedate the person, it just failed to affect them. There are likely biological and psychological reasons for this rare lack of response. Despite popular media's overwhelming emphasis of ayahuasca's visionary experiences (Gearin and Calavia Sáez 2021), not all participants experienced visions during their ceremonies at Pachamama Temple. Roughly 28 percent described experiencing "many intricate and clear visions," 36 percent described experiencing "a few intricate and clear visions," 26 percent "only vague patterns and colors, nothing very intricate or clear," 6 percent "maybe some faint imagery," and 4 percent saw no visions. There was wide variations in the kinds of visions that occurred among guests during each ceremony I attended at the retreat. Some described complex and vivid visions during ceremonies where others had only seen faint patterns. This suggests the capacity to see visions is not simply based upon the particular brew served but on the person consuming it too.

The perceived healing benefits, presented in order of most common, included obtaining an increased self-confidence; less anxiety and a greater ability to deal with stress; overcoming trauma and troubling past experiences; relief from depression; overcoming alcohol dependence and other addictions; processing grief; and gaining purpose and stronger life goals. Many guests considered these positive outcomes as resulting from the ayahuasca retreat activities in general, but also in particular from specific, often-intense personal ayahuasca experiences. They described visions of animal and plant spirits, mind-altering interactions with the Shipibo healers, journeys through alternate worlds, and appearances of visiting relatives and significant others. They were more eager to talk about their personal ayahuasca experiences than to answer questions related to their motivations to attend the retreat, personal benefits and outcomes, or the challenges of integrating back into ordinary life afterwards.

Their descriptions of healing experiences sometimes entailed undergoing an ontological crisis. This included awe towards the vividness of the experiences and the encounters with spirit entities, Shipibo healers, and colorful

FIGURE 3.3 Integration discussion with Pachamama Temple attendees discussing their ayahuasca experiences, Peru, winter 2019. (Photo: Alex Gearin)

other dimensions. These ontological crises reflect the results of a recent study that examined whether psychedelic use may promote changes in metaphysical beliefs. Examining 886 survey responses—primarily by people in the United States and England, with 90 percent identifying as white—researchers demonstrated how psychedelic use appeared to shift beliefs from materialist to spiritualist perspectives, sometimes through the "ontological shock" of the psychedelic experience itself (Timmermann, Watts, and Dupuis 2022). Following are two examples from my research at Pachamama Temple that are representative but not exhaustive in illustrating the often-shared perspective among guests that ayahuasca can evoke seemingly impossible visions, an ontological shock, and that the Indigenous healers were crucial to this evocation.

EXAMPLE 1: ARTHUR

Arthur is a thirty-six-year-old French man working as product manager at a life science journal. He described how the ayahuasca ceremonies at Pachamama Temple helped him overcome anxiety and appreciate what is important in life. It was his second time attending an ayahuasca retreat. He explained that he received healing by "shocking" his sense of self and myopic reality.

> [Ayahuasca] creates a sort of shock that separates us from our ego that we are constantly grasping. While in this state we are able to learn extremely valuable lessons that can take years if not decades for most people. Ayahuasca also helps us to see the bigger picture. It is as if it was allowing us to zoom out and remove the mind limitations that are preventing us from seeing what matters most.

Arthur described perceiving spirits a few times in his ayahuasca visions. One story included a giant insect-person hovering over him and communicating to him. "The conversations [with the insect] were pleasant and full of surprising insights," he remarked. The creature explained to him why it was important for him to always remember his purpose in life. When he asked the spirit creature why it had not told him this earlier, the visions "flashed back and went through my life very quickly and I saw books, movies, and other experiences that were trying to pass me the same message." He explained how in his most

126 GLOBAL AYAHUASCA

important vision he saw himself waking up from a kind of illusory dream which then triggered an experience of cosmic unity.

> Life was just a joke and all the stress, emotional pains, and fears that we all have were just made-up things. I felt super free and happy, then later the vision became different and it was like I realized that I was just *one* with all people. My girlfriend and I were actually just one. The vision then went deeper and my ego completely disappeared. I was everything and nothing at the same time. I felt amazing and it was the scariest moment in my life too.

Arthur described how following the retreat he felt more relaxed and less anxious during everyday stressful situations, including at his job back in France. The retreat, he explained, also made him feel more introspective and wanting to avoid large crowds, which he was not sure was a good or bad outcome. Overall, ayahuasca made him realize that "life shouldn't be taken too seriously, and we are all part of one super soul." The wondrous ontological rupture of interacting with insect spirits and dissolving his ego into the collective soul of humanity made him grateful to ayahuasca and to the Shipibo healers. He specifically chose to drink ayahuasca with Indigenous specialists because "they have a deep experience with the medicine . . . [and] thousands of years of knowledge." He added, "I think it would be difficult to find non-Indigenous specialists that can create the same experiences." From his perspective, his visionary experiences of drinking ayahuasca were generated by the Shipibo healers.

EXAMPLE 2: JENNIFER

Jennifer is a forty-six-year-old fitness trainer and life coach from England. She was attracted to Pachamama Temple because it "seemed professional, well organized, reliable, traditional and true to the culture." She heard from a friend that it emphasized the "traditional way" of Shipibo healing. Her motivation to attend the ayahuasca retreat included a desire to overcome long-term grief and emotional pain, which she had been unable to cure through ordinary health care services. Jennifer had become sharply critical of allopathic medicine and its "old-fashioned thinking and training." Psychotherapists and psychiatrists, she suggested, "rely too heavily on medication and don't recognize the mind-body connection." She thinks that physicians are not trained to make people truly healthy and are "based on minimums rather than optimums." Jennifer expressed a preference for drinking ayahuasca with Indigenous rather than non-Indigenous specialists and was concerned about modernization eroding the brew's healing powers and making the Indigenous healers more like "us" and less like "them."

> When you take something out of context, it can easily get modernized, updated, and slowly watered down with other customs. For me, there is good and bad with this, but I feel more aligned with staying traditional, at least to the variety of Indigenous cultures that have utilized the medicine over a long time. I feel uncomfortable when Westerners begin to microdose as it seems to me to be a Western allopathic model. . . . I prefer to try new practices in a traditional way to experience what has been found to work/heal over many centuries. Using the medicine and understanding its strength and meaning is so important, but it's also part of experiencing another culture rather than bending a practice to "our" culture. To me, the only way to preserve these cultures is to use them as they have been forever.

A sense of timeless, archaic wisdom is popularly projected onto the Shipibo healers by the guests. The ayahuasca retreat was a space to heal Jennifer's emotional problems; to help her become "unstuck" and hopefully excel beyond average health. She described how the visions she experienced were shaped by the maestros and their *icaros*.

> I must confess that I didn't like the *icaros* at first! But after the first ceremony, I came to love them. . . . I found them magical, comforting, clarifying, reassuring, and uplifting. I think you always align with different energies in a different way. I loved Maestro Jose's enthusiasm and dancing, Maestro Manuel's patience and reassurance, and Maestra Francesca's soaring voice. They each took me to different places and showed me energies and parts of myself that I never knew were possible. I was also excited when Mama Maria was in the house [*maloca*].

Disrupting her existing ontological commitments, ayahuasca revealed the impossible as felt, seen, and possible. Jennifer described a range of visions.

This included monkeys and other "jungle creatures traveling up through [her] body from the floor," a range of "guardian spirits" that were protecting her, and many other "light, fun, playful characters" that she found difficult to describe. Outlining her most important or beneficial ayahuasca experiences, she wrote how each ceremony presented a certain theme:

> The first ceremony was around grief. The sadness, guilt, and burden, I felt deeply. It made me feel heavy and tired. It clearly showed that I had a choice, and it depended on my actions and responses. This also opened up an avenue of enquiry outside of the ceremonies. The second ceremony was around being light, playful, and childlike, seeing the magic in things again. The third illustrated how self-judgment kept me in indecision and paralysis. The fourth showed me how to accept, help/love, and how I sometimes fought people without realizing they were actually on my side. It also gave me an insight into meditation that I hadn't had before despite studying and teaching mindfulness. I learned how to simply sit, breathe, and receive. It also opened up further exploration and access to meditation afterwards.

Jennifer's second ayahuasca ceremony involved rejuvenating a kind of childlike wonder and "seeing the magic in things again." This occurred after experiencing a period of heavy grief and guilt during the ceremony and before further psychological lessons about the self and its relations with others. Overall, she described a deep gratitude towards the Shipibo healers for "guiding [her] soul" and enabling her to heal "through radical acceptance." Stepping outside allopathic medical traditions and into a marvelous visionary world deemed untouched by modernization, Jennifer described gaining a range of healing insights and personal transformations. She positioned her ayahuasca retreat among her wider trajectory of cultivating the self with meditation practices and yoga.

A common thread weaved throughout the Pachamama Temple survey responses included the notion that the Shipibo healers were instrumental in shaping guests' visions. Here, minds melt and the emotional intensities of the guests and the healers become expressed and exchanged. It was not uncommon for healers to occasionally struggle during the ceremonies and become weak in their ability to sing joyous and elated *icaros* for the guests. When a healer, dosed on ayahuasca, became weak, another healer would sing a special *icaro* to them to help boost their spirit. The ceremonies included affective dimensions of what Anna Tsing (2015) called a contamination of diversity, whereby the pain and suffering and the hope and joy of the healers and guests, cultivated at different vantages of global modernity, intermingled and overlapped.

But not all differences mixed in the heightened perception and altered space of ayahuasca tourism ceremonies. The guests were generally unsure how to respond to the suffering of the healers conceptually let alone practically. Guests traveled far and invested considerable money and hope in receiving healing from the spiritual masters of the rainforest. They sometimes placed the healers at imaginary heights grand enough to heal their troubled modern conditions and high enough to place the distress of the healers beyond their comprehension. Shamanic tourism encounters, short and sometimes loaded with expectation, can evoke confusion and indifference among guests. The moral distance between a suffering Shipibo healer and confused guests during the ayahuasca ceremonies was reflective of the wider modern condition in which we increasingly "deal with people in purely abstract and instrumental terms" suspended by the commercial webs of modernity (Wilkinson and Kleinman 2016:10). The guests' tendency to be in awe of the Shipibo healer's plant spirits and *icaros* but remain largely ignorant about their systemic conditions of social suffering involves dealing in primitivist imagery in the reproduction of an instrumental relationship.

Shamanic tourism retreats in Peru are permeated by intentional wonder. The healers themselves become objects of wonder by performing dramatic songs that help alter the ayahuasca experiences of the guests. The visitors arrive having consumed wondrous discourses about the brew and having imagined the potential of exceeding expectations into an Indigenous cosmovision. The kinds and intensities of awe that occur at these settings are made possible by arrangements of psychoactive molecules, selves, and societies that assemble in global spaces of healing. The visitors were often looking for trytamine-rich psychedelic brews and a window onto other ways of life. As a vortex of mysteries and alternate realities, ayahuasca marvels those who are courageous enough to stick with it. While sensitive to the social and cultural scaffolding of the setting, ayahuasca can evoke a place-based atmosphere of wonder and visionary experience. Foreigners arrive in the Amazon rainforest to drink ayahuasca with Indigenous specialists and to encounter a horizon of self and society. This becomes part of the place, during the retreats.

Some visitors arrived more balanced while others displayed naive romanticism and projected intense fears and hopes onto plant spirits, session leaders, and mysterious Others in visions. The wonder of ayahuasca can empower "cultish" behaviors of uncritically following a community leader's pronouncements. Ayahuasca encounters that involve cheating, manipulation, sexual abuse, and other intense moral issues have not been addressed in this chapter. But an examination of wonder in such contexts is worthy of study (see Peluso 2014; Wright and Ross 2021). Some Australian ayahuasca drinkers explained to me that sexual abuse will never happen in their ceremonies because they are protected by plant spirits. Yet the mystery of ayahuasca and its plant spirits can also weaponize unethical acts. For example, one infamous facilitator would harvest protected Acacia plant species—whose populations were severely diminished—for making ayahuasca. He proclaimed that the spirits of the plant species told him in a vision that it was okay to harvest them.

The next chapter delves into Australian ayahuasca groups in detail. The approaches are still shaped by primitivist ideals present in the global, spiritual-wellness ecosystem, but they also edge towards belonging or community, wherein extended forms of sociality shape the visionary experiences and their associated narrative practices.

FOUR

NATURAL MEDICINE
IN AUSTRALIA

Following the pattern of many other creation stories around the world, aya-huasca allegedly first arrived in Australia in the hands of a special person descending from the sky. Terence McKenna (1946–2000) was an American speaker and author who toured many Western societies in the 1990s advocating for psychedelics. He is granted myth-like status in today's psychonautic underground (St. John 2024). In 1997, he flew from his home in Hawaii to conduct a series of talks across Australia, including a seminal appearance at "Beyond the Brain" in Byron Bay. McKenna brought with him a cutting of the ayahuasca vine, which was apparently the first time the plant had touched Australian soil.

McKenna had arrived with new botanical wonders and a long-established critical sensibility towards mainstream society. His views positively reform some of the ideas discussed by the American historian Theodore Roszak in *The Making of a Counter Culture* (1969), when some youth in 1960s North America were finding the liberatory impulses of consciousness-altering techniques against conventional cultural and social life. A few decades later, McKenna boiled the message down to an aphorism, that "culture is not your friend," which he explained to auditoriums packed with people eager to learn his psychedelic knowledge.

McKenna had a profound intellect and entertaining knack for storytelling. His descriptions of psychedelic shamanism, pharmacology, cultural cri-

131

132 **GLOBAL AYAHUASCA**

tique, and phenomenology captivated vast crowds at universities, public halls, and outdoor music festivals, which now endure on YouTube and other media platforms. His has been the most sampled voice remixed in psytrance electronic music, "becoming chief bard to the neo-psychedelic counterculture" throughout the 1990s and beyond (St John 2012:115).

Poetically expressing the mysteries of psychedelic use, McKenna's talks and popular books represent a key source of psychedelic wonder discourse. He prized DMT—the alkaloid in ayahuasca brews—as the most potent and astonishing of all psychedelics. In *Food of the Gods*, McKenna wrote,

> Under the influence of DMT, the world becomes an Arabian labyrinth, a palace, a more than possible Martian jewel, vast with motifs that flood the gaping mind with complex and wordless awe. Color and the sense of a reality-unlocking secret nearby pervade the experience. There is a sense of other times, and of one's own infancy, and of *wonder, wonder, and more wonder.* [italics added] (McKenna 1993:258)

McKenna was invited to Australia by a small psychedelic reading group, and shortly after his tour, one of the organizers, a white Australian in his late thirties called Darpan, began to train with brew that was posted from McKenna in Hawaii. After three months of intense self-initiation, Darpan went on to spearhead the Australian ayahuasca scene across various corners of the country. By 2003, he and a small network of specialists were offering semipublic ceremonies in multiple locations, and by 2019, he had become one of the world's most prolific facilitators by personally conducting over fifteen hundred ceremonies to ten thousand or more people in covert locations across much of Australia, Europe, and other parts of the world.

Darpan brings a theatrical approach to ayahuasca. In 1976, he graduated with honors in psychology and dramatic arts from an Australian university and worked as an actor while singing in the rock bands The Divinyls and Die Laughing. Afterwards, he spent years studying spiritual crafts, including meditation with the controversial Indian mystic Osho and holotropic breathwork with the psychedelic psychiatrist Stanislav Grof. In the decades after meeting McKenna, Darpan trained with specialists in Brazil in Santo Daime and in Peru and Ecuador in vegetalismo and shamanistic approaches. But, in light of all these influences, he said that ayahuasca told him, during an

FIGURE 4.1 Australian ceremony facilitator Darpan in front of Shipibo fabric covered in neoshamanic utensils, northern New South Wales, Australia, 2012. (Photo: Rak Razam).

initiation, to conduct ceremonies in his own way. This meant administering ayahuasca to facilitate the natural energies within people and to cleanse and reconnect them to the spirit of the natural world.

At "Beyond the Brain" in 1997, the esteemed psychonaut McKenna was pleasantly interrupted by the smell of the vapors of DMT spreading through the room from the lungs of someone who had just inhaled its vapors. Australia has a large natural repository of DMT in its native acacia trees, and a psychonautic subculture of scientists, botanists, artists, and spiritualists had mobilized during the late 1990s and early 2000s. They experimented with local and foreign psychoactive plants and designed new organic formulas to imbibe (Tramacchi 2006; St John 2017; Van Kuelen, Tramacchi, and Williamson 2010). They also gathered to share knowledge and exchange at specialized cultural events, such as Entheogenesis Australis in Melbourne, and on the popular Australian internet forum The Corroboree. However, this early psychonautic period quickly became unknown to many ayahuasca drinkers in Australia.

134 GLOBAL AYAHUASCA

Ten years into the new century, drinking ayahuasca had crystallized into a unique approach that was mainly attracting people from New Age and alternative healing networks less interested in psychonautic experimentation than in healing trauma, discovering their Higher Self, and connecting with Mother Nature. A novel healing movement had formed with special attitudes and styles of drinking ayahuasca and relating to the experiences it evoked. Darpan explained the shift to me in 2012:

> When I started this work eighteen years ago, I'd only get the freaks, people on the fringe, alternative people, like me. But now my groups are large with the whole spectrum. I have people in their eighties and people in their teens and everywhere in between. We host up to eighty people in the ceremonies in Melbourne. Buddhist monks, doctors, lawyers, psychiatrists, sociologists, a lot of professional people, and a lot of people who just trust the plants, who trust nature and have a good intuitive sense of it. Some people come to me to drink ayahuasca who have never even smoked a joint [cannabis], maybe only drink a glass of sherry occasionally, and that's it.

It is hard to accurately measure the amount of people who drink or have drunk ayahuasca in Australia, given its illegal status and the privacy of many groups. I estimate there are several thousand or more. When I began ethnographic fieldwork in 2011, new ayahuasca retreats, or "circles," were emerging regularly with many facilitators having learned with Indigenous specialists in Amazonian Peru and Brazil. These ceremony facilitators would, in turn, apprentice new facilitators in Australia. There were several large, interconnected retreat networks operating across the country, plus many smaller insulated groups. To my surprise, a large portion of the hundreds of ayahuasca drinkers I encountered in Australia did not participate in, and often did not know about, the psychonautic subculture of chemical experimentation that had recently germinated ayahuasca healing circles there.

During my fieldwork in Australia, most people came in search of healing and meaning or connection, and those who were motivated by spiritual, creative, or other pursuits nonetheless tended to incorporate healing terminology into their ayahuasca narratives. During dedicated "sharing circles" at the retreats, people described a variety of afflictions that were motivating them to

FIGURE 4.2 Ayahuasca ceremony space and environment, northern New South Wales, Australia, 2012. (Photo: Darpan)

FIGURE 4.3 Integration ceremony with participants discussing their ayahuasca experiences, northern New South Wales, Australia, 2012. (Photo: Darpan)

136 GLOBAL AYAHUASCA

drink the brew. These ranged from marital problems, a lack of purpose in life, and sexual abuse trauma to chronic back pain and astigmatism. A greater sense of afflictions that people in Australia seek to cure with ayahuasca will be explored further on. But, to first get a sense of what united these diverse seekers and afflictions, it helps to consider a contextual dilemma that they often expressed.

URBAN DISENCHANTMENT

The ayahuasca brew was transplanted to urban Australia as a special remedy for healing a spiritual disconnection from nature. Darpan distilled this view: "The main illness I've been working with is the split in the Western psyche, the individual, between themselves and nature," he explained. Here, the retreats were typically conducted in natural environments, away from human settlements. They were places to imbibe sacred plant medicines and experience the visionary powers of nature coursing through one's body, hopefully bringing healing to the soul. Urban and metropolitan spaces were abandoned for the restorative embrace of natural environments. This quest to overcome a split between humans and nature was premised on the view that major lifestyle parts of modern societies were causing suffering by creating an artificial separation from nature. Healing was achieved by drinking the brew, surrendering and allowing nature and the cosmos to flood consciousness, which can inspire visceral sensations of purification and wild encounters with a deeper nature.

This spiritual thirst for nature has occurred in other non-Indigenous contexts outside Amazonia. In urban Brazil, for example, drinkers felt a sense of being "deprived of contact with nature" and overcame this deprivation with "the sacred plants . . . ayahuasca" (Virtanen 2014:73). The motivations of shamanic tourists in Peru involved seeking "personal self-awareness, including contact with a sacred nature, God, spirits, and plant and natural energies produced by ayahuasca" (Winkleman 2005:209). Such visitors explored "ecology via ayahuasca visions" (Brabec de Mori 2014:216) and perceived Indigenous peoples and knowledge as "the last repository of a primordial ecological vision" (Losonczy and Cappo 2014:109). Fashioned by a primitivist perception, the visitors encountered a primordial ecological realm positioned as "the antithesis of Western civilization: pre-industrial, premodern, natural, exotic, spiritual, sacred, traditional" (Fotiou 2014:163). The ayahuasca groups in Australia shared some of these similar features with other places. However, as noted in the Introduction, Indigenous Amazonian healers rarely traveled to Australia due to the country's strict visa and travel policies. This may have given a creative freedom to the circles Downunder.

Generally speaking, a pathological division between society and nature—including between the inorganic and organic—appears at the heart of many new ayahuasca healing modalities across the planet. In Australia, modern society was described as suffering—in a pathological sense—from a lack of authentic spirituality and healing that ayahuasca and natural environments could provide.

Researchers have suggested the brew recuperates individuals who are disenchanted by modern societies (Kaplan 2011:19; Tupper 2009:120; Partridge 2005:96; 2018). In doing so, they pit ayahuasca against a key strand of modernization theory. Historical processes of modern rationalism, materialism, and capitalism provided a remarkable mastery of the world at the grave expense of eroding existential grounds of meaning, according to social theorists. In his tome *A Secular Age* (2007), Charles Taylor suggested the modern erasure of enchantment has buffered and dislodged the self from wider cosmic orders, leaving it subject to a historically distinct malaise. The inability of spirits, gods, or the supernatural to compel the self is accompanied by a wider vacuum of meaning, he argued, in which "our actions, goals, achievements, and the like, have a lack of weight, gravity, thickness, substance" (2007:303–307). In Max Weber's terms, individuals of industrial capitalism are progressively disenchanted into cogs in the machinery of rational pursuits aimed at precision, steadiness, and speed, becoming "specialists without spirit, sensualists without heart" (Weber 1992:124). Considering what was lost to such an instrumental modernity, Stephen Kalberg suggested that religion entrenched the premodern world with ethical foundations and "coherent constellations of values that address fundamental questions concerning the ultimate meaning of life" (2005:29). The idea of recovering aspects of a premodern world animates much of the global spread of ayahuasca drinking, and certainly among neoshamanic and Amazonian tourism contexts that enact features of therapeutic primitivism. Neoshamanic practices can bring to lived experience a meaningful and porous cosmos coming from far beyond the existential vacuum of modernity.

Ayahuasca engaged such crises of meaning through an infusion of the cultural with the chemical. When ingested, its alkaloids can enhance the perception of meaning or "cause things to appear dramatically more meaningful than they would otherwise seem to be" (Hartogsohn 2018:1). As Benny Shanon explained, "[I]t is very common for [ayahuasca] drinkers to feel that they suddenly understand why things are the way they are, to find deep, heretofore hidden, meanings in verbal expressions and in texts, to discover the true sense of their own lives" (2002:243). When the drink meets the neoshamanic cosmology, such an enrichment of meaning has special existential import. Psychologist Ralph Metzner explained that "the real beauty of the teachings of ayahuasca spirits is that they can help provide meaning, purpose and direction to one's life" (1999:97). Ido Hartogsohn situated the meaning-enhancing side of ayahuasca and other psychedelics "in the broader cultural context of late modernity's struggle to make sense and meaning of life in increasingly atomized, individualized, and stress-ridden societies" (2018:3). Ayahuasca has been popularly consumed to reenchant a world of capitalist disenchantment (Kaplan 2011:19), which can also be observed in how neoshamanic cosmology has pitted a toxic society against a healing natural world (Gearin 2017). The ayahuasca plant spirit became popular as a natural medicine existing beyond the disenchantment of society. Here, it can help people overcome crises of meaning and discover who they *really* are.

The idea of modern disenchantment, however, has been critiqued by social theorists who provided important corrections, which, I argue, can help us better appreciate ayahuasca drinking in places like Australia. Pointing out how most people in the "modern West" believe in some form of charms, magic, or the supernatural, Jason Josephson Storm (2017) untangled theories of disenchantment and modernity. He interpreted Max Weber's iconic notion in terms of its literal translation, in which modern disenchantment was never fully achieved. What is important, instead, are processes of disenchant-ing (or *de-magic-ing*). These disenchanting efforts have served various political constituencies, including the truth of secular science against the apparent il-

lusions of religion; the church pronouncing its creeds against primitive super-
stitions in the colonies; and new spiritualist revivals emerging against those
they deemed hoaxes and false prophets (Josephson Storm 2017:306). As a historical process, accusations of disenchantment have spun with cyclical powers
of liberation and domination that are actualized along colonial, economic,
and intellectual lines. As described in Chapter 2, the harsh conditions and
inequalities of the colonial rubber industries in Amazonia did not disenchant
Indigenous workers but emboldened ayahuasca sorcery (Taussig 2010) and
spawned millenarian uprisings coordinated by shamanic leaders (Wright and
Hill 1986). The rationalization and specialization of industrial capitalism has
produced stressed and restless workers but not necessarily disenchanted workers. The disenchantment thesis has been further scrutinized by scholars that
illustrate how modern life includes a vibrancy of secular enchantments (Bennett 2001) and how capitalism itself operates like a quasi-religion with myriad
mis-enchantments (McCarraher 2019).

But many academics and proponents of ayahuasca, across the globe, write
as if the common mood of modernity is without the wonder of enchantment.
In addition, it should be noted that both enchantment and disenchantment
have suffering and struggle built in. Malaise and suffering can appear in the
lives of people depressed by disenchantment as well as in those lives that are
saturated by charms, spirits, and the supernatural.

BENEVOLENT NATURE

Ecological environments could be the most enduring balm for urban restlessness. In Australia, people tended to agree that nature, or the bush, is a
sacred and necessary context for authentic healing to occur with ayahuasca.
Ceremonies in urban settings were deemed inappropriate and could block
the spirit, limit experiences, and even open the drinkers to dangerous spiritual and psychological harm. "All of the functions of society take me away
from having a profound ayahuasca experience," Nick told me. He was an
avid ayahuasca drinker and nurse working in Melbourne during 2012. Nick
was passionate about the brew and often eager to express his gratitude for the
healing he had received from it. He explained that ayahuasca should be im-

bibed in "sacred circles" in natural environments where "things don't get in the way; they work with the experience." When we met, he was saving money to quit his job and leave the rat race to buy land in subtropical northern NSW to grow psychedelic plants and conduct his own ceremonies.

He once drank ayahuasca in a suburban house in Melbourne and encountered visionary "energies from people on the streets, electromagnetic frequencies, and the density of the city," which disturbed him. Cities are "toxic places full of mental distractions, material addictions, self-interest, and ego indulgence," he explained, and added, "The average person is so far removed from any element of living that could be described as normal or natural that most people do actually suffer from some form of mental disease, but that is the new normal." After a few hairy episodes of drinking ayahuasca in a home in an urban area, he now only drinks in natural environments, outside the city.

The bush is where ayahuasca ceremonies *should* happen. Drinking in a city apartment, an urban house, a secluded industrial estate, or anywhere among the machinic hum of the metropolis was profane and spiritually dangerous or even reckless.

The reverence for nature that is shared by many ayahuasca drinkers reflects the wider global trends of eco-healing found in forest bathing and other nature therapies. There is good reason to spend some time outside cities (Qing 2018; Plevin 2018). Natural environments can reduce stress, boost the immune system, and restore well-being (Hartig et al. 2014; Bowler et al. 2010). This has led some physicians to write "nature prescriptions" or give patients a written recommendation to spend time in nature (Kondo et al. 2020). Examining what has long been folk knowledge among urban ayahuasca enthusiasts, Sam Gandy and colleagues (2020) suggested that exposure to natural environments can complement psychedelic therapies.

It is unclear what exactly makes spending time in nature so healing. Biologist Edward Wilson (1984) suggested an evolutionary affiliation between humans and other lifeforms defines an innate "biophilic" psychology, conservationist ethic, and aesthetic attraction to nature. The wonder of natural spaces—such as shimmering waterfalls, melodic bird calls, and aromatic flowers—appears to contribute to their mental health benefits (Kanelli et al. 2021). Alluding to the sensory changes induced by psychedelics, Aldous Huxley famously suggested that the substances could "cleanse the doors of perception" (1954) and assist the beauty of nature to radiate with enhanced colors, sounds, and smells, including sometimes for several days afterwards. Psychedelic practice can help attune the senses to their environments or umwelt (Tramacchi 2006:26).

Spiraling fractal designs are common features of the psychedelic sensorium. The designs are also ubiquitous in nature, such as in leaves, tree branches, waves, and seashells. Fractals are mathematical structures that appear at different scales. The physiology of the brain is fractal in nature, which led Ary Goldberger to hypothesize that fractals in Gothic architecture and art could represent an "externalization of the fractal properties of our physiology in general, and of our neural architectures and neuro-dynamics, in particular" (Goldberger 1996). The dazzling fractals people see on tryptamine psychedelics—including ayahuasca—may also reflect basic structures of brain physiology that mirror wider design principles of nature.

Observing the wondrous shape of fractals in nature can have a calming effect upon the mind for some people (Sternberg 2009:35). Although, the fractals can take on an energetic and pounding wonder at a "bush doof" outdoor psychedelic festival that is less calming and includes more social experiences with the substances, such as dancing. For some Australian ayahuasca enthusiasts, the pulsating fractal designs of their deep visions indicated special healing processes. In the safety of a well-held space, they perceived morphing patterns in synesthetic flows of sensory-bodily sensations that encouraged purging and the releasing of "stuck emotional pressure." Visionary fractals were sometimes described as an expression of the interconnected spirit of nature that would heal and purify the body.

Alice, a Chinese Australian in her mid-thirties from Sydney, described her fractal ayahuasca visions in a way that would be intuitive to many drinkers in the country. When I first met Alice in 2012, she had quit a corporate job in the city and was living in a remote area among lush green hills north of Brisbane, while assisting her boyfriend's art business. She had drunk ayahuasca more than a hundred times, mostly for healing childhood family trauma. But she also described how ayahuasca helped her overcome an "obsessive angst with finding my purpose." "Now I am much more relaxed about my journey; trusting in myself and what is right for me leads me effortlessly along," she added. When I asked if the spirit of ayahuasca is male or female,

142   GLOBAL AYAHUASCA

Alice highlighted how the fractal designs of her visions embodied a feminine sentience of nature.

> For me, ayahuasca is female. It is more usual than not for me to feel her as a presence. Sometimes [during a ceremony] I hear her voice when I ask her questions. Sometimes when I ask for help she will just come in and I will have an amazing insight or see a vision. Sometimes we just work as one on an instinctual, energetic level and I feel the process of letting go. I love the fractals of psychedelics. For me, they are often made up of luminescent, feminine eyes that see into my being. Sometimes I just feel her all-encompassing love and compassion and nurturing of my being, and sometimes I become one with that in my consciousness and can tap into her network of living beings.

She connected the fractals with the restorative balm of Mother Nature. When I asked if ayahuasca had healed anything in her life, Alice listed a range of health benefits and then highlighted that the brew had changed her perception of nature.

> Yes! My eyesight has improved. My breathing is easier. I went from taking tramadol for period pain to taking nothing. It brought attention to my unhealthy relationship with my body, which was riddled with pain in my back, neck, and shoulders. I am now mostly pain and painkiller free. . . . I have let so much anger and emotional pain from my childhood trauma go. It has been healing my intimate relationships. The medicine [ayahuasca] has also been healing my relationship with the earth. I now consider my natural environment as one of the biggest supports in my life and I feel compelled to nurture the environment.

For ayahuasca drinkers and non-ayahuasca drinkers alike, the healing that comes from spending time in natural environments is probably due to multiple factors. This would include the sensory exposure to beautiful vistas, soothing sounds, and aromatic flowers, and the biological exposure to healthy air and microbial dimensions. Also welcome to many would be the psychological relief that comes from stepping outside the sociocultural sensorium of urban environments. Existing at the social edges and with countercultural attitudes, ayahuasca neoshamanism groups find healing and restoration in the fractal geometry of their visionary eco-worlds.

At an outdoor cultural festival called "EntheonGaia" that attracted over a thousand punters to a tropical valley in northern Queensland in 2012, leading Australian ayahuasca facilitators were present (EntheonGaia 2012). They conducted workshops and talks about natural medicines, shamanism, consciousness, and an imminent Great Awakening that many people at the event were talking about. "We live in the age of prophecy, of miracles and telepathy," a speaker explained on the microphone, echoing the lyrics of a song commonly sung during ayahuasca ceremonies in Australia. It was December, during the exact year and month that countercultural icon Terence McKenna had prophesized a utopian spiritual awakening would occur (Hanegraaff 2010; McKenna and McKenna 1993; St John 2024). The event was joined by Terence's brother, the ethnopharmacologist Dennis McKenna, who is a long-term friend of Darpan, Australia's key facilitator.

Given the large emphasis on ayahuasca at EntheonGaia, some attendees playfully lamented that the festival should have been called "EntheoAya." In an autobiographical talk, "Ayahuasca: Reflections on a Road Well-Travelled," Darpan spoke to a captivated crowd of several hundred people spread out across the grassy field. The "core teaching of ayahuasca," he explained, is "self-acceptance, and through this basic realignment The Madre can heal most maladies on earth, including depression, abuse, and even war. It heals through reconnecting your soul with nature, because we have been dislocated from the natural world and our divine nature. The intuitive soul has been virtually lost under the humdrum of modern society."

Ayahuasca spread through corners of the Australian imagination at the center of a therapeutic spirituality located in nature, beyond the disenchantment of society. "We are nature," Darpan continued. "We are observing ourselves when we observe nature. Ayahuasca is a medicine that reconnects you to the great mystery of that larger part of who you are." However, overcoming the chasm between the self and nature, and learning to fully trust the spirit of ayahuasca, is not necessarily easy. Whether attempting to heal from a recent divorce, the distress of an intense workplace, trauma related to serving in the Australian military, or chronic back pain from an unknown injury, learning to "let go" and not resist allowing Mother Ayahuasca *in* during the ceremonies *provides the* difficult path of authentic healing. In a more extreme philosophy of healing described by facilitators in Australia, the powers of the brew were sometimes put to the test against society itself. The Australian facilitator Jules described it as follows:

> Western society is sick and ayahuasca goes to the heart of it. Ayahuasca visions are all about the interpersonal realm, how you are relating to others, the connections you have with others. . . . A lot of people discover a deeper sense of connection through ayahuasca, a connection with themselves, the planet, the cosmos, each other, the plants; because people live with such a disconnection from the earth. I have my own path of understanding my disconnection and wanting to connect myself to the cosmos, to other people, to the plants, to the natural world. It's a deep sense of healing. I've never got to the point that I feel like it is a finished product. . . . The plants say, "You think this behavior is okay because everyone else is doing it or because society has sanctioned it, but actually what you are doing here is fucked, and it's causing you pain and other people pain." . . . Most people are so alienated and disconnected and the plants are getting through this and giving feedback.

Drinking ayahuasca plants in Australia did not emerge in a cultural vacuum. It resembles the countercultural perspectives of New Age spirituality and its cultural criticism towards conventional society and politics (Hanegraaff 1996; Brown 1997). Such ayahuasca drinkers aim to heal distress and sickness by imbibing a natural antidote sometimes said to heal the trauma of society itself.

The idea of escaping the drudgery, malaise, and alienation of the city for an authenticity found in the bush has a long history in Australian settler society. A whole century earlier, in the 1890s, intellectuals and bohemians in urban Sydney and Melbourne idealized the bush as a place of radical egalitarian values. Their creative works about the bush were shaped by colonial legends of courageous pioneers exploring the harsh environment. The bush legend has successfully gripped the national imagination since federation in 1901, exhibiting varying iterations and values. However, as David Carter (2017) explained, the bush has always been where the authentic and quintessential Australian will be found.

Those who drink ayahuasca in the Australian bush are also searching for a natural authenticity beyond urban life, beyond the ordinary. Whereas most of the classic bush legends depict pastoral landscapes, and are therefore based upon wild spaces that have been tamed or converted to farms, the spirit of ayahuasca is pristine, free from human mastery, and radically uncorrupted by civilization. Connected with the spirits of wild plants and animals, Indigenous Amazonian healers, and in other cases angels and extraterrestrials, Mother Ayahuasca appeared as an outsider and profound Other to urban Australia. Benevolent and caring and permeating the natural landscapes, she represents a salubrious alternative to the colonial motifs of Australia's bush myths. However, Des Tramacchi cautioned against neoshamanic groups that are coming from settler societies but are inscribing their psychedelic spirituality onto unceded Indigenous lands (2017). At the World Ayahuasca Conference in Ibiza in 2014, a famous white Australian ayahuasca facilitator gave a talk about drinking the brew and exploring the Aboriginal Dreamtime cosmology. The conference organizers, after being lobbied by different people, decided to not upload the facilitator's talk to YouTube, like they did for the other presentations. While people of all stripes across the planet drink ayahuasca and perceive anacondas and jaguars glowing in Indigenous Amazonian lands, the brew's extension to Australia brings the neoshamanic sensorium into a new and more heavily contested environmental cosmology.

Several key ayahuasca specialists in Australia emerged from a psychedelic subculture of outdoor electronic dance events called psytrance "bush doofs," which began in the late 1990s (St John 2001; Luckman 2003). Among this subculture, the urban mythological template of the bush is recast into an electronic dancefloor surrounded by glowing art designed to interact with the altered experiences of taking LSD, psilocybin mushrooms, and other psychedelics. With its playful and spiritual merging of dance music, creative spaces, wild dress codes, and natural environments, the ideas of recreation, celebration, and spirituality blur at the bush doof (St John 2015). Des Tramacchi described how a sense of psychedelic spirituality helped connect the "doof community to the landscape and allows the occurrence of spontaneous mystical bonds with nature" (2001). Some bush doofers emphasized the "connectedness and communal enlightenment achieved by eco-rapture—that is, the feeling one gets from dancing and stomping upon the earth" (Haebich and Taylor 2007:76). At such events, participants consumed psychoactive chemicals very similar to what is in ayahuasca brews (and I have heard of bush doofs including ayahuasca ceremonies before and after the event). However, many ayahuasca drinkers typically differentiated their practices from psychedelic festival events by describing the brew as "spiritual not recreational," even though bush doofs embodied spiritual philosophies of nature.

Ayahuasca Australiana can be differentiated from the psychedelic milieu of bush doofs by virtue of its emphasis on healing, ceremonial norms, psychedelic dosage, and musical styles. Once an ayahuasca ceremony has officially begun, participants should not talk or interact in the space, but rather, "hold space" to better allow everyone to have their own journey. Drinking the brew in the bush—in natural environments, but usually indoors—attendees are immersed in loud music that colors the dark room with an inner world of personal visions and changes in mood. Here, the dosage of the psychoactive substance and the ceremony emphasis on the individual are both at increased levels compared to the bush doof. Whereas the bush doof dancefloor is a space of swarming bodies and collective effervescence, the ayahuasca ceremony is more individualized, private, and otherworldly (Gearin and Calavia-Sáez 2021). The ceremonies open visionary portals of personalized and enchanted worlds with plant spirits, gods, aliens, lost memories, traumas, and higher selves.

Prior to the proliferation of ayahuasca groups in Australia at the turn of the century, the bush doof accommodated a vibrant subculture associated with smoking the isolate compound DMT. Des Tramacchi did a pioneering study on the spiritual and experiential dimensions of the compound in Australia. As outlined in *Vapours and Visions: Religious Dimensions of DMT Use*, many users "emphasised the sense of awe and wonder that accompanied their DMT 'voyages'" (2006:107). Their reasons for consuming it were "entheogenic, or spiritual, or religious" yet with an idiosyncratic style and "relative lack of ritual elaboration" (172). The ayahuasca networks in Australia

SITTING CEREMONY

On a Friday afternoon in the winter of 2013, twenty-seven people, including myself, were gathering from across eastern Australia and from as far as New Zealand, making our way to John's opulent and secluded retreat center to participate in an illicit form of spirituality and alternative healing. More than half of the attendees had traveled directly from work, and most stayed at the retreat for two evening ceremonies and left on Sunday afternoon. After several hours of being stuck on the highway, bumper to bumper, I eventually arrived at the retreat nestled among mountains outside a major Australian city. Daylight was ending. I joined some of the others in John's personal lounge room and sat around an enclosed fireplace next to a large bookshelf populated with texts on transpersonal psychology, classic poetry, New Age healing, and psychedelic art.

The crowd of early arrivals, roughly a dozen people, had separated into several fluid conversations, with people occasionally moving around the room. I got talking with a couple in their early twenties who were nervous about drinking ayahuasca for the first time. "Do people ever stay in the visions, like, don't come out of the journey, forever?" Chris asked me, referring to the duration of the effects of ayahuasca, his eyes pinned to my response. "I have never heard of that happening," I replied. Lucy, a middle-aged woman from Israel who had consumed ayahuasca more times than she could recall, was listening to our conversation and switched her position on the couch to face us. She had been a regular attendee at various other Australian ceremonies organized by a related group. Tonight, however, she had traveled several hours by plane to attend this retreat. With a maternal and welcoming gaze, she told the young couple, "I remember the first time I journeyed. I was more afraid than before going to mandatory army training. Then I actually drank the brew and realized it offered me a way of transcending my own inner terror."

The words seemed to calm the couple. "People forget that ayahuasca is a medicine," Lucy emphasized to us. "La Madre [ayahuasca] purifies and aligns us on a deep level. It is a very natural thing." Our conversation was absorbed by those sitting with Lucy and a discussion began about types of healing people had received from the brew, narratives that included curing depression-anxiety, astigmatism, and musculoskeletal problems. Concomitantly, on the other side of the room, several men, regular attendees, were discussing which artists and sci-fi films best illustrated the contents of their visions.

Most attendees were white Anglo Australians, but also present was a Chinese-Australian, a Japanese, an Israeli, and a white American. Ayahuasca retreats in Australia were not cheap and therefore tended to attract older clients who, during 2011 to 2014, could afford the \$300–\$600 AUD for two nights of drinking the brew. At this particular retreat, attendee occupations varied: a tennis coach, an ecologist, a retired war veteran, a tattoo artist, a chef, a graphic designer, a musician, a nurse, and a nutritionist.

Healing with ayahuasca was approached as a holistic process. While the social gathering and ceremonial practice was typically restricted to the weekend retreat, drinkers described the period shortly before and after the weekend as equally important for healing. For usually three days prior to and three days after the ceremonies, participants were asked to follow a special and healthy diet and to avoid sexual behaviors (Gearin and Labate 2018). By temporarily reducing salts, sugars, meats, and other foods, and eliminating or diminishing high-arousal activities such as sex, television, and alcohol, the ayahuasca drinker is "preparing their mind and body in the same way one might prepare a temple for an esteemed guest," Darpan explained to me, on another occasion. Psychologist Benny Shanon argued that practices of dieting and prior psychological "cleansing" were necessary for evoking the marvelous qualities of ayahuasca.

> With Ayahuasca, the impact of cleanliness is concrete and evident. For a person to experience the wonders of Ayahuasca in all their magnificence, she or he has to be cleansed. If one's body is not clean (for instance, if one is not careful in observing the dietary precautions before the Ayahuasca session), one will purge and vomit. If one's psyche is not clean and one carries psychological matters that have not been confronted and properly dealt with, one's experiences under the intoxication will reflect personal

conflicts and concerns. . . . Only when both body and psyche are clean will the mind be ready genuinely to profit from what the brew can offer and experience what might be characterized as "the world of Ayahuasca." (Shanon 2002:300)

In Australia, drinkers described how a short *dieta* or dieting process undertaken prior is psychologically challenging and how mastering this can help them to hone their attention on their reasons for drinking the brew. For example, Michael, a high school teacher, explained to me,

When dieting, I associate my intention with the dietary sacrifices in terms of using them as a reminder. As I reach for anything that is restricted and remember that "I can't have that," the immediate following thought is "remember your intention." Then when confronted with the sudden and intense flavor of the medicine [ayahuasca] in ceremony, my body takes it as the signal to go seeking the chosen intention actively during the session.

Ayahuasca drinking was often described as "work," and it can be a very demanding practice. People described how the preparatory diet period included challenging feelings, dreams, and slight alterations in ordinary perception that later become pronounced during their ayahuasca visions. The diet period starts to blur the normally-rigid boundaries between the mundane and the sacred, and also helps shape the coming visionary experiences and healing narratives. The effects of psychedelic substances can be influenced by the users' expectations and socialization (Dupuis 2022a). The bodily practice of dieting helps to build the person's expectations, including their "intentions" or reasons for attending the retreat, into the somatic habits of daily life, whether the person intends to try to heal trauma or find their true self.

With the sun falling over the horizon, everyone finished their herbal tea and privately donned all-white clothing. It was time to enter the ceremony hall. Walking in the large room, my senses were captured by the space. The lighting was dimmed. Several candles were alight. Aromatic vapors of the South American fragrant wood *Palo Santo* saturated the air. Soft harmonic music was playing. In the middle of the room were two large Amazonian Shipibo fabrics upon which a small shrine was centered where participants could place their own sentimental objects to charge with spiritual energy. The shrine included fresh flowers, semiprecious stones and sigils, candles, aromatic resins, and a big plastic bottle encasing the brown liquid.

We all sat on the ground, making a large circle that faced the central shrine, an arm's length apart from each other, mounted on mattresses and large pillows, each with a plastic vomit bucket. This is the most common spatial organization of ayahuasca ceremonies in Australia. Some groups split gender, with men and women on opposing sides of the ceremonial hall, facing each other across a middle shrine area. But mainly, the circles mix genders and people gravitate to sit near their companions or family members. The ceremonies are casually described by drinkers as sacred circles. Drinkers "sit circle" and define desirable ceremonies positively as "powerful circles" and undesirable or dangerous as "cowboy circles" that are "not held well." One third of the diameter of this circle was reserved for the ceremony facilitators, one male and two females, who were surrounded by high-quality instruments and equipment. The ceremony hall had expansive views over rolling green hills. Surrounding us were the sounds of cicadas, the wind rustling in the trees, the occasional bird call.

Standing upright with a calm and confident poise from years of qigong and meditation practice, Joseph was the ceremony facilitator and central point of responsibility. He walked around the group welcoming new members and making jokes with some of the regulars, asking them in a thick Australian accent if they chose the best cosmic pad to launch into the universe tonight. Joseph is a white Australian, in his early fifties. He was trained to facilitate ayahuasca primarily by his own drinking practice, he told me. He had less appreciation for Indigenous ayahuasca traditions compared to what can be learned "directly from the plants." His approach is "more in the psychedelic therapy tradition of the West than the native sorcery traditions of the Amazon," he added. Many facilitators doing ayahuasca ceremonies in Australia identify themselves as specifically "not shamans but facilitators," highlighting their supportive role in helping the attendees activate their own spiritual and therapeutic potentials. One facilitator described himself as a "guide from the side, not a sage on the stage." This relational position reflects a wider constellation of individualism in which each person is a contained vector of visionary gnosis.

NATURAL MEDICINE IN AUSTRALIA   151

Joseph first decided to drink ayahuasca about a decade earlier in a desperate search for healing after being discharged from the Australian military with post-traumatic stress disorder. He had tried "every conventional therapy [society] had offered." But ayahuasca was shockingly powerful. After being cured, he desired to learn from experts and drank with Indigenous healers from Ecuador and Peru. But he found these approaches "somewhat underwhelming." Expressing a kind of primitivist antiwonder, he told me, "The Amazonian shaman comes from a culture where life is mainly centered around the lower three chakras [bodily spiritual nodes]. The key issues of interrelating with people and surviving from day to day are basic tribal issues of family and are about power."

Joseph returned from South America to Australia to develop his own style, isolating alone in remote hills to brew and drink ayahuasca for weeks. That was his true ayahuasca initiation. But his approach is not without its critics. Some influential facilitators, who undertook ongoing "plant diets" under the guidance of Indigenous specialists—often in the Peruvian Amazonia—described Joseph's approach as spiritually naive and dangerous.

Joseph was introduced to ayahuasca at Darpan's ceremonies, where he observed how to hold space and serve ayahuasca. He once employed Darpan's special invocations at the beginning of his ceremonies, but after learning that Joseph refused to "do dietas" and train with Indigenous masters, Darpan eventually stopped endorsing Joseph's ceremonies, prompting Joseph to create his own ceremony invocations.

Despite his suspicion of Indigenous practices and a disagreement with his quasi-teacher, Joseph captured a large market and wielded respect from hundreds of ayahuasca drinkers in Australia who regularly frequented his retreats. He also served ayahuasca to some of the most well-known global advocates, including prominent scientists, social media influencers, film makers, and military veterans, whom he referred to as his "medicine family" and "medicine brothers and sisters."

Joseph's approach is part of a wider phenomenon that has come to be known as "spiritual but not religious." The words "spiritual" and "religious" were synonymous before the twentieth century, but gradually they became separated, with the spiritual now marking a social phenomenon whereby metaphysical life is increasingly privatized (Fuller 2001). In popular Western parlance, the word "spiritual" tends to refer to a "personal and private realm of thought and experience," while "religious" is used to describe the "public realm of membership in religious institutions, participation in formal rituals, and adherence to official denominational doctrines" (Fuller 2001:5). The passion of those who identify as spiritual and specifically not religious is often based upon a distrust of orthodox religion matched by a deep reverence for individual spiritual sovereignty.

Such a passion is present among ayahuasca drinkers in Australia who make jokes about the Brazilian ayahuasca churches (such as União do Vegetal) that have strong Christian and doctrinal elements. Joseph proclaimed that members of such churches "do not have a direct line to ayahuasca" because "the tradition gets in the way and teaches people to give their autonomy away" instead of helping them "learn self-responsibility." To be spiritual and not religious, here, involves placing a radical sovereignty upon the self and the uniqueness of its consciousness, including against tradition and doctrine.

During an important visionary experience in his "initiation with the plants," Joseph asked ayahuasca if he was ready to hold space and serve the brew to others. "She answered me. Oh boy, did she answer me!" he explained. "I was thrown into a spiritual sickness for weeks. Nightmares. Fear. Pain. All the trauma of flying helicopters at war came back to me. . . . It's challenging to convey my initiation in a rational sense," adding that decades of Taoist meditation and martial arts practice had helped prepare him for ayahuasca. But the instructions to serve the brew, he said, came from "learning to navigate the medicine [ayahuasca] space yourself." Luis Eduardo Luna (1986) noted this attitude about the shaman's direct relationship with the plants among some vegetalismo healers who suggested that ayahuasca initiation is ultimately a solo endeavor. Joseph learned his ayahuasca trade straight from the brew, which he said prepared him for serving it and holding space. He added,

> I don't know what other facilitators experience; I can only speak from my own background. When I drink ayahuasca, I experience enhanced sensory input. Knowing how to use that in a group you're facilitating is the trick. Often, I feel like I am simply responding to a need—the need, whether that be for healing or learning or whatever—the need comes from a place of oneness. My job is to help people integrate into that oneness.

With everyone seated comfortably in a circle, the lights dimmed, and the atmosphere sweet with aromatic fumes, the quiet recorded music was turned off and Joseph began the event by officially welcoming everyone.

Popular ayahuasca retreats in Australia had regular attendees and a sense of ongoing social belonging, but they also had a high turnover of new participants drinking for the first time. Joseph would always give an "introduction talk" to the group, which allowed new attendees to feel his "energy" and build trust, so they could better "let go" and allow the experience to unfold better. He spoke, "This is an ancient global tradition spanning millennia . . . from the Amazon . . . Ancient Egypt . . . and the Ancient Greek Eleusinian mysteries." He described some chemistry of ayahuasca and its basic phenomenological effects, highlighting that "people can be having very different experiences to you, so it's important to respect that." Setting social conventions, we should refrain from speaking or interacting in the ceremony space but instead approach the evening as a "private introspective meditation."

Everyone was silent. A few people took a long slow breath in, and then out. Following Joseph's introduction, we were invited to individually speak our "intention for the journey" or reasons for participating in the ayahuasca retreat. An email sent to all participants a week before had prepared us for this. We were told,

> The aim of these ceremonies is for healing and transformation and the intent each individual brings is of utmost importance. Your intention may be to receive knowledge, expansion, insight, clarity, release, healing. . . . The respect and focus you bring affects the whole, so we ask that you come prepared mentally, emotionally and physically.

The "intentions for the journey" expressions that people articulated moments before they drank the brew were often animated by the Socratic dictum "How ought I live?" One participant said, "My intention is to heal my inner masculine and discover my purpose, discover what I *should* do with this precious thing called life." The intentions were spoken aloud often as indirect or direct requests to Mother Ayahuasca. Examples in this ceremony included "to heal some recent life challenges," "to journey in bliss and joy," "to heal lifelong sinus problems," "to surrender to whatever the mother [ayahuasca] wants to show me," and "to realize my divine potential." As described further

154 GLOBAL AYAHUASCA

on, ethical expressions might not appear as "I ought," "I should," or "my purpose" during the intention narratives, but they were more likely to appear the next day during the "sharing circle" when drinkers integrated their visions in the light of ordinary sociality and consciousness. More on that later.

First, Joseph officially "opened the space" by reciting an incantation that included a directive to pursue reflexive knowledge:

> Since the dawn of time, we have gathered around fires, in stone circles, temples, and pyramids to explore the mysteries of light, life, and love. Inscribed above the portal of the ancient temple of Apollo at Delphi were the words: know thyself. We gather here tonight in the footsteps of our ancestors on this same eternal quest for self-knowledge.

The room was dark. I could barely see the silhouettes of others. Joseph finished by spitting sacred aromatic liquid—*Agua de Florida*, a cologne used by ayahuasca healers in Peru—over the altar in the four directions. The flowers and Amazonian fabrics and altar in the center of the circle were softly illuminated by candle, the only source of light in the room.

Ayahuasca does not taste very good. But a recorded ambient song began on cue with cheeky lyrics repeating in a soft and female tone, "We taste only sacredness, we taste only sacredness," signaling it was time to drink about 30 milliliters of the bitter brew. Attendees took turns to receive the drink, kneeling in front of Joseph, often clasping their hands in gestures of prayer. We were asked to visualize our personal intention while holding the small glass before drinking. After drinking, some coughed and twisted their faces in response to the foul taste. Small pieces of raw ginger were available to chew, yet many avoided it and described the taste as "not so bad" or, much less commonly, with a positive appraisal such as "warm and nourishing." One special person described how midway through a ceremony, when he returned to have a second cup, he was "journeying so deep" under its strong effects that the brew tasted like "sacred ambrosia, sweet and heavenly," adding, "I let it sit in my mouth, in awe, feeling the light enter me." But this is unusual, as are the cases when people vomit seconds after drinking the brew and are offered another cup to attempt to keep it down. Typically, attendees smiled after drinking, placed a hand on their chest, gestured in prayer, or bowed slightly in gratitude to the facilitator, before returning to their place in the circle. After everyone drank, the facilitators and musicians drank too.

Normally, everyone in the space, which can include everyone at the retreat property, such as caretakers and cooks, had consumed ayahuasca. Some facilitators say that it is necessary for them to drink the brew to better support the group's energy and choose what songs to perform. The idea that ayahuasca can enhance musical abilities was widespread. Others commented that personally imbibing while facilitating ceremonies could help to release some of the collective "psychic pressure" in the ceremonial space.

Once everyone had drunk the ayahuasca, there was not a lot to observe ethnographically given the darkness and emphasis on experiencing inner visions. The music connected the drinkers to a shared level of experience, but such a union was usually transcended by the inner visions of each person. Perhaps the most social aspect of the ceremony was the vomiting. The purgative effects of ayahuasca were relatively common. When someone vomited, and particularly if it was intense and roared out accompanied by moaning, this could easily induce others to vomit and perhaps see haunting visions too. Such purging often occurred in waves or rounds that lasted five minutes or more, after which everyone calmed to silence and the music gained supremacy again. Some ceremonies only had a few purging sessions, whereas others felt like someone was purging the whole time. Afterwards, people described diverse visions as if they had just returned from a totally unique journey, whether through the natural world, into a greater cosmos, or to their own biographical past.

If drinking ayahuasca is a journey, then music is the vessel. Typically, live music was performed at the Australian ceremonies, but sometimes recorded music was played too. When an attendee described the ceremonial music as powerful, special, challenging, or "not my thing," it was sometimes synonymous with their feelings towards the ceremony itself. At several different retreat groups, during the next morning, drinkers would complain to the ceremony facilitators about a certain song that they did not think was ap-

156   GLOBAL AYAHUASCA

propriate or good. Some facilitators would reply by telling the person that their resistance to the song was a symbol of an underlying spiritual resistance and psychic block that ayahuasca was attempting to help them overcome and heal. The disapproval of the music by attendees was described by facilitators as an opportunity to overcome spiritual sickness. The selection and performance of music appeared to be one of the most involved tasks of the facilitators. Accusations about the inappropriateness of the music may seriously impinge upon reputation.

Some specialists described being told by the spirit of ayahuasca to perform or play certain songs at certain times during the ceremony. They suggested these intuitive abilities assisted people in healing. In parallel, attendees reported uncanny synchronizations between a particular song and the corresponding visions they experienced at that moment. It appears that the eclectic music at Australian ayahuasca ceremonies has helped to elicit a diversity of visionary worlds. Darpan explained,

> The music you play in circle tends to evoke the traditions they resonate with. So if you play Bhajan chants, you'll probably see Hindu deities. Sound is the pathway into those realms. The astral realm is a multilayered tapestry of realities—the upper celestial realms, deities, angels, you have the human realm then you have the demonic realm, the lower realms or the underworld. Depending on the songs, you can direct which way you're going into those worlds.

A popular songbook of 117 songs written by Australian ayahuasca facilitators for singing in ceremonies includes an aesthetic range divided, with approximately one quarter of lyrics with Eastern religious themes (Hinduism; Buddhism), one quarter South American themes (mestizo ayahuasca; Santo Daime; and Indigenous Amazonian *icaros*), and one half with New Age ayahuasca therapeutic themes (about Mother Ayahuasca, Gaia, and healing). Ceremony specialists made use of various musical equipment—analogue and electronic—including guitars, microphones (with amplifiers and quadraphonic speakers), hand drums, rattles, harmoniums, harps, chimes, electronic synthesizers, computers, and live music software.

Music at the beginning of ceremonies tended to be ambient and instrumental and was more quiet and gentle, as the participants silently prepared or waited for the ayahuasca to kick in. Once the heights of the visions or psychoactive effects were present, the music was dramatic and louder and then softer and calmer, over approximately twenty-minute sequences, alternating back and forth between tension and release. The psychoactive effects of ayahuasca, drinkers explained, came in waves of intensity, and the music sometimes modulated these visionary waves. During the final hours, participants tended to be more reflective while integrating the dramatic aspects of their experiences. Yet, against this neat and general picture, ayahuasca can be unpredictable. Some drinkers described becoming visionary only towards the very end of the session. Many ceremonies finished around 2:00 or 3:00 a.m., but some continued longer in order to "process the energy in the room." These extended evenings and reactions could be due to a range of reasons, including the brew's strength and how many booster cups were consumed, participants' dietary practices or lack thereof, the levels of visionary enthusiasm or affliction in the room, or even just the proclivities of the musician-facilitators.

The rules of a ceremony were described as holding space. Ceremonies described as not being "held well," among those I participated in, included higher levels of expressed distress that included screaming and vocal aggression. Removing interaction during ceremonies seemed to minimize or contain communicative channels of distress in the group. Drinkers expected to possibly encounter challenging psychic materials, confront visions, or have a "difficult journey," and this process was honored as courageous steps towards healing. But in ceremonies deemed "not held well," emotional challenges could overwhelm participants with continuous and infectious distress manifesting among the entire group. In one of the worst ones I witnessed, the facilitator was hiding with head under a blanket while one older woman was thrashing about at risk of physically hurting herself, while a young man was off wandering outside experiencing alchemy by ingesting dirt from the remote, rural driveway. The facilitator later explained to the group that it was a rough ceremony partly because the plant was unhappy that he had harvested it. He had brewed a rare acacia species that is better not named, because the natural populations are so low, and this somehow haunted the event, from his perspective.

The social individualism of ayahuasca neoshamanism makes it difficult to outline clear cartographies of place-based visionary experiences. As I have described elsewhere (Gearin 2015; Gearin and Calavia Sáez 2021), the ceremonies permitted and somewhat encouraged individuals to be creative in visionary experience and their healing journeys on the road to transformation. Sharing circles were replete with different ayahuasca experience narratives, including about encounters with plant, animal, and other nature beings; gods from the pantheons of the world religions, with Buddhism and Hinduism dominant; aliens and interplanetary guides; family members and work colleagues, politicians, and celebrities; fantasy, sci-fi, and cartoon characters; visionary sensations of biological functions; and visionary narratives of vast landscapes, portals, cities, and alternate worlds. In Australia, people commonly said that ayahuasca "shows you what you need to see." But what you need to see was potentially very different from what others needed to see. Drinkers had direct access to a cosmological wellspring of personal significance.

In Australia, ayahuasca appeared in many visionary forms. It was described to me as a person ("she," "Madre"), a thing ("it," "medicine"), a domain ("the aya realm"), a drug ("on aya"), an experience ("the experience"), or simply "aya." These different concepts of ayahuasca helped people understand aspects of a very different way of approaching mental health, whether concerned with therapeutic, psychedelic navigational, or interpersonal parts of life. Experiences deemed most important, though, were often marked by an encounter with a sacred and benevolent person named Mother Ayahuasca. She typically appeared in natural form, such as a plant or an animal, or in some cases, as all of nature. Drinkers would ask each other how much they felt ayahuasca during a particular ceremony, as if her presence waxed and waned over the months. Ayahuasca also accompanied people in everyday life, during integration—as explored in Chapter 6.

The next section provides two in-depth examples of ayahuasca drinkers in Australia. The first explores the visionary experiences of a long-term participant. The second explores a novice drinker who had only consumed the brew a few times. Both cases demonstrate the potential wide diversity of visionary experiences that one person can experience with ayahuasca.

EXAMPLE 1: KATE

The first time Kate drank ayahuasca was shocking and profound for her. On the Sunday afternoon after a retreat conducted by Darpan in secluded mountains outside Melbourne, Kate drove several hours back to her suburban home and lay on the floor in the middle of her lounge room for hours. She was astonished by her ayahuasca experiences and by the fact that hardly anybody she knew had any idea that such a thing was even possible. "I had no idea that there were other dimensions and realms of existence beyond my concept of reality and my waking reality until I had ayahuasca," she explained. Kate told me that she still received new insights from this particular ayahuasca experience six years later.

An Australian born to immigrant parents from Greece, Kate was in her early forties in the early 2010s and working in the public sector as a graphic designer. She learned about ayahuasca from a friend who originally thought it might inspire her art. But she received far more than artistic inspiration. When we met, Kate had drunk ayahuasca over a hundred times and was regularly flying across the country to facilitate ceremonies by singing music. Reflecting on her introduction to the brew, she said,

> It was life changing. . . . Ayahuasca became my spirituality . . . or actually it is not my spirituality but my contact with spirituality . . . not an identity but a relationship, a learning arena, a place to learn about myself and how the universe works, how I integrate with the universe and become more connected with life. . . . I can love people better and fuller now.

In the beginning, Kate only attended the ceremonies once every six months. But gradually over several years she learned to "navigate the medicine space better" and then started attending retreats once per month (and drinking both nights of the monthly retreats). She explained that if she did not drink for several months, she found herself becoming antisocial and selfish and feeling "dulled down a bit." The longer she went without the brew, the more she forgot the "feeling intensities" of the experiences, which only became apparent again upon her returning and "dropping into the medicine space."

Over several months and retreats, Kate shared with me dozens of aya-

160 GLOBAL AYAHUASCA

huasca visions she had seen. The diversity and variety are almost as astonishing as the narratives themselves. While the experiences are her "personal treasures," "divine gifts," and "precious healing insights," she rarely described them outside the retreats, and particularly not with people who had never drunk ayahuasca. Kate was quite extroverted in social spaces, but she approached ayahuasca "like an introvert" because it "is a personal inner journey," she explained. The more she drank the brew, the more the visions and realms appeared to her as reflections of her own inner psyche and not as external realities beyond herself. But she was still somewhat agnostic about this.

She described how an old traumatic incident became a symbolic theme across some of her ayahuasca experiences. Fifteen years prior, she was in a life-threatening car accident and had broken seventeen bones in her body. With ayahuasca, she traveled back to the accident, witnessed herself trapped in the car, and reassured her younger self that everything will be okay. Her chronic pain had reduced, which she attributed to the ayahuasca ceremonies. Returning to the accident was just one reoccurring experience among a variety of other ayahuasca "journeys of going back to all the times I experienced crisis in my life. . . . [These] journeys into the past refract through time to heal me now and make me more comfortable with all the things that hadn't gone the way that I wanted in my life." Journeying into the past with ayahuasca is something different compared to just ordinary remembering. Kate said that when simply remembering things with her imagination, she remains an observer of the past, yet with ayahuasca, "It's like I can actually go back and slip into my body in that place and time and have the emotional experience first-hand and that feels more healing than just observing." Coupled with the enhancement of mood and embodied participation with the visionary state, experiences of the past were particularly meaningful to non-Indigenous drinkers (more on that in the Conclusion).

Following are five of Kate's ayahuasca experiences, which I recorded during retreats or in the days afterwards. She described encountering (1) Mother Nature, (2) an alternative family in another dimension, (3) solving world peace and finding the source of existence, (4) biological sensations and purification, and (5) how music and emotion shape her experience.

1. I have had really strong Mother Earth experiences, like the spirit of the Earth, or the Earth as Mother. I've had a lot of experiences like this. It feels like a feminine energy belonging to the planet comes up through me, through my body. I've had journeys where I feel like I am Mother Earth and my breasts are full of milk pouring out over the earth. But I also have a lot of intergalactic visions beyond the earth.

2. I've had a recurring vision where I've got a family, a husband, and three blond-haired children in a great big house, and I arrive thinking, "Oh yeah, I forgot about this." It's like I've got another life, somewhere else, and I know a whole lifetime of it, being there, but I haven't dropped in on that one for a while.

3. I've had experiences of solving world peace and all sorts of whole world revelations. . . . I was terrified but then in ultimate bliss when I found source. I never imagined that so much love could exist. I remember coming out of it saying . . . that was like having fifty thousand orgasms at once but without it being sexual. . . . It blew my mind that so much love existed, and that there was a place in me, and everywhere, in everything, that was love. I literally felt loved by everyone on earth. . . . I watched the universe begin, plants and life-forms emerge. It showed me time and eternity, the planets and how everything was created. . . . It was phenomenal. . . . I got a fast track of the whole entire history of the universe. . . . It showed me how I can unmake everything, and actually that I had to unmake everything. It's like Big Bang theory. The universe explodes outwards, but in the ayahuasca realm it creates a vacuum and vortex back into it. Everything gets sucked back into the original source, and then it comes out again with the opportunity to get it right this time. It is really a matter of getting it right this time. I was so scared. I had to unmake all my relationships with my family, friends, and the world. They get turned in and out like the visuals and the body feelings, and then my personal relationships come back into shape or are made anew, better, clearer, with more room for love.

4. I sometimes see the medicine going into every cell of my body and it's almost like machinery, the mechanical parts of your cells going *sh, sh,*

162 GLOBAL AYAHUASCA

sh, sh. . . . It's like healing cells, cleaning them up. Sometimes I get this feeling of peristalsis, like my whole body is like an intestinal tube and that there are these spasms, almost all of it pushing my body, there's pressure, in my head as well, and it pushes, it's like, *vvwooOO*, or *shwwvvvoOO*, like it's squeezing me. I don't like the feeling. It could be a sign of me resisting. But I usually feel a hundred times better after.

5. I can feel yellow and white and orange filling up my consciousness and with that comes feelings of love, well-being, and bliss, and I can just go with the colors and patterns or I can form it into a beautiful female or male figure. . . . Once there was a huge masculine feeling in the music in the *circle* and my visions transformed into a huge mechanical circular saw, going *zhhhhh*, looking like it wanted to cut me up, and I thought "that's a bit fucking intense." There were thousands of circular saws and it felt very masculine. Then, it faded away with the next song. I don't see it as an evil spirit. It's just the darkness morphing into something that I can give a name to. It's all really energetic. I would say that the things I experience, whether they are scary or happy, it's all about energy and emotion. She [ayahuasca] pushes me around to try to get me to a place of understanding to know what I am going through. There is a deep intelligence behind it.

When I kept probing Kate to describe more of her visions and in greater detail, she laughed. She was amused and somewhat surprised by my scholarly interests in the visions. Over the years, the more she drank ayahuasca, the less she tried to make ultimate sense of it.

Now I just let it be. It's all doing what it needs to do, and going where it needs to go, and I trust that it works. I don't have to understand it on an intellectual level because you can never understand it with our own brain capacity. It's beyond the nuts and bolts of our ordinary reality to comprehend.

The ineffability of ayahuasca had reduced her desire to talk about it. This reduction was amplified by another pressure, that of privacy. In 2012, after six years of drinking ayahuasca, she had never told her parents or work colleagues about it, because she suspected they "probably do not understand

NATURAL MEDICINE IN AUSTRALIA   163

altered states" and would develop "wrong ideas about it and get worried or look down at me." Kate's most powerful healing and her deepest lessons from ayahuasca involved cultivating a more authentic self when among others, she explained. But she preferred to covertly show the benefits of ayahuasca in action. The visionary experiences were her private treasures and divine gifts.

EXAMPLE 2: MICHAEL

At the end of a retreat in south Queensland, I talked with Michael about his introduction to ayahuasca. A white, twenty-six-year-old postgraduate student studying languages and living in Sydney, Michael had only drunk ayahuasca a few times, but he had a longer history of psychedelic use. He said that ayahuasca was more healing compared to LSD and psilocybin mushrooms. Michael preferred to drink ayahuasca with local Australians rather than what he called the "imported styles" from Indigenous Amazonia. He favored the range of music that Australian facilitators played in ceremonies, which he described as "kind of real world and away from the deep ayahuasca realm" that Indigenous styles of music evoked for him.

Michael and I spoke about his ayahuasca experiences. His response is worth noting in detail to get a sense of the visionary intricacies in Australia and the ways in which godly, alien, and ineffable figures can occur alongside mundane perspectives of family and daily life:

> You notice changing sensations in the body. Changing sensitivities. You feel a lot more energy starting to rush through you. I typically perceive a sense of light in my consciousness. My mind becomes a lot brighter with my eyes closed. You could say that it's like more energy on a physical level because if you were drowsy it is likely to push all that away, really brighten your mind and bring you up. You get thrown into a more immediate environment and your thought patterns change. They tend to be uninfluenced by what you were doing earlier that day, or that sort of stuff seems to fade away and you are thrown into a more active relationship with something, and what it wants to show you and the thoughts that it is reflecting back to you. You drop a lot of baggage as the plant begins to kick in.

"What type of baggage?" I asked.

It just takes you away from your more mundane thoughts you might have been having earlier that day: work, eating, all that normal chit-chat we've got going on in our minds. . . . Things in the room start morphing and changing, shifting. Everything will start to breathe. The floor might start to undulate. Colors might rapidly change. If there are reds and blues in the room, they might start to become yellow and alternate. Your senses start to blend and vibrate. It can ripple further and then part of the room might become a being, a creature, in the room with you. Thoughts start to arise that you wouldn't have otherwise had without drinking the brew. When you start to delve into those lighter realms, there is entity contact, and that sort of thing. If you break through to that kind of level, usually you are so astonished you are not thinking much more about what you cooked for dinner last night.

You are brought to a much more immediate and direct encounter. . . . What ayahuasca tries to show us is that we have a connection to much higher planes of existence and realities. . . . When you are in those high-dose breakthrough realms, it shows you how you are connected to the rest of the universe, and connections to things almost on an atomic level and with the forces of nature. But then it will work down back through you with the interactions you have with your friends and your family. It shows you where you might be going wrong there, or what might be a nice gesture to help put those things in line. Because when those things are in line it helps everything else. When you have some sort of relationship or contact with, let's say, an intergalactic being that you can only really contact through a deep meditation with ayahuasca, it's going to show you how to do that more effectively. It also helps with what's going on at a more earthly level. It will point you the right way. It takes you to some really abstract places and then tears you down to, you know, be better to your mum [he laughs], things like that.

In Michael's liberal description, features of everyday life are transcended shortly after drinking the brew when the "plant begins to kick in" and then they later reappear, after wild and otherworldly visions, in more mundane realizations such as "be better to your mum." However, he had never told his

NATURAL MEDICINE IN AUSTRALIA   165

parents about this. "They would be mistrustful of any benefit I said I got from it and assume it had intoxicated me and now I was just being neurotic," he explained. He also preferred not to speak much about his experiences with his friends, even though they did not stigmatize psychedelic usage. Most people, he thought, would not understand it, and talking about it with them can diminish the power of the experience and even "do a disservice to ayahuasca." He continued,

> It's a personal thing. You come out of a retreat and it might make you more social, more open, warmer, more patient, but when you are there and working with it, it's very personal, it's your own trip, looking at what's going on with you. But that will go on to affect others afterwards.

Michael encountered "galactic entities" and other foreign beings while modulating perceptions of worldly affairs and reigniting family and social virtues. Ayahuasca can help suggest a "nice gesture to put those things in line" and "point you the right way," he said. After only a few ayahuasca sessions, Michael approached the brew with a spiritual conviction forged out of his psychonautic past. For several years prior, he had been experimenting with very large doses of LSD while listening to the 1960s US psychologist Timothy Leary's audio journey "The Psychedelic Experience," which is inspired by *The Tibetan Book of the Dead.* But he still found ayahuasca more powerful and healing compared to that. Ayahuasca took him outside the ordinary, which then threw open his view of aspects of family life and other topics, but especially his mother, now seen in the presence of Mother Ayahuasca. These kinds of spiritual experiences occurred in natural environments, outside the city and beyond ordinary sight. They often came with a blast of light and color, beauty and wonder that was partially celebrated by drinkers by the insights and virtues it offered to everyday life.

Ayahuasca became localized to Australian society during the turn of the century as a potent visionary space outside urban life, everyday routines, and ordinary consciousness. The wonder and awe of ayahuasca experiences, here, expressed a countercultural view of modernity that is present when Mother Ayahuasca transports the soul beyond the city and purges sickness ascribed to society and family while also promoting critical attitudes and values, whether towards allopathic medicine, educational histories, or the media. If modernity and ayahuasca were at odds in neoshamanic Australia, then the secular approaches I encountered in China built ayahuasca into modernity with a very different attitude and approach. The next chapter looks at how the allure of modernization appears to have shaped these nominally secular ayahuasca experiences.

FIVE

BECOMING MODERN IN CHINA

Eager to experience a deeper connection to nature, find relief from mental afflictions, and venture beyond the disenchantment of society, ayahuasca drinkers across the globe have helped to revive Indigenous shamanism in Peru, Brazil, and Colombia and spawned a range of new approaches across South America, Europe, North America, Australia, and elsewhere. Different kinds of ayahuasca use have received considerable scholarly research, but one topic that has barely started to be discussed is how Chinese culture might interface with the global psychedelics boom. Offering a partial view on this, this chapter examines how a psychoactive brew made its way to mainland China at the center of a nominally secular and remarkably original style of use.

Through an ethnographic sketch, I examine how ayahuasca was used by young Chinese professionals searching for holistic wellness, self-cultivation, and a competitive edge in capitalist environments. Many of the attendees I met at the ayahuasca healing centers in Peru or the spiritual wellness retreats in Australia were searching beyond society for an enchantment deemed lost to modernity, whereas those I encountered in China during 2019 to 2021 approached the brew as a means of developing a greater mastery over modern life. The use of ayahuasca and other psychedelics to "optimize," "boost," or "enhance" staff performance in corporate contexts, which I observed in China, is also a theme of psychedelic use in parts of North America, Europe, and elsewhere. Between 2018 and 2023, popular business media outlets, such

168 GLOBAL AYAHUASCA

as *The Economist, Business Insider,* and *Fortune,* published on ayahuasca for improving productivity, team cohesiveness, and corporate decision making—a topic deserving scholarly attention.

Although current research is patchy, it appears there was a vibrant religious past of psychedelic use in ancient China among shamans, Daoists, and others (Li 1975; Needham and Lu 1974). Fan Pen Li Chen (2021) suggested some of the "spirit mushrooms" described in historical Chinese documents dating back two thousand years were likely psychedelic varieties. For instance, the occultist intellectual Ge Hong (238–364 CE) described how the "black cloud spirit mushroom" could "enable the body to live for a thousand years without aging, ride on clouds, communicate with heaven, and see ghosts and spirits" (Chen 2021:21). Three hundred years later, spirit mushrooms helped Daoist masters "ride on clouds with phoenixes," "communicate with spirits," and "enable one to grow feathers and wings" (23). Shamanistic practices were severely diminished by the Confucianist agendas of the Han Dynasty (206 BCE—220 CE) and its focus on secular affairs, politics, and society.

More research is waiting to be undertaken on the potential or probable continuation of psychedelic use from ancient to modern China (Needham and Lu 1974:121). The early twentieth-century spiritual master Xiao Changming described undergoing three years of training in mountains in Hunan province, which included "eating a magic mushroom that gave him incommensurable powers" upon which "he was instructed by the Cloud Dragon Sage to teach his method and save mankind" (Palmer 2012:178–179). It is not clear if his mushroom method was imparted to others, but his impact on society was widespread. He frequently provided wisdom and spiritual services to Chinese Nationalist Party elites and there is evidence he provided spiritual counsel to Mao Zedong's mother (Palmer 2012). More recently, a variety of psilocybin mushrooms were consumed by the Yi in Yunnan, who described how they "look blue in the hand" and regarded them as "the little people" (*xaio ren ren*) (Arora 2008). While working and living in Fujian, south China, in 2018 I was told some Daoist masters in the area used special plants to promote inner sight (*nei guan*).

There are many unknowns surrounding past uses of psychedelics in China, and there are also significant pressures to keep the practices private. The first pressure is the government's draconian antidrug stance, which is reinforced by nationalistic wounds inflicted by European imperialists during the nineteenth-century opium wars. The second overarching pressure is the government's historical emphasis on the secular against the religious. Modern Chinese society would appear particularly ripe for reenchantment, given that it underwent such an intense period of secularization during the twentieth century.

The ayahuasca use I recently studied in metropolitan China represents a hypermodern and nominally secular approach. To help illustrate this, first a brief look at twentieth-century Chinese modernization can help to indicate the fertile ground upon which ayahuasca became so compatible with corporate life and an enterprising spirit. Chinese society was the subject of dramatic reforms and revolutions during much of the twentieth century. The religious-type activities that permeated premodern China and its social institutions became singled-out, categorized, and under assault by nationalist elites who placed "religion"—a newly appropriated institutional category—in opposition to political, economic, and cultural efforts (Goossaert and Palmer 2011). It included a sometimes brutal and often "relentless disenchantment of social life" (Yang 2008:8) accompanied by the sacralization of the Maoist secular state. After Mao Zedong's death in 1976, an era of repression towards religiosity receded. The revival of Daoism, Buddhism, Christianity, and spiritual sects during the 1980s coincided with widespread capitalist reforms, economic "opening up" to global trade, and the proliferation of consumer markets. Today, religious and spiritual activities exist within a fast-paced society saturated by capitalistic demands, consumeristic desires, and workplace pressures.

With a nod to Weber, Arthur Kleinman (2011) suggested that this new environment of capitalistic materialism is a leading source of disenchantment in contemporary China. He explained that the "quest for religious meaning" and the "popular hunger for religious values and sentiments is sought after to confront a secular world that is increasingly seen to be hypermaterialistic and wildly commercial," adding that the "hyperpragmatism of everyday political life is also a stimulus for this quest" (273). Yet diverse spiritual quests in modern China have been stimulated not as a reaction against a secular and commercial world but through spectacularly absorbing capitalist sensibilities. As Adam Chau (2006:2) explained, the classic disenchantment thesis is too simple in China, given the widespread occurrences of magical rituals, offerings, and prayers to help with commercial, economic, and social challenges. In instrumental fashion, worshipers may call upon deities to miraculously secure a new job, resolve a business dilemma, cause rain, diagnose medicine, or reveal the winning numbers of a lottery. The thirst for spirituality in China is also popularly quenched by the magical achievement of modern-world mastery and not simply from a divine fountain of meaning outside or lost to modernity.

The utilitarian ethos of ayahuasca I examined in China shares a general attitude with these aspects of modern Chinese religiosity. Here, ayahuasca is drunk by individuals not to overcome a malaise of modern meaning and discover the purpose of life, but to help execute a greater mastery over worldly affairs. The wondrous visions are animated less by a crisis of meaning than the demands of a programmatic modernity. Those who drink ayahuasca sometimes measure the value of it instrumentally by its capacity to inspire actionable changes to workplace and corporate contexts, and such pragmatism can shape their ayahuasca visions and otherworldly experiences, as demonstrated below.

This Chinese approach would likely come as a surprise to many, but not all, Euro-American ayahuasca enthusiasts. In parallel, very practical applications of the brew have long been observed in South America where specialists try to find lost objects and discover the plans of enemies (Luna 1986:60), cleanse the body for improving hunting perception (Shepard 2004), contemplate temporal correspondences between astronomical and ecological patterns of animal behavior (Reichel-Dolmatoff 1997), and inspire artistic creations (Gebhart-Sayer 1985). These instrumental approaches highlight the uniqueness of the Euro-American neoshamanic contexts, which I place Australia largely under. In these neoshamanic contexts, the motivation is often to overcome modern disenchantment and find emotional relief, existential meaning, and verification of the truth of spirituality or a natural order beneath ordinary reality. But is ayahuasca, in the West, really responding to a vacuum of meaning that modernity sucked out of life? Scholar Jason Josephson-Storm (2017) examined how most people among middle and upper classes in Western societies throughout the twentieth century believed in charms and displayed magical thinking. So even if modern disenchantment is less a condition than a perpetuating mythos, it contrasts sharply with the type of ayahuasca drinking I observed in China.

Before outlining how Chinese drinkers successfully executed on their neoliberal lives through the visionary brew, it's important to know that my interview methods (as outlined in the Introduction) employed targeted strategies. After learning that some upper-middle-class Chinese workers were seeking wisdom from ayahuasca for their careers, I mostly interviewed these types. Thus the chapter is not attempting any grand essentialism about the localization of ayahuasca in China. It is mostly designed to expose how neoliberal values, in a Chinese context that is nominally but not really secular, can intersect so sharply with the mystery and wonder of the brew.

Ayahuasca drinking in China overlaps with the *shen xin ling* or Body-Heart-Spirit milieu and its reinvention of New Age spirituality. Some of the Chinese drinkers I met regularly attended *shen xin ling* workshops and activities in search of holistic wellness and spiritual inspiration. Anthropologist Anna Iskra demonstrated how the New Age in China was inspired by a "returning" of aspects of Chinese, Japanese, and Indian religiosity back to Asia from Euro-American countercultural networks (Iskra 2021). These cultural reflows first emerged in China during the 1980s and 1990s, particularly from the United States, through Taiwan and Hong Kong (Iskra 2021:90). Historian Paul Farrelly examined the careers of two key Taiwanese New Age teachers—CC Wang and Terry Hu. Although it is unclear the extent to which psychedelic neoshamanism entered mainland China during the 1980s and 1990s, 9 of the 101 Taiwanese New Age books published until the year 2000 were about Native American shamanism (Farrelly 2017:219). Farrelly noted that "an underground interest in Amazonian-derived entheogenic shamanism" was emerging in Taiwan in the 2010s (316), which is a topic worthy of study. A translation of the psychedelic ethnobotany picture book *Plants of the Gods* (Richard Evans Schultes and Albert Hofmann, 1979) was published in Mandarin in 2010 by Shangzhou Press in Taiwan. Originally written in the late 1970s by a Harvard University ethnobotanist and the Swiss chemist who discovered LSD, the book's overview of ayahuasca and plant shamanism represents the first major Chinese translation on the topic. A decade later in 2021, the Taiwanese New Rain Publishers released a Mandarin translation of *DMT: The Spirit Molecule*, an iconic book written by American psychiatrist

Rick Strassman (2001) about his studies into the key psychedelic alkaloid in ayahuasca. The book received a new cover art with an edited image taken from the surrealist cult film *Holy Mountain* (1973) by Alejandro Jodorowsky, thus recasting the psychiatrist's clinical research as more artistic and edgy than the mystical experience depicted on the book's English version. A reading group in Hong Kong published a 2019 'zine about a public event in the city where panelists discussed psychedelic books from North America and Europe. The group included local artists, students, academics, musicians, bankers, a yoga instructor, and an asylum seeker (Zheng Mahler 2019), suggesting that the substances were attracting people from across society. In the psychonautic underground in mainland China, political sensibilities and the surveillance state appeared to have shaped a young Beijing man's terrifying DMT experience (Gearin 2023a), however it is unclear how common this mode of psychedelic use is in the country.

The ability of ayahuasca to be compatible with different pursuits—whether for therapeutic modalities, mystical devotion, corporate inspiration, hunting prowess, artistic skills, or military "sympathetic magic"—is due to its shapeshifting sensitivities. This includes its subtle and overt resonance with

FIGURE 5.1 Mandarin translation of the American cult book *Plants of the Gods*, published in 2010 by Shangzhou Press in Taiwan.

the intentions and metaphysical beliefs of the participants, as well as the social and environmental contexts. These variables were described by early psychedelic researchers as the psychological "set" and the social and environmental "setting" (Leary, Metzner, and Alpert 1964; Hartogsohn 2020). With this in mind, this chapter explores the inner experiences and nominally secular cosmology of an emerging kind of ayahuasca use. For most of those I interviewed in China, modern life was not presented as the pathological antithesis of enchantment, like in the countercultural worlds of the Euro-American contexts. Ayahuasca addressed the restlessness and malaise of the Chinese workers by clarifying and healing parts of themselves that can improve their leadership and other skills and promote happiness at home.

BRIDGING THE GAP

Ayahuasca is typically translated in Chinese as "dead, vine, water" (*si teng shui* 死藤水), which is somewhat reminiscent of the Indigenous Quechua terminology of "aya" meaning "spirit," "soul," and "deceased ancestors," and "huasca" meaning "vine" and "woody rope." It is difficult to know when ayahuasca was first introduced to Chinese society. Françoise Barbira Freedman (2014:141) noted that Indigenous ayahuasca shamans were traveling to Beijing at the turn of the twenty-first century. Part of the difficulty in mapping the history of ayahuasca in China is due to the strict drug laws and risks of punishment that have generated stricter codes of privacy among some users.

The ayahuasca brew is prohibited in China, and it recently appeared on official government social media news accounts. In early 2021, a Beijing police article on Weibo (the largest microblogging platform in China) described a person being arrested for possessing ayahuasca in China. The article included a propaganda infographic with skeleton hands reaching over the heading: "New Drug. Dead Vine Water Is Coming!" (*xin xing du pin, si teng shui laile*). The Quechua meaning of ayahuasca as "spirit" and "ancestors" was twisted into a creepy image of death. Underneath was an illustration of a Mazatec Indian dancing and wearing a large, feathered headdress, accompanied by the text, "Ayahuasca is a medicinal plant from the Amazon rainforest. It has been used for hallucinogenic activity in religious rituals." The police described the arrested person as "addicted to the illusion created

174   GLOBAL AYAHUASCA

by the ayahuasca," "out of touch with reality," "similar to autism," and with a reference to the American sci-fi film, said the person "confessed to living in a world like *Inception* . . . sometimes he can't distinguish between dreams and reality and is worried he will do extreme behaviors." It finished by stating, "But now he faces the severe punishment of the law!" Around the same time, a pattern of similar articles about ayahuasca appeared across China on more than a dozen social media accounts of local police stations.

Given the sensitive nature of writing about ayahuasca practice in a society with very strict drug prohibition, the following ethnographic writing required a delicate approach. I have minimized or anonymized some important details, such as specifics of the retreat location, life histories of participants and organizers, and the workplaces of the participants. But, to my surprise, such concerns were not shared by a considerable number of the ayahuasca drinkers I spoke with in China. When speaking with Zhang, an executive at a large multinational firm, I was struck by his disinterest in the risks. He said, "Technically, it is not illegal, because it's just natural plants," and "If you're a good person, helping society, I believe you will be okay." He, like many others, was not very interested in my response that alkaloids in the brew were in fact illegal in China. By contrast, Ting Ting, a manager at a large technology firm, spent fifteen minutes at the beginning of our interview in raw hesitation, questioning me about my intentions and research methods. She asked how long the data would be kept, exactly where I intend to publish, how I will protect her identity. She wanted to contribute to the research, adding, "It's important to share these stories. Ayahuasca has helped me. It's helped many people here." But the dangers she sensed were real, and even though we spoke mostly about how ayahuasca had helped her career, she was reluctant to identify the company that employs her. Our conversation hovered at a much more abstract level than usual, suspended above a fearful cloud of persecution. Her words, like the ayahuasca visions she described, were only partially able to integrate into discourse. Such an ineffability was not only spiritual or phenomenological in nature but veritably punitive and constituted by the constraints of China's draconian drug policies.

What appears to have been the only ongoing commercial ayahuasca business operating in mainland China was largely cultivated by one person. Luke, a young and energetic ayahuasca specialist from Europe, had conducted hun-

FIGURE 5.2 Antidrug propaganda about ayahuasca, produced by the "Beijing safe" police account on the social media platform Weibo, 2021.

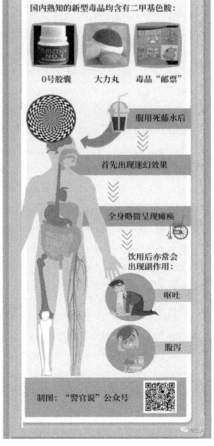

dreds of ayahuasca retreats in China across six years, involving hundreds of participants, many of whom were Chinese participants, though some were foreigners. In the beginning, mainly foreigners attended, and then over time, more Chinese nationals came. Transnational flows of knowledge and practice that draw from the heterogenous South American traditions of ayahuasca use were visible in Luke's use of ritualistic music, aromatics, and paraphernalia. To help gather knowledge and training in the craft of serving ayahuasca, Luke had made more than ten visits to Brazil and Peru to learn from Indigenous Shipibo healers, urban Daimistas, and Uniao do Vegetal ayahuasca specialists.

Yet, setting himself against such traditions, Luke described his approach as secular. "I have great respect for the different ayahuasca traditions," he told the fifteen mainly Chinese attendees at a retreat shortly before everyone drank the brew. "We have our own way. It's not the shamanic approach, or religious approach, but the therapeutic approach, the secular approach." Luke described the events as specifically "sessions" and "processes," rather than ceremonies or rituals. The sanitization of ayahuasca into a secular framework is remarkably novel. It presents, in theory, a weakening of the enchantment of ayahuasca. But in practice, such sanitization can be merely cosmetic or superficial. For instance, when needing to make a crucial decision in his business or personal life, Luke personally drank ayahuasca to seek counsel from the inner intelligence of "the plants." Furthermore, there was no strict codification of secular belief at these retreats. Participants described encountering spirits, gods, and other worlds in their visions and Luke made no effort to correct them along secular lines. Spiritual practitioners are often obliged to justify themselves in modernist contexts (Goossaert and Palmer 2011:304), and describing ayahuasca drinking as secular and therapeutic gives it a modernist bent, which was Luke's explicit intention. As partially included in the Introduction, he told me,

> To bring the plants [ayahuasca] to the modern world, sometimes it needs to be translated. If you start talking to a manager from a company who is very square-minded about power animals and *mariri*, he is going to think you are crazy. My background is more aligned with companies and corporate mindsets. I talk more in terms of anxiety, depression, purpose, mission, conflict. . . . When they don't see you wearing feathers, when you speak in a language they understand, the outcome is better.

Presenting the practice as secular also helps dislocate it from an association with religious communities or consensual moral universes and makes it more individualistic, pragmatic, and instrumental.

When I began researching Luke's networks in 2019, he was developing a "portfolio" of retreats in Beijing, Shanghai, and Shenzhen. "We have different packages and services all designed to help people transform," he explained. This transformative business included a core product, titled Bridging the Gap, which aimed to take clients beyond a functional state and enhance their vocational abilities. It was a leadership program designed specifically to help corporate managers, entrepreneurs, and CEOs to advance their careers and live happier lives. It included workshops, coaching sessions, and two or three group ayahuasca sessions spread across three months, and it cost 60,000 RMB (approximately $9,000 USD). Clients were supported by Luke and retreat staff in an overall goal, "Bridging the Gap," wherein they sought to align an internal self, called the Monk, with an external self, called the Suit. The Monk self was related to "spirit, heart, purpose, and intuition," and the Suit self to "occupation, material belongings, ego, and mind." Group sessions of drinking ayahuasca helped individuals perceive and understand the gap between their two selves. Subsequent coaching sessions and knowledge seminars helped the client "take action" to close the gap between the two inner selves and "implement change" in their workplace and domestic life. This all results, hopefully, in a "Suited Monk."

The clients pursue happiness and integrity by aligning the Monk and the Suit. The objective is both personal and vocational, and the coaching and workshop activities help clients "integrate what they experience in the session with ayahuasca to their companies," Luke explained to me. "Ayahuasca creates a powerful inner awareness, and this has a high premium for managers constantly trying to overcome blind spots," he added. Switching conveniently between secular and spiritual language, the program includes references to Daoism, Buddhism, and other "ancient techniques made practical" that are defined in relation to the Bridging the Gap philosophy. In doing so, the approach shares with cognate religious practices in China that "create new compositions out of selected elements of tradition—elements often selected for their perceived compatibility with modern, secular values" (Goossaert and Palmer 2011:304). The Monk is attuned to an intuitive and ecstatic "flow" of

GROUP SESSION

As I arrived at the ayahuasca event, I was surprised by the large walls that surrounded the housing estate. Two security officers watched over the small entry. Inside were elaborate and perfectly detailed gardens, multistory villas, and remarkably clean and new streets. A shining Porsche drove past. Gardeners were busy working. For those not enrolled in the larger Bridging the Gap program, the one-evening ayahuasca retreat costs 2,000 RMB ($300 USD). These individuals usually attend for personal healing, curiosity, or spiritual exploration, and they share the event with the Bridging the Gap participants. Luke encouraged all participants to receive an included yet optional one-hour coaching session with him approximately one week after the ayahuasca session to help them better integrate the retreat into daily life. Everyone had been given mandatory "homework" to do before coming to their first ayahuasca session. These "exercises to do before the Process" consisted of emailing the organization seven different drawings done by pencil. Each newcomer had to draw a family, a person, an animal, a house, a person under the house, a tree, another tree. Then, after doing all the drawings, they had to write a short fictional story about the second tree they had drawn. These were always kept confidential. Luke explained to me that the exercises helped put the clients into a reflexive state and activate their visual imagination, which can help the ayahuasca work better. Plus, he analyzed each person's drawings and stories as part of a screening process to try to remove people who were not motivated for authentic healing or authentic spiritual reasons, he said. The high cost of the events and coaching program gives an indication of the class status of the participants. One Chinese woman had recently purchased an apartment in the expensive French Concession district in Shanghai. Another was married to a mathematician who ran a blockchain company. Most participants were upper-middle-class, Chinese working professionals between twenty and thirty-five years of age.

BECOMING MODERN IN CHINA   179

People arrived in the early afternoon, and we began the retreat by sitting in the "process room"—where the ayahuasca drinking would take place after dark. We drew with colored pencils our "intention for the process" onto pieces of paper and arranged them onto the room's walls. Luke's confident and analytical mind was on full display as he shared with the group the latest science about the therapeutic properties of ayahuasca. "Ayahuasca is a tool. It can help you know yourself better. That is all," he told us. Before the ayahuasca session, everyone was taken to a neighboring park for group activities designed to "let go of the stresses of work and life." This included hugging a stranger in the group for two minutes, followed by talking with them about how it made you feel. Looking into the eyes of a stranger in the group for two minutes, and finally, after other activities, we paired up, preferably with someone we did not know, and took turns being blindfolded and led for ten minutes through winding paths, descending stairs, and across roads. These exercises, Luke said, are good for creating a sense of trust and support in the group. The blindfold exercise helps participants to learn to "let go" and face the darkness, similar to drinking ayahuasca, given that the "visions appear from darkness and are guided by music and what feels like an outside source." As a drinker myself, this made intuitive sense to me. At the same time, the pre-ceremony activities somewhat reflected corporate team bonding techniques with a psychedelic and consciousness-altering bent.

Returning to the process room as the sun set, the group donned white clothing and closely lined the walls sitting on yoga mats, each with a pillow, bucket, and eye shades. As the group sat in a large circle, a rope was passed around and each participant spoke their "intention for the process" while knotting the rope. Shortly after, everyone drank the brew. A glowing large salt crystal was on the floor in the middle of the room, surrounded by sage leaves, *Palo Santo* fragrant wood, a piece of ayahuasca vine, and a pine cone. One wall was decorated with Amazonian Shipibo fabric, a large Chinese script for driving away ghosts (next to a figure of the Daoist deity *guan yu*) and an image of a Tibetan Buddha, which were all above Luke who was observing the group over an online Spotify music playlist and DJ musical equipment.

The music was loud. The lighting very low. The session went for four to six hours. The music included Indigenous Amazonian *icaros*, high-energy male and female Italian opera, 1980s Chinese popular music about friendship and

180 GLOBAL AYAHUASCA

family, South American folk ayahuasca music about sacred plants, Persian and Middle Eastern religious chants, and classical Indian music. During the evening, Luke's playlist exposed the participants' visionary bodies to a polysonic cosmopolitanism.

Three cups of ayahuasca were offered over the course of the evening. Everyone had the first cup. Most people had the second cup. But few had the third. Most participants lay down and explored inner visions. When someone purged, vomiting into their bucket, Luke would move over to them and smudge them with aromatic sage smoke, or sometimes the Amazonian fragrant wood *Palo Santo*. Sometimes he massaged their back in an attempt to induce purging. He also used a range of aromatic liquids that Peruvian shamans use, including Agua de Florida. He circled the group and rubbed the strong aroma on the participants' hands and told them to apply it to their own face and neck.

During the session, some people cried, some vomited, but most of the time everyone was silent and still. Attendees found themselves navigating inner scenes and worlds that were sometimes spectacular and strange but other times were very mundane and secular, often concerning family or about issues in their jobs. In the most general sense, for the dozen Chinese entrepreneurs and corporate leaders I interviewed or spoke with about their visions, ayahuasca was a medicine. Purifying the body through purging and visionary experience opened the psyche to an enduring state of "flow" in which the inner self and outer self—the Monk and the Suit—operate as one. Such an ideal state was marked by less stress, enhanced creativity, workplace success, and overall happiness and satisfaction in professional and personal life.

During the morning after the ayahuasca session, everyone met at 8:00 a.m. in the process room for a one-hour ecstatic dance session designed to "integrate into the body" the healing transformations from the previous night's session. We then lay on the ground and followed a guided meditation that culminated with visualizing throwing fears, hatred, and pain into an imaginary fire in a cave, embracing our ambitions, and breathing light and awareness into our own body. After a quick breakfast meal, everyone joined together for a three-hour-long "integration circle," which is the final part of the retreat. The "intention" rope was passed to the last person who had made a knot. They undid their knot and verbally shared what happened in their ayahuasca experience and how they felt. Many described gratitude for the experience

BECOMING MODERN IN CHINA   181

and feelings of elation, including insights and convictions about changes they now wanted to make in their lives.

EXAMPLE 1: TING TING

Ting Ting, a Chinese woman in her early thirties, started drinking ayahuasca in 2018 for personal and professional reasons. It had helped her in deeply personal ways, she explained. As briefly described in the Introduction, Ting Ting grew up in a large city in China and moved to a first-tier city after completing her university studies. She was partly motivated to move to the city to escape the distress of her father being diagnosed with a terminal disease and given less than two years to live. About a decade after her father had passed, she attended an ayahuasca retreat in the city attempting to heal feelings of guilt, shame, and sadness.

Her ayahuasca healing experiences, while including deep family topics, also had an impact on her perception of her job at a large technology firm. She described her company as fast-paced, competitive, and challenging. Her goal was to increase her salary and advance her career by doing good work and getting noticed by senior colleagues. This required a social tact that ayahuasca assisted her in cultivating. In one telling vision, Ting Ting witnessed her co-workers in a wondrous vision of workplace rationality that was not dull or lifeless, but vital, energetic, and scary.

> After I cried for two or three hours [over my father's death], I then puked a little bit. I was working on my own journey. I started seeing snakes and my co-workers. So, if you open a watch, you will see how it works on the inside. You will see all those wheels working in an organized way, working at a fixed pace. I was seeing this, but it was not metal wheels. They were snakes, turning around, in fixed rotation. All of them are moving in a clockwise direction and there is one in particular on top of all of it, and it's looking at me. Sometimes it gets really close to my face and then it goes back to the workings. It was black and yellow, and the snake is my least favorite animal. So it was scary, but I wasn't too afraid. The snake would let me know that it's watching me with its tongue, then it would return to the clock's workings.

By witnessing her colleagues and a clock entangled with snakes, but not feeling terribly afraid, Ting Ting confidently encountered a scary otherworldly scene that entangled workplace environments, mechanical time, and animal sentience. In this case, ayahuasca made her porous to an invisible cosmic realm that spun to the cogs of workplace life.

Such a porosity of perception provided psychological insight. Ting Ting explained that "the vision of the snakes reminded me that I am sometimes as alert as a snake. I am very quiet, usually, but I am very sensitive to changes, sound, or any disturbance to my life. So, that's what I got from that experience." In a different vision, she saw dozens of red lanterns floating up to the sky, each with a face of someone she loved or someone she despised, including her workplace colleagues and her new and old friends. The vision taught her to "let go of other people's opinions easier." She explained,

> When I saw the lantern, I thought, it's not their hope to make me sad, but I choose to be sad. It's all on me. So, as the lanterns floated away, I was able to let some of my frustration and anger or unsatisfied feelings go with those people. Some of those people are in my company, working with me every day, or some are friends I sometimes see during the weekend. . . . People who don't believe in me, I now don't see them as a threat to blocking me from progressing in my company, and I don't let their opinion bother me as much now. The ayahuasca helped me feel it's not personal anymore. I realized their advice is not always compatible with my expertise and development.

By closing the gap of an inner and outer self through insightful visions and releasing "negative energies" from her body, Ting Ting felt that she had improved her management techniques and excelled further at her job. Following the Bridging the Gap philosophy, she purged afflictions ascribed to her family history and to her perceptions of workplace relations. This purging and visionary experience appeared to bring an embodied grace and confidence to her workplace life. By encountering visions as personal psychological material that required interpretation, her ayahuasca drinking was aimed at healing family issues and excelling at work.

EXAMPLE 2: WANG

Wang, a thirty-four-year-old, spent the first half of his life in California as a Chinese American, and then moved to China after college to study business management at a leading Chinese university. Shortly after his studies, he married a local Chinese woman, had a child with her, and began working as a manager for a Chinese company in a second-tier city. After living there for twelve years, he approached ayahuasca for personal and professional reasons, including to help remove his anger from home and from the workplace.

He had been increasingly stressed as an executive manager at a fast-food franchise. The business was excelling, partly on the basis of his management efforts, and he was finding it difficult to cope with the new challenges and responsibility that came with opening more stores. Business language and thinking permeated his approach to ayahuasca. He described the retreat group bonding activities as "like a good job interview" when the hiring committee takes you out of the office into a park and the group can "network together" and "informally exchange." Wang kept attending ayahuasca retreats because they provided him with a lasting sense of calmness and peace that he said helped him be more tender and perceptive as a father and husband and more successful as a manager and business coach.

Wang's intentions for drinking ayahuasca were primarily to deal with the stress of work and to control his temper. His ayahuasca narratives followed a pattern that intersects with the Bridging the Gap philosophy. The beginning of the sessions were usually mentally challenging, disorienting, and otherworldly, but eventually he "reache[d] a certain level" or had a "new ego death" and then the rest of the session involved graceful periods of exploring worldly affairs. He narrated a violent and otherworldly experience that gave way to a period of visionary grace directed at his workplace challenges. At the start,

I was just an observer, like an audience member, watching. I wasn't scared. I wasn't worried or anxious. Physically, I did feel sick. I was seeing the same thing if I opened or closed my eyes. It was violent. Small and large creatures were climbing the walls, kicking and punching each other, and flying around. There was blood and water in the air. Ancient symbols were glowing on the walls, and trees and plants were growing out of them. The sensation, the smells, it was very real. The ceiling I remember vividly. It was open to outer space, and there was no sun, but I could feel a warmth like the sun.

Then, shortly after vomiting, he achieved a state of visionary peace and "flow" in which he felt confident to tackle challenges and "turn the positive energy into something applicable." In a state of grace, he realized his pride had been affecting his management skills in negative ways that made the business operate less efficiently. He was failing to address performance issues with key managers and HR staff. Rather than expecting them to simply follow his orders, he now desired to manage with less pride and better listening. He visualized the designs of the planned new restaurants. He could navigate around the space "like in a video game" whereby he wondered whether the customer experience was dull and needed more investment in the short term. Ayahuasca helped Wang appreciate a potential lack of meaning, a dullness, that should be improved with more natural light, colored furniture, a more pleasing design, in order to attract repeat customers. "I visualize some of my challenges [during the ayahuasca session] and think, okay, tomorrow morning I want to make this decision and I want to start rolling out this execution. It's very detailed and very clear."

Wang described his otherworldly visions as "strange" and "entertaining" but expressed a motivated wonder towards the worldly aspects of his other visions. Following the Bridging the Gap model, his ayahuasca sessions involved a release of negative emotion followed by a unity of grace and reasoning, intuition and rationality, spirit and success. The stress of the workplace was discharged in strange and violent visions that enabled a renewed spirit to permeate his workplace decisions and attitude.

EXAMPLE 3: FEI FEI

As mentioned earlier, not all attendees at Luke's ayahuasca sessions in China were undertaking the Bridging the Gap coaching program. Some participants attended simply for the ayahuasca retreat. These included individuals seeking to improve their vocational or workplace mastery, but also those focused on healing or spiritual inspiration related to other issues entirely. The following is a more in-depth account of another angle that focuses on ayahuasca healing and Chinese identity.

Fei Fei, a Chinese woman in her late twenties, attended an ayahuasca retreat in a first-tier city to heal her troubled sense of identity. She had grown up in a small village in a poor family in rural Shandong province. As the top-performing student in her final high school year, Fei Fei was expected to receive a prestigious scholarship to a leading university in Beijing. When she arrived at the waiting room where a handful of the best students from her school were selected to interview, she immediately noticed a low-performing student and painfully realized the opportunity had been rigged. The student's father was a top official in the local government and he had used his *guanxi* (social connections) to procure the scholarship for his own daughter. This early encounter with corruption and injustice distressed Fei Fei.

During her undergraduate studies at a top Chinese university, she became the deputy dean of the student union. She described the hierarchical nature of the union as a "mini-China" wherein people higher up the ranks became increasingly "demoralizing and inhumane" to those below. Fei Fei then went to the United States for postgraduate studies. There she learned for the first time about the Tiananmen Square massacre of 1989 and other disturbing Chinese histories that had been hidden from her back in China. She underwent a "personal transformation" in the United States, learning about Chinese history and studying academic texts on critical thinking. While living there for five years, Fei Fei increasingly came to disdain not only the widespread corruption and authoritarianism in China but also her own Chinese identity, from which she felt increasingly alienated. The inner conflict was amplified when she returned to China for work and to be closer to her family.

After living back in China for around one year, she attended one of Luke's ayahuasca retreats following a recommendation from a friend. During the "sharing circle" the morning after drinking, Fei Fei described with the group a series of experiences she had had the night before. The experiences displayed some key tensions. She shared her story of feeling confronted by returning to China and related this to "disturbing" visions she had had the night before, which included scenes of Chinese gangsters smoking cigarettes and driving dirty trucks, and crooked Chinese matchmakers wearing feudal clothing. During the ayahuasca session, the menacing visions eventually gave way to beauty when Luke played a popular Chinese song from the 1990s about love and family. She then encountered wondrous Chinese Daoist goddesses flying through the clouds and happily playing music. It reminded her of her previous love for Chinese aesthetics. She had never seen such beauty, and it also invoked her teenage passion for literature. For Fei Fei, the ayahuasca session had exposed a deep rift in her identity and provided a therapeutic recuperation in which the self—split across societies and cultural worlds—came together in a new level of appreciation. I spoke with her again six months after her original ayahuasca session. She was still grateful for how the session helped her "remember the beautiful side of Chinese culture" and had introduced her to new friends.

ENCHANTED RATIONALITY

If Weber was around today and aware of the Bridging the Gap approach to ayahuasca in China, he would have been puzzled. He had never closely studied the phenomenology of mysticism and generally conceived of it as antithetical to rationalization (in the bureaucratic, or efficiency means-to-ends type). He suggested that mystical experience, in its "orgiastic" and "ecstatic" forms, led away from rationality given its ineffability and excessive otherworldly orientation (Weber 2009:290). Yet the ayahuasca use I encountered in China involved ecstatic visionary experiences in which everyday action was rationalized and encountered through the integration of the spiritual and the mundane, or the Monk and the Suit.

By cloaking a business coaching model in a spiritual experience, the Bridging the Gap practice shapes the visionary exaltation of ayahuasca to the demands of capitalist life. The wondrous gnosis of the visions is harnessed to inspire attitudes and perceptions compatible with worldly business affairs. Describing the benefits in corporate contexts, Luke explained that Bridging the Gap "changes the quality of your decision making in alignment with your unified self." In contrast to neoshamanic ayahuasca practices in Western societies that focus on otherworldly primitivist visions associated with nature and Indigenous spirituality to confront a meaning crisis of modern life, this practice in China takes a different approach that is nominally secular and overtly embraces modern life in the pursuit of worldly visionary experiences and workplace mastery. While some have argued that ayahuasca has become globally popular by liberating modern souls from the disenchanted iron cage of instrumental rationality, a novel and inverted scenario was occurring in China. Here, entrepreneurs and executive managers rationalized ayahuasca experiences in the hope of achieving a competitive edge.

The practice of unifying the Monk and the Suit with ayahuasca drinking disturbs classic theories of modern disenchantment. In this case, the overcoming of disenchantment is not pursued to revive religiosity, but rather to achieve corporate objectives and tackle business challenges. Ayahuasca provided Wang with an inner visionary environment to enhance his management skills and to workshop his customer service ideas. Self-discovery and existential questions, such as who or what he is, were less important than becoming better at what he is doing. In this context, the consequence of disenchantment is not a malaise of modern rationality, but a hindrance in conducting business. The secular Suit requires a synthesis with the intuitive and visionary Monk to generate a happy and successful life in capitalistic environments that extends into one's existential being. Similarly, when Ting Ting derives meaning from her visions, that meaning orients a rational way of life, aligning attitudes and embodied comportment to enhance her management skills.

The Bridging the Gap approach represents a pragmatic and instrumental style of drinking ayahuasca. But unlike Chinese popular religious practices described by Chau (2006) and others, it is stripped of the capacity for miraculous intervention (or magical efficacy) and approached as a humanistic endeavor. The emphasis on "integrating" or unpacking visions into daily life downplays the enchantment of ayahuasca by placing agency squarely upon the individual person, and not upon gods, spirits, or the supernatural. The value of the otherworldly experiences, in this nominally secular approach, is measured by its capacity to inspire actionable changes in everyday life, including in workplace and family contexts. The participant is ultimately responsible for achieving worldly affairs, and he or she draws upon the otherworldly for cultivating the self towards these ends.

By ascribing the vistas of ayahuasca to the inner workings of the psyche, the Bridging the Gap practice is made amenable to a liquid modernity that pivots upon individual flexibility, responsibility, and desires. The rise of individualism in modern China presents a psychological problematic in which the liberated psyche faces new sets of challenges that manifest as particular structures of feeling (Kipnis 2012:7). The visionary use of ayahuasca here by a young professional class raises these new challenges to ecstatic heights. Contradictions of Chinese modernity manifest in the afflictive experiences that ayahuasca drinkers purge, purify, and release from their bodies. A religious telos was pursued not against the hyperpragmatism of everyday life, but within it, within a unification of the Monk and the Suit, where religious sensibilities and rational action assemble a coherent image of the modern self.

Such evenings of drinking ayahuasca have little in common with the popular image of drug use as indulgence, excess, or escape. Ayahuasca visions in the Chinese group are not animated by a rebellious spirit of degradation and wildness aimed at perturbing consciousness against the perfunctory routines and disenchantment of society. The gnosis of the visions is directed functionally, not critically, at society. It involves altering consciousness not to transcend the everyday but to triangulate and enhance the perception of it.

When ayahuasca or similar psychoactive substances become a visionary technology employed to advance business life, they enter a brave new world in which the secular and ecstatic combine as precursors to a pharmacological modernity. Similar to practices typically discussed in anthropology as trance, shamanic flight, or spirit possession, the Bridging the Gap program recasts ayahuasca into a good example of the "magic of modernity itself" (Meyer and Pels 2003:34). Whereas Birgit Meyer and Peter Pels discussed examples that cover how secular and rational practices resemble magic, witchcraft, or shamanism—whether in American politics, university science labs, or corporate media boardrooms—the examples of Wang, Ting Ting, and Luke's Bridging the Gap approach to ayahuasca inverts the formula. These ayahuasca drinkers embark upon intense and strange states of consciousness widely associated with religiosity and magical thinking to inspire what they deem rational changes to secular life. They are not hoping what happens in the visions will "magically" change their business affairs. But the business affairs can be triangulated by wondrous inner experiences that offer actionable insights onto the workplace. Nonetheless, there is still an acknowledgment of agnosticism structured into the Bridging the Gap approach and the participants' relationship to ayahuasca, among those I interviewed.

As the previous chapters demonstrated, ayahuasca visions are astonishingly varied when considered in the global context. Many participants in Australia found an enchanted refuge in a visionary nature that illuminated against the perfunctory routines of urban life. Chinese drinkers transformed a secular inner self and uncovered their "blind spots" in the hope of advancing their careers. In Peru, Shipibo attempted to entice the spirits of plants to share healing songs to cure the troubled visions of foreigners. The variation certainly does not end here either.

The visionary worlds of ayahuasca appear to multiply as the brew spreads across the planet. Given this diversification, any attempt to bring the visions into a productive global conversation may appear futile. Other global theories have turned out to be provincial perspectives projected to universal levels, such as the notion that modern disenchantment is the main stimulus for the burgeoning interest in ayahuasca. Yet the widespread sense of ayahuasca re-enchanting a spiritual void of modern life—common among neoshamanic Australians and international visitors in Peru—does allude to a disturbance in existential vitality that is very real for many people.

SIX

INTEGRATION AND SOCIETY

Not only are there many different depictions of ayahuasca experiences across the planet, there are also sharply different perspectives on what it means to narrate the experiences to others. Some Indigenous approaches have emphasized keeping ayahuasca experiences secret (Harner 1972; Rubenstein 2012). For Shuar in northwest Amazonia, speaking openly about a powerful spirit ally that was gained while drinking ayahuasca risked causing the ally to leave the body. Narrating the experiences could weaken their intrinsic powers. Among urban practitioners of Santo Daime and Uniao de Vegetal in Brazil, it can be inappropriate to share elaborate stories about personal ayahuasca visions (Labate and MacRae 2010). William Barnard (2022) described how the reluctance to narrate such experiences may help Santo Daime members sustain the wondrous qualities of the brew and even guard them from egoism:

> It *is* probably good spiritual practice to treasure the sanctity and profundity of our [ayahuasca] spiritual experiences; to not casually throw them around; to not cheapen them by speaking of them carelessly or flippantly, especially if we are, knowingly or unknowingly, using our descriptions of these *wondrous inner gifts* as a way to subtly or not so subtly puff up our ego. [italics added] (181)

Against this backdrop, cultivating and sharing narratives of ayahuasca experiences is a major healing activity in the burgeoning commercial use of the brew. Ayahuasca practices in these loosely categorized global networks—what

I termed "global ayahuasca," given its overlap with the wellness industry—widely promote the benefits of narrating ayahuasca experiences. They emphasize the value of interpreting and verbalizing experiences in dedicated group activities, psychotherapy encounters, or coaching relationships, as a means of gaining lasting healing and benefits.

While the narrative styles among global ayahuasca drinkers are diverse, the therapeutic emphasis on narrating a visionary self situates the practice among wider allopathic health care practices such as psychotherapy and psychoanalysis. Ayahuasca drinkers are now protagonists in their own visionary realms, whether they seek spiritual enlightenment, healing from trauma, corporate success, or encounters with Mother Nature. The sometimes abrupt transition from ayahuasca retreats back to daily life has been called the "integration" phase or process, which often means making new meaning by generating special narratives about the experiences. In its simplest definition, "to integrate" means to combine something with another thing to make a whole. Ayahuasca integration involves taking the gifts, blessings, or insights derived from ayahuasca experiences and using them to inspire a positive change within oneself. These changes could be therapeutic, existential, artistic, work-related, or even political and antiestablishment in nature. In addition to narrating the visions, other popular integration techniques included doing art, writing poetry, composing music, getting a massage, doing nature therapies, or attending counseling. Yet the most common practices, often incorporated into retreat programs, involved drinkers narrating their visionary experiences and sometimes decoding the meaning in group activities with others listening on.

In today's psychedelic marketplace, there are integration therapists, groups, coaches, gurus, and apps to assist in this process. Psychedelic consumers are surrounded by a plethora of options for undertaking "the real work" of unpacking into everyday life whatever was realized or shifted during the psychedelic session. Anthropologists, including myself, have been deeply interested in understanding how social contexts can shape psychedelic experiences (Dupuis 2021a; Langdon 1979; Luna and Amaringo 1999; Gearin and Calavia Sáez 2021). However, ayahuasca drinkers, and other psychedelic users, appear more interested in the opposite. They are deeply committed to exploring how visionary experiences can have an impact on their daily lives, which is the essence of integration. Just as there can be a curious feedback loop between attributes of social context and the features of psychedelic experiences (Hartogsohn 2020:7–8), learning how to live in light of the gnosis of psychedelic visions can include addressing contradictions in routine life, which can inform future visions.

Reflecting on how people in the United States find meaning amidst chaos, Gay Becker (1997) emphasized the role of storytelling. Stories can help to restore a sense of order when faced with upheavals like tragedy, disease, or loss. In this light, storytelling helps people cope and offers a means of constructing a renewed sense of self in a transformed lifeworld. This is echoed in Claude Lévi-Strauss's (1977) iconic examination of Cuna curing songs. He perceived the songs as helping to instill psychological and supernatural order amidst the chaotic storms of illness and suffering. Many therapeutic narratives involve stories that ultimately aim at restoring a sense of order and harmony over chaos. Yet, by contrast, Michael Taussig (1987) demonstrated how ayahuasca drinking in the Putumayo of southern Colombia appeared to encapsulate the chaotic brutality of colonialism. In this example, the mythic realms and ayahuasca visions were symptomatic of disorder itself rather than simply something that counteracted or harmonized it.

Through analyzing descriptions of psychedelic experiences, scholars have spawned various meta theories in psychology and the social sciences. Psychiatrist Stanislav Grof (2008) characterized psychedelic substances as nonspecific amplifiers of psychological processes. While this can accommodate a wide affective and cognitive range of the states induced by psychedelics, it overlooks the impact of social dimensions on the visions. Previously, Claude Lévi-Strauss described the substances as amplifiers of collective cultural concerns and social discourses (cited in Dupuis 2022a). However, Lévi-Strauss's structuralism failed to account for social change or to grant sufficient agency to the person. The idea that ayahuasca visions simply reflect social worlds overlooks each person's capacity to potentially reshape the conditions of their existence. To neglect the personal and contingent aspects of ayahuasca visions in favor of the ways they mirror social structures risks sliding into a "dark determinism"—wherein systemic conditions leave no room for theorizing subjective agency (Beihl and Locke 2017:xi). The challenge is to strike a balance by analyzing the person in the social and visionary experiences they inhabit, navigate, and help to animate.

This chapter explores the relationships that people form with ayahuasca during everyday life. Examining "integration" practices among drinkers in Australia and in China, I use a contrasting approach, one that is not based upon delineating essential differences or similarities. While there are similar integration experiences across these two contexts, the aim is not to substantiate any sweeping or essentialist theory. Rather, I explore how different models of integration can reflect different relationships to modernity. While demonstrating this, the analysis considers the presence and power of ayahuasca visions in everyday life—while also acknowledging the absence, limits, and detachment of the visions from ordinary affairs. It explores the tension between the interior dimensions of the person and the exterior conditions of their social existence, between the unseen and the seen, the personal and the societal, and the subjective and the objective. As will be discussed, ayahuasca's power and presence can be based on altering and dissolving such boundaries—whether through integration efforts, divine synchronicities, or in Amazonian contexts, sorcery. The invisible interiority of the person that ayahuasca renders visible comes entangled within the social and cultural environments that can shadow, inspire, and pervade the visions.

Whether at ayahuasca retreats in Australia or China, or among shamanic tourism centers in Peru, integration narratives often included wonder discourse. Experiences of awe may occur during the integration discussion circles, but in my observations, this was rare and less likely to occur than expressions of wonder or astonishment. During the drinking sessions themselves, experiences of awe were much more common, depending upon the person, dose, and session. Importantly, during the drinking sessions, participants oscillated in and out of different moods and states of consciousness. Navigating deep states of wonder, awe, fear, dread, confusion, equanimity, gratitude, joy, and other emotional responses was common and varied among the groups I researched. If we define wonder and awe across a spectrum between an epistemic emotion (wonder) and an ineffable emotion (awe) then a key practice of integration resided in the creative exchange between the two. Wonder sometimes appeared imbued with the same ineffable hues as awe but at a lower intensity and therefore was perhaps better equipped for living meaningfully with ayahuasca from the perspectives of ordinary situations and mundane demands.

Before analyzing the ethnographic materials, this chapter first considers the origins of ayahuasca integration practices in psychedelic therapies of the 1950s and 1960s in North America and Europe. Early psychedelic therapists placed great emphasis on integration, which they defined in at least three ways that I categorize as intrapsychic, relational, and cultural. I then explore how contemporary ayahuasca integration practices in countercultural Australia reproduced this earlier emphasis but encompassed the three models within a holistic concept of the person pitted against issues of modern society. This is then contrasted with a deep analysis of one enterprising ayahuasca drinker in China, where integration efforts involve an attempt to positively address moral contradictions of capitalist subjectivity. The chapter concludes by considering the lack of "integration" concepts in Indigenous Amazonian approaches.

AFTER THE VISIONS

Whatever the properties of an individual's psychedelic experience, it is common to hear enthusiasts exclaim that such properties are squandered if the person does not actively incorporate them into their daily life. This principle animates many clinical psychedelic therapies and ayahuasca retreat programs alike. In the clinical space, the experiential value of consuming the substance has become more utilitarian in the sense of aiming to influence everyday life—such as by achieving goals of psychopathology reduction. The notion of integration is widely employed to communicate this ideal, but as several researchers have noted (Earleywine et al. 2022; Gearin 2023b; Gearin and Labate 2018:191; Sloshower et al. 2020:15), it is loosely defined and lacks theorization. It appears that psychologists, psychiatrists, and therapists have struggled to define psychedelic integration precisely because it requires theorizing the interiority of persons within the messy social and cultural environments they inhabit. Before scaling the analysis to consider social and contextual elements of integration practice, first the psychological elements are introduced, given their importance in 1960s clinical psychedelics.

Ayahuasca practices at the commercial retreats across the globe appear to share many similarities with the clinical psychedelic therapies. They both involve an introspective approach to visionary navigation followed by a narrative emphasis on interpreting the experience during the days and weeks that follow. They both follow a rough triad model or process. It includes (1) the participant undertaking a period of preparation, maybe several days in duration, whereby they change their social behaviors and mental activity to get ready to consume the substance, (2) the psychoactive ceremony or drug session itself, and (3) an integration or aftercare period which can last days, weeks, or longer. In psychedelic-assisted therapies, the preparation encounters help the therapists understand the patient's condition, build rapport and trust, and prepare the patient's expectations and personal "intentions" for the session. The model pivots upon the middle phase, also known as the "dosing session," when patients undergo extraordinary and often intensely meaningful experiences associated with the mystical and religious (Richards 2016). Clinical literature has highlighted the need for patients to undertake integration activities after the dosing session. If "set and setting" is the most enduring concept in psychedelic therapy (Hartogsohn 2020; 2016)—which focuses on the social, psychological, and environmental factors that shape psychedelic experiences—then the notion of integration is perhaps the second most pressing, although some would say more important.

Psychiatrists and therapists administering the substances in the 1950s and 1960s in North America and Europe highlighted the importance of integration. Stanislav Grof, a Czechoslovakian psychiatrist, pioneered LSD psychotherapy during this period by conducting more than four thousand sessions (2008:13). He emphasized integration techniques such as psychotherapy, group therapy, special breathing modalities, artistic expression, and even having the patient watch a video recording of their psychedelic experience after the session to give them a "more objective point of view" (147). Psychological insights that emerged during challenging psychedelic sessions should be paired with aftercare techniques, he argued, to "facilitate the integration of the material and its application to everyday life" (147). This shares some similarities with the general aim of psychotherapy and counseling to generalize benefits achieved during the therapy session into everyday life (Walsh 2012). But high-dose psychedelic approaches involve unique requirements for integration given the dramatic changes in mood, perception, and experience—

let's call it mystical and shamanic—that can occur during the dosing session.

Early researchers were less than clear on how much integration was needed or desired, other than to recognize that different patients required different degrees, and that, generally, more is better than less. Grof highlighted that "sometimes the integration of the session takes days or weeks" (2008:147). American psychiatrist Sidney Cohen suggested "the months following the LSD treatment are most important" (1965:192), and American psychologist Betty Eisner commented "some of the more important effects of drug sessions, especially with LSD, can occur as long as six weeks to three months after the sessions" (2002:103). Concerned about the risks of unregulated psychedelic therapists treating patients without adequate aftercare, Cohen warned about services that finish when the therapeutic process is actually just beginning (1965:193). These early researchers emphasized the importance of tailoring integration services to different mental health needs, suggesting that integration should not be approached as a one-size-fits-all set of therapeutic practices.

The term "integration" has at least three definitions across both early and current research in psychedelic therapy. The first, which was particularly overt in the early period, refers to the interiority of the patient's phenomenological experience and the coming together of different parts of the personality (Cohen 1965; Naranjo 1973; Eisner 2002), including through bringing together psychological insights, memories, and affects with altered bodily and sensory experiences. In this intrapsychic model, mental health is pursued by helping the person reintegrate parts of the self that have been fractured by life experiences. The second kind of integration, which appears in the early psychedelic therapy literature but has become the most common definition today, refers to transferring positive mental or spiritual gains from the drug session to endure across everyday life (Walsh 2012). If the first type concerns a person's inner harmony, the second concerns the challenge of bringing this harmony to the relational demands of family, work, and habitual realities. The third and final definition, which is less common in both the early and current contexts, refers to the broader cultural and legal challenge of incorporating psychedelic use into society in beneficial ways. This includes histories of persecution and moralized views about the dangers of prohibited drugs that apparently lacked medical and spiritual value.

These three levels of integration—intrapsychic, relational, and cultural—

represent different dimensions and can have different goals, yet their distinctions sometimes blur or collapse in the lived experiences of ayahuasca drinkers. Integration has been difficult to sharply define because it requires accounting for the complexities of each individual's psychological life within their varied realms of social and cultural specificity. The following analysis will eventually illustrate how integration can entangle the instrapsychic, the relational, and the cultural with lived experience, depending upon the person and context.

THREE MODELS, ONE PERSON

The intrapsychic model of integration I observed in Australia resembles ancient religious descriptions of the state of grace. Roy Rappaport considered William James's notion that grace "is a psychic reunion in which war among parts of the self is replaced by a harmonious and enthusiastic concert of the whole self working in peace as one" (1999:383). Integration of the self or personality was a major goal of ayahuasca drinking in Australia. People attempted to recognize the totality of themselves, including their less-desirable traits and behaviors. Building upon the psychology of Carl Jung, they worked to "integrate" their "shadow" by encountering afflictive ayahuasca experiences—whether monsters, demons, unpleasant memories, or past moral transgressions—as parts of the self that *needed* to be "integrated" in some capacity, that is, recognized or even understood.

The shadow self was construed as a maladaptive and pathological subconscious with habits that required deep recognition to overcome and stop them from unwittingly shaping everyday life. "Ayahuasca heals by bringing that which is unconscious into the light of awareness. It can bring up any kind of trauma or repressed experience or feelings," explained Darpan, the Australian facilitator. He recommended people simply witness their visions and not react, judge, or resist them. This was repeated by ayahuasca drinkers across Australia through the navigational adage "resistance is persistence." To observe the confronting or grotesque aspects of ayahuasca experiences without reacting to them will cause "the energy to dissipate and resolve," he added. The hope is that this will reduce a person's shadow self from having an unconscious negative influence. Darpan explained to me, "In ordinary 3D reality, we project our highest qualities and our highest self onto gurus, healers, masters, just as we project our lowest aspects of our being onto people we demonize, judge, and blame. Ayahuasca is a brilliant panacea to bring some neutrality to this very dynamic process." This implies that there are core psychological dynamics shared between ayahuasca experiences and ordinary life circumstances. The experiences unfurl psychological habits by embodying them in extraordinary and other ways.

Darpan told his clients to approach his ayahuasca ceremonies as a meditation activity that aims to reunite the mind and the body and to reconnect the person with nature. Recommending they approach challenging ayahuasca visions with a detached, introspective mindset takes the practice beyond the intense social approach of sorcery-healing in Indigenous Amazonia and reinvents it with principles taken from Eastern spiritual practices, or more precisely, from the globalization of mindfulness. Historian Anne Harrington's (2008) work detailed how mindfulness techniques from Eastern religions were reframed scientifically in the 1970s. The drive to alleviate stress through mindfulness was adopted as a remedy for sicknesses ascribed to modern lifestyles, and embodying some similar critical angles to what ayahuasca neoshamanism would later include. The young American meditation teacher Jon Kabat-Zinn popularized mindfulness as "the regular, disciplined practice of moment-to-moment awareness or *mindfulness*, the complete 'owning' of each moment of your experience, good, bad, or ugly" (cited in Harrington 2008:220). Echoing this mindset, Darpan asserted that ayahuasca offered personal revelations, helping people "take responsibility for all their feelings, thoughts, and actions, and indeed [their] very reality." He suggested that the more people attempted to suppress their shadow selves, the more these qualities would become strengthened and habituated, not only reoccurring in ayahuasca visions but featuring during life crises and high-stress situations.

This understanding forms the basis for integrating the shadow with ayahuasca in Australia. The evening experiences can become a topographic map of affective habits and the psychedelic moral dimensions of the self. They can provide insights and experiences that people *should* encounter in a somewhat detached state of mind, Darpan encouraged. He called this "the witness state" and said that learning to navigate ayahuasca in this observational state, and then integrating the experiences afterwards through talking about the visions, or expressing them through other means, can lead to healthier and happier lives.

Another integration theme discussed and practiced in Australia was the need to unify the mind and the heart, with the former sometimes associated with the ego—hubris, self-absorption, and mental chaos—and the heart with love—compassion, forgiveness, and prosociality. In this intrapsychic model, the heart is considered above and beyond the mind. Australian author Rak Razam (2009; 2014) described how drinking ayahuasca teaches that "the mind is the control room; the heart is the temple." Similar to the medicalization of mindfulness, integrating the shadow self or integrating the mind and heart with ayahuasca are intropsychic and spiritually humanistic pursuits.

Unifying the shadow self with the conscious self, and the heart with the mind, reflects the notion of integrative holism in psychotherapy (Goldfried, Pachankis, and Bell 2005) and of religious grace in Christianity and Western esoteric traditions. Considering how William James and Gregory Bateson approached grace as a marriage between the discursive and the nondiscursive, Roy Rappaport argued that a lack of grace is therefore a problem of language itself. "The alienation of parts of the psyche from each other," he suggested, are "a consequence of the elaboration of discursive reason concomitant with the emergence of language [and thus] grace can only be achieved by reuniting elements of the psyche that language sets at odds" (Rappaport 1999:384). Grace, here, is the result of integrating nondiscursive and ineffable states with the discursive and verbal.

> In the state of grace, and in religious experience generally, non-discursive feelings, emotions, and presentiments grasp, envelop, or pervade objects of discursive thought. The numinous and the sacred unite to form the all-embracing Holy. The term "holy," sharing as it does its etymology with "whole," is appropriate for the designation of that which encompasses and integrates both the discursive and non-discursive aspects of human experience. (Rappaport 1999:384)

To integrate an ayahuasca experience during a social sharing circle can help ground the ineffable into narratives of the person becoming whole or "holy" in the classic religious sense. But for many people, ayahuasca is far from graceful. If the troubling and disordered consciousness of ayahuasca experiences represent symptoms caused by a confrontation with the obstacles to grace, then the verbalizations of disorder should have some resemblance to how and in what ways language sets elements of the psyche at odds with each other. Although grace can involve an unreflective and intuitive flow with a given situation, the possible casual dimensions of grace's absence include how language practices intersect with social and cultural settings.

Some common visions and integration practices of global ayahuasca have religious roots. The goals of drinking ayahuasca to merge with "All Nature" and "Mother Ayahuasca" or to undergo psychedelic ego dissolution reflect classic mystical experiences described by William James and others—such as the unification with God. As another example of this influence, the neoshamanic goals of intrapsychic integration reflect "the Holy" as the coming together of different aspects of the psyche, including the nondiscursive and the discursive, the heart and the mind, the shadow and the light, the self and the higher self. In this intrapsychic space, the psyche's lack of integration equates to an unbalance between two poles of the person's interior. It is characterized by a lack of grace, disturbing visions, and a sign that suffering and healing remain a challenge and that more integration is needed. Along these lines, it seems that talking with others about ayahuasca can help them to solidify and unify different holistic models of the self.

The second kind of integration found in early psychedelic therapies of the mid-twentieth century—which concerned the relational challenge of generalizing any benefits from the psychedelic experience across everyday life—is central to global ayahuasca. For many people, "integrating," "downloading," "anchoring," and "grounding" ayahuasca experiences into daily life is the ultimate path to benefiting from the brew. If someone requires more integration, they are typically recommended to drink less or have a longer period of abstinence between retreats. Integration can become a barometer for how often to drink ayahuasca and how to live in a balanced and correct relationship with the brew.

To better understand this relational integration, first it helps to consider more about the narrative-making social practices that surrounded ayahuasca, because this is recognized as probably the main way to integrate ayahuasca. When I first began researching in Australia, I was immediately struck by the enthusiasm of people to meet and talk with me about their experiences. Given the illegality of the brew and its spiritual nature, I had wrongly assumed that it would take substantial time to build trusting relationships with people for them to feel comfortable to open up. But I had serendipitously tapped into an established process of storytelling that existed at the core of many ayahuasca retreats across the globe. Speaking about their experiences with me gave drinkers an opportunity to continue their healing processes and grapple with their wondrous experiences in a new kind of social space and at the ayahuasca retreats themselves.

Handling the insights and the changes in view that ayahuasca can bestow is a challenge that can be encountered very differently, depending on context and other factors. In Australia, integration efforts were diverse. They were formalized during the retreat programs and informalized in everyday life. Informal acts were described as "organic," "natural," and "intuitive." Kate, a regular drinker, explained, "The teachings are countless and endless. They happen all the time, including when you least expect it. You might be walking down the street thinking about something else and a [visionary] journey from six months ago drops into your head." Peter, another regular drinker, shared his approach to integration: "I can't contain my journeys as they are like a book unfolding in front of me." Daily life is perceived in the presence of ayahuasca sessions and their wonders and other worlds.

Ceremony facilitators often cautioned that if someone is not doing integration, they will most likely not receive lasting healing from the brew. They also cautioned that Mother Ayahuasca can recognize when the drinker is not making an effort to integrate the insights, and *she* will respond by only providing superficial experiences to the drinker. Darpan explained to me,

> Unless you are integrating it into your daily life it is as worthless as a dream. But if you take what you have learned from the medicine and start to apply it daily into your life, whatever it is, it could be a simple thing like learn how to manage your own anger, and stay on the program with that. The mother [ayahuasca] notices, she knows, because you are dealing with a divine intelligence, and she will give you more and more beautiful

energy to work with. But if you're not [integrating] all you will get is some fractals and nice colors and nice feelings. And she will say "pffft, come back when you are serious" . . . it's about anchoring visions. I just see the [ayahuasca drinking] sessions as a microcosm for life. It's school. You go there to get the insights then the real work starts after the session when you are doing daily life. People forget that, they think, "Oh we are going into session to do the work and now I am just going back to my ordinary job." No, it's the other way around. That's the school, this is the real job, to integrate it into life.

Ayahuasca drinkers tended to view the several days after a ceremony as a particularly good time to be integrating. It may be more challenging precisely because the temporal gap between the visionary and ordinary lifeworlds is smaller, the embodied mind more open or the realms more porous. Previous emotional and behavioral patterns may become visible given the sudden change in mood and the insights that ayahuasca can help inspire. With the veils porous shortly after the ceremonies, the ayahuasca drinkers typically joined for a morning sharing circle to narrate their preceding night's experience.

Sharing circles and similar integration activities are aimed sharply at the self. Similar to psychotherapy, they are based upon a depiction of the self that places a radical responsibility upon the person narrating their own situation, desires, and needs. Psychiatrist and anthropologist Laurence Kirmayer (2007) illustrated how psychotherapy had historically helped to reinforce individualist values along these lines. Examining Western contexts of psychotherapy, he described how failing to attain sufficient autonomy may be cast as psychopathological. Healing in this context, he argued, was pursued through learning to recognize desires and needs and achieve greater self-control. Kirmayer compared this egocentric perspective to models of selfhood in China, India, and other places where the self is decentered and where family, community, and ancestral obligations may overdetermine persons.

Australian ayahuasca integration provides a curious example to considering how social contexts can influence the boundaries of the person. The evening ceremonies inspire dramatic somatic, sensory, and cognitive experience, characterized by a dissolving self—whether into Mother Ayahuasca, psychedelic nature worlds, or God. The normal boundaries between self and world are abandoned during wild times that transcend language. This is followed by integration efforts that help to establish or reconfigure the dissolved boundaries between self and other, self and world, and self and society. As I have explored elsewhere (Gearin 2015; Gearin and Calavia Sáez 2021), the narrative social crafts of ayahuasca integration sessions reproduce individualistic values by placing epistemic, moral, and cosmic autonomy firmly on the individual's oration of their visionary self. Through the discursive norm of only listening when others are narrating their visions, it emphasized each individual's particular visions, goals, traumas, and healing. The cosmic ego-dissolving properties of ayahuasca can help reproduce an autonomous self equipped to define, narrate, and heal itself, while "holding space" to reduce opportunities for their own experiences to be influenced or explained by others. This gives integration an expressive individualist value that can have an impact on how meaning derived from visions is lived with in daily life. Integration, defined as transferring spiritual gifts from the ceremonies to the everyday, is partly an attempt to push against the individualist orientations that fragment the cosmos into eight billion people by testing and concretizing new existential visions of the self in social spaces.

The third and final model of psychedelic integration analyzed here involves the process of legitimating and incorporating ayahuasca and related substances into mainstream society against histories of criminalization, demonization, and pathologization. I term this "cultural integration." In aiming to understand this in Australia, it helps to compare ayahuasca use against common perceptions of other kinds of psychoactive substances. As outlined earlier, the unpleasant ayahuasca experiences were framed by drinkers as afflictive shadows of the self that required integration to promote healing. In this approach, people experience ayahuasca in a diametrically opposed moral landscape to how other illicit psychoactive substances were framed in the popular Australian imagination. This contrast was particularly true when I was doing research between 2011 and 2014. The recent boom in the medicalization of psychedelic therapy has begun to shift public opinion towards appreciating the benefits of psychedelics. But among the wider social imagination of Australians, when I collected data, ayahuasca was associated with other "illicit drugs"—such as cocaine, heroin, MDMA, and LSD—and carried charges of criminality, immorality, and pathology.

Australian medical professionals described ayahuasca as a "recreational drug" that can cause brain damage and other pathologies. These views were relatively common across Australian society during the early 2010s. They were televised through the moral authority of physicians speaking on Australia's most popular free-to-air television news program, Channel 7 News. In August 2012, the program aired a five-minute story with sensational language that described the apparent health dangers and illegality of ayahuasca and other psychedelics. The story began, "Sydney medical experts are warning of possible brain damage from hallucinogenic plants apparently used by South American medicine men." Ayahuasca, the story continued, "is being used in secretive ceremonies across Australia." The New South Wales attorney-general Greg Smith warned, "We are concerned with stamping them out as much as possible, restricting their use, and further growth." Despite that emerging scientific evidence at the time had demonstrated the relatively non-toxic effects of ayahuasca (Grob et al. 1996) and genuine psychological benefits (Bouso et al, 2012), Dr. Gordian Fulde of St. Vincent Hospital claimed that with "hallucinogens you've surrendered control of your brain and may also be leading to permanent brain damage." In no small irony, St. Vincent Hospital has now become a trail-blazing Australian context for clinical trials that are testing the therapeutic potential of psychedelic substances (Cole-Adams 2021). The prohibitionist and pathological depictions of ayahuasca by Dr. Fulde and Channel 7 indicated a stark moral inversion between those in Australia who drink ayahuasca and those who feared and condemned it.

Ayahuasca was not a "drug" but a "plant medicine" and "plant spirit." Against public opinion, they understood their use of ayahuasca *not recreationally* but with relational, spiritual, and healing concepts. This sets the practice at moral odds with the public perceptions of psychedelic drug use described above. While medical institutions and the general public have perceived heroin, cocaine, and ecstasy as offering pleasurable experiences with subsequent detrimental effects to health and moral character (such as addiction, dilapidated bodies, criminality, and desperation), ayahuasca drinkers in Australia described unpleasurable immediate experiences (vomiting, disturbing visions, and emotional turmoil) with subsequent positive effects to well-being and moral character. Comparing Indigenous views of ayahuasca and alcohol in the Peruvian Amazon, Peter Gow (2012) commented how alcohol was perceived to produce a hangover in the morning after drinking it whereas ayahuasca resulted in feelings of elation, a desire to work, and good fortune in the days following. Similarly, peyotists in the Native American Church said that drinking peyote causes the hangover to come first or during the ceremony and then positivity and health benefits come after (Jay 2019:28). For the Australians I studied, the brew was not an intoxicating escape from the shadow self and its repressed suffering body but provided illuminating encounters with it, the goal being to purge or overcome the troubles of a shadowy world. The illumination of the shadow was cultivated through a shared need to integrate the challenging and marvelous experiences.

What I would now like to highlight is how these three definitions of integration—intrapsychic, relational, and cultural—at times conflated in the practice and thinking of ayahuasca drinkers in Australia. In this context, ayahuasca experiences provided a source of daily moral empowerment that became pronounced in oral performances in the sharing circles as expressive well-being and visionary poetics. The integration narratives included a wide range of hopes, fears, and desires. The overcoming of challenges in family life was perhaps the most common worldly theme. People described visionary encounters with plant spirits, angels, monsters, aliens, other worlds, and much more. But whenever the person interpreted these otherworldly experiences psychologically, it was typically in relation to their interpersonal life, moral dilemmas, and traumas they linked to different parts of themselves and their pasts.

Ayahuasca, in this context, can be seen as a kind of social medicine. The quest to integrate ayahuasca sometimes involved a reevaluation of one's social relations and social obligations. For Judith, a white thirty-five-year-old social worker, the healing she received from ayahuasca inspired her to divorce her husband. She described having postnatal depression for years while living under his violent and abusive rule. Her battle with depression included suicidal thoughts, but she felt determined to live to care for her child. During an

206 GLOBAL AYAHUASCA

ayahuasca ceremony in hills outside of Melbourne, she purged intensely for thirty minutes while experiencing a dizzying array of haunting imagery. This was followed by a remarkable sense of peace which formed an empowered new view that emerged weeks after her retreat:

> Prior to taking aya, I had no idea who I was, what my morals and values in life were, what I wanted to do or be, and I was thirty-four-years old and married with two toddlers. After taking aya I left my husband, went back to school, moved out, endured being dragged through the legal system by my ex and have never looked back. Why? Because I have that knowing inside that aya gives.

She understood the unraveling of her escape from her husband among a wider healing and awakening process facilitated by ayahuasca.

> The voices in my head were so loud and constant, twenty-four-seven, for months. I was so scattered and hopeless then. About four hours after [drinking] aya the voices stopped, and all I can say is that I felt like I was liberated, but I couldn't work out what I was liberated from. It was about three weeks later that I realized I was liberated from all the negative beliefs I had about myself. Liberated from my parents and the false beliefs and fears they instilled in me, and liberated from my ex-husband. I was no longer responsible for anyone but myself and my children and whilst I used to know this intellectually, I didn't know it with certainty, with every cell in my body. I have always looked to others for answers. I no longer always do that as I now have access to a knowing that I didn't have before, as no one had taught me. I also have more compassion for people who are angry and fearful and dominating as I can now see how they are just in pain and don't love or accept themselves.

Judith found a source of moral strength in the spirit of ayahuasca and the natural world. As it did for others in Australia, *ceremony* provided her with insight and healing from the transcendental embrace of Mother Ayahuasca. All that which was painful, immoral, confusing, or sick in society could become exposed and some of it hopefully healed by illuminated benevolence. Healing, as described during integration circles, was directed towards family disputes, sexual violence, childhood bullying, trauma from war, injustices at work, and other afflictions. The brew opened people to healing dimensions of nature positioned against society and its many ills. Ayahuasca drinkers in this context were more likely to express a dissatisfaction and disenchantment with society (Gearin 2017).

Judith's first ayahuasca experience, which she described as "weird but the most important experience in my life," entailed a kind of spiritual union with ayahuasca that would be familiar to others in Australia. "I watched myself and Mother Aya make love (not sexual) through our chests, both our souls weaving upwards like the plant itself . . . whilst I was watching this happen, I was actually feeling it." In the days and weeks afterwards, this unifying with Mother Ayahuasca sometimes hovered in her mind during daily life and acted as an emotional resource to "integrate" when faced with challenges. "When I am feeling sad," she explained, "I always think of that experience and try to get that feeling back." The moods and insights from ayahuasca were waiting to be reflected upon and absorbed. Judith's experience demonstrates how the three models of integration noted before can be lived as one. First, integrating of the shadowy, haunting, and marvelous dimensions of the self was healing for her. Second, divorcing her husband and making changes to ordinary life in light of the ayahuasca experiences was emphasized. Finally, integrating the feminine spirit of nature against the problems of society was present in her narratives and experience.

Many I interviewed in Australia were hesitant and often unwilling to talk about their ayahuasca experiences with nondrinkers due to fears of ridicule, discrimination, and even persecution. Negative kinds of legal and medical perspectives about "hallucinogens" combined into a uniquely disenchanted view that alienated the practice of drinking ayahuasca and suspended it beyond civil society. Such alienation further authenticated the intuition that society was existentially toxic and disenchanted and that ayahuasca and the spirit of nature are powerful antidotes to it.

For Judith's ayahuasca drinking, healing came premised upon a polysemic notion of integration that threaded psychological, social, and cultural aspects into a composite image of well-being. This shared composite represented health and the person drinking ayahuasca to purify their body-mind

208 GLOBAL AYAHUASCA

and to come into better alignment with nature. The three-layered models of integration reflect different parts of her new source of moral strength and healing.

SEEING THROUGH PARADOXES

Ayahuasca drinking in China reveals unique examples of how social contexts can inform psychedelic experiences and the efforts people undertake to integrate them. This section undertakes a long ethnographic analysis of one ayahuasca drinker to glimpse at how the experiences can enhance career development while wrestling with moral contradictions in Chinese family and workplace contexts.

It was a cold morning in the early winter months of 2019, and I was in Shanghai's French Concession district waiting to meet Chao for a discussion about ayahuasca. It was the first time we had met. A successful corporate manager in his late thirties, Chao arrived in a sleek black van with his personal driver at the wheel. As we meandered through the opulent streets surrounded by Art Deco architecture and aligned with bushy London Plane trees, a legacy of the late eighteenth century, we discussed how surrealist art traditions shaped Chinese propaganda posters during the Maoist era. We spent several hours at a local café discussing his ayahuasca practice while his driver waited patiently in the parked van. Chao's demeanor, characterized by an ease and smoothness in his tone and body language, exuded a competence befitting his position as general manager of a large multinational company.

Chao explained that his time was very precious but the reason why he occasionally took two days away from work and family to drink ayahuasca was to become a "better person in all ways; I feel like I'm a better dad, colleague, a better husband, manager, because of ayahuasca." He was not compelled to share ayahuasca visions stories with his wife, parents, or colleagues, even though the visions were often about them or were interpreted by him in light of them.

Chao approached ayahuasca similar to how he approached the religious shrine in his home, which hosted Doaist and Buddhist deities whom he prayed to daily. The brew was, ultimately, a personal and private source of faith and connection with the cosmos. He learned the practice of constructing a shrine in his home from his parents. "I adhere to those beliefs, because as a child growing up, it made me feel good," adding, "Those objects, ideas, and prayers help me go into a deeper state with ayahuasca." Chao does not discuss ayahuasca with his parents because they are "China parents" who are more interested in "very practical questions, like have you eaten enough, rested enough, or how is your job?" Yet his ayahuasca drinking is aided by the spiritual practice he adopted from his parents. As demonstrated below, the brew opened a portal that emanated significance grounded in family and elements of Chinese religiosity.

For Chao, and perhaps most others regardless of context, ayahuasca drinking can be challenging. His most recent retreat had been especially challenging due to a series of difficult events. In the span of one year, his mother, mother-in-law, and father-in-law had all been diagnosed with cancer. His father-in-law died, and to make the loss worse, one of his closest friends had also died that year, the victim of "a senseless act of gun violence" in the United States. The last interaction he had with his friend was a petty argument, which added a layer of guilt and confusion to his grief. Amidst this turmoil, Chao sought refuge in his job.

During an ayahuasca session with Luke, he encountered a giant monster that blanketed his eyes with darkness. He recognized it as a "terrifying shadow of guilt for working too much. . . . When I faced the monster, it all came out in a purge." Chao found some relief vomiting the shadowy figure of guilt into a bucket. "I was no longer blinded by darkness. I could see clearly what I needed to do," he explained. The next day, after leaving the retreat, he went home and called his mother-in-law and apologized for his absence. He also made a conscious effort to spend more time and good mood with his family.

But gaining these relational insights into his family came as something of a surprise to Chao. He was initially attracted to the retreat's unique blend of spiritual practices with a corporate mindset that prioritized vocational success and satisfaction. The Bridging the Gap philosophy at the core of the program harmonizes spiritual principles and professional hurdles with visionary experiences, coaching sessions, breathwork activities, and other services. As described in Chapter 5, the narrative model of this approach is designed to help people navigate the tensions of integrating into a capitalist world while

210 GLOBAL AYAHUASCA

balancing familial obligations and higher values and purpose. For Chao, aya-huasca revealed to him hidden dangers underlying his professional drive.

He was general manager for a prominent global firm that assists brands to adapt to the Chinese market, and he finds his work satisfying. To maintain his privacy, I intentionally described his company in vague terms. His clientele included Ubisoft, Porsche, UBS—"almost any brand," he shared. He finds passion and meaning in the challenge of "creating a rigid structure that can solve the ephemeral and fluid challenges of different situations and clients." But he also carried an ambivalence towards his work and a need to do more good in the world than he was with his job. He told me how he once arrived at an ayahuasca retreat feeling burdened by the constant pressure to achieve financial growth for his company. Speaking of his work but also the world in general, he shared in frustration, "Right now we are stuck in this weird race of GDP. Everyone is looking for more growth. When you are searching so hard for growth, it leads to stupid projects." When he first decided to drink ayahuasca in China, like everyone else who attended Luke's retreats he was asked to create a personal intention plus a special question. "We had to ask the universe a question we wanted answered in the context of our careers and personal development," he explained. His was, "How do I impact the world in a positive way as a professional?" He worried that his lifestyle and work-place were ultimately built upon a predatory global system that is harming the planet and humanity's potential to survive. Several months after his initial ayahuasca experience, he was still thinking about the experience intensely and pondering this worry about his impact in the world. He said,

> I've been successfully climbing the corporate ladder for years. I hit the numbers. I am given the rewards. I can afford to dine at any restaurant, go on expensive holidays, all of that stuff. But I feel like I am contributing to a system that is not aligned with the progression of earth. . . . If we don't fix our human system in the next couple of decades, we might not be able to continue. This is hard for me to accept. I love humanity and I hope we are not a virus to this planet. . . . I am part of this economy, we all are part of it, but this economy needs to transform and alter and adhere back to the laws of nature, but how do you do that? This is the biggest question for myself and the rest of my community.

INTEGRATION AND SOCIETY 211

Chao was confronted by the challenge of living in a contradictory world, saying, "It's impossible to not contribute to ecological destruction, global wars, and other atrocities . . . we are in the trenches. We all buy things, pay taxes, we are all part of the big system whether we like it or not." Against this concerned backdrop, drinking ayahuasca showed him marvelous visions of pristine futures that included godlike realms of beauty and wonder. The following visions, he explained, inspired him to want to do more good in the world.

> I remember every single detail like it was yesterday. It will never leave me. The taste in my mouth, the ash, and the little bit of acidity in the back of the throat when you drink it. The music was so necessary to the experience. Sometimes it was a tribal shaman chanting and when I heard that, it triggered a vision and I was sitting in a campfire of these old ancient beings. It felt as though they were timeless beings. Visually it looked very old. I kept feeling like I was experiencing something that was timeless. I kept seeing what looked like subatomic particles. The mesh of the building blocks of life. If I let go a little bit and relaxed my eyes, I could get down to the details of how things were linked together, almost like fractals, it was weird, it was insane. It was so . . . it was like being born again, the things I saw were miraculous. I still get choked-up when I talk about it. It was so powerful.

For Chao, the timelessness of his ayahuasca visions illuminated a sacred ecological reality beyond a destructive growth mentality. Reflecting on perceiving timeless beings sitting around an ancient fire, Chao found faith in humanity against fears that we are an inherently destructive species killing the planet. "To have unblinded faith, I really struggle with that. I am a deep skeptic," he added. This visionary faith enabled him to resolve the moral contradictions of participating in a global and capitalist world that is bent on destruction and exploitation.

> We are in the grind, but we are trying to do something better. My business colleagues and myself still haven't found anything. We talk about it sometimes, "like, you know, we are still not impacting the world, we are just making our numbers." I watch the news and I see people doing all this

> awesome stuff, and I keep thinking to myself, how do I get there? That's one of the reasons I took ayahuasca, the plants, not to give me the path but just to get a sense, a notion, of what to do.

Attempting to bring eternal visions and idealistic values into the everyday terrain of workplace and domestic life is not necessarily easy. Since his awe-inspiring ayahuasca experience, Chao created a consultancy fund to help clients who want to create sustainable businesses designed to benefit the world. Ayahuasca, arriving to China as a narrative practice that involved integration groups, changed Chao's views of narrative and humans. He shared that ayahuasca had given him hope by deepening his view that humans are but narrative machines.

> Although the process, the plants, didn't give me like "here's the answer," what it showed me was very clear and everything suddenly made sense. We are psychological machines that make stories. Everything has a value to it and everything has a story to it. That's how humans survive. So, for me, that gave me peace, and a little bit of hope towards my virtually inconsequential time on this planet.

Ayahuasca provided Chao with a faith to continue working hard despite or because of his moral dilemmas of capitalist subjectivity. The ayahuasca retreats in China took him into mercurial states of perception and experience that ultimately evoked a greater flexibility to juggle contradictory values and opposing life demands. These contradictions primarily included (1) his need to seek financial growth for his business and his desire to help create a sustainable ecological world, and (2) his need to attend to his family with more time and emotional resources and his desire to work. The brew inspired different facets and new angles on his psychic challenges of family life and corporate work.

Chao's quest to become more flexible and impute the visionary into the ordinary reflects psychedelic therapy's wider ideal. The promotion of psychological flexibility has become a core goal of psychedelic-assisted therapies and their integration techniques (Watts and Luoma 2020; Sloshower et al. 2020) and a model for predicting mental health benefits of psychedelic medicine use (Close et al. 2020). The phenomenological effects of the substances have been described as a hyperplastic "pivotal mental state" (Brouwer and Carhart-Harris 2021) and a "hot" phase of psychological chaos wherein beliefs and mental models are relaxed (Carhart-Harris et al. 2014). This malleability is thought useful for personality transformation, including in situations of social crisis (Carhart-Harris et al. 2014:9). The parameters and restraints of such flexibility bring into focus the social and cultural sides of psychological life, given that this is where the successes and failures of integration are forged. Neural plasticity and psychological flexibility, therefore, are not simply amoral, therapeutic goals, but must be assessed in relation to the social and cultural contexts that they push against, enact, or reproduce. This is because sometimes the need to resist psychological flexibility or psychological adjustment is the good ethical response. As Martin Luther King said in his 1968 address to the American Psychological Association,

> There are some things in our society, some things in our world to which we should never be adjusted. There are some things concerning which we must always be maladjusted if we are to be people of good will. We must never adjust ourselves to racial discrimination and racial segregation. We must never adjust ourselves to religious bigotry. We must never adjust ourselves to economic conditions that take necessities from the many to give luxuries to the few. We must never adjust ourselves to the madness of militarism, and the self-defeating effects of physical violence. (King 1968:10–11)

Foregrounding psychological flexibility as an inherent good without addressing the social conditions which enable or pressure such flexibility risks reproducing a problematic individualism that can obscure important social issues.

Just as the brain and mind appear to enter entropic states of chaotic neurological signals and relaxed beliefs under the effects of psychedelics, cultural and social domains can become subject to their own orders of flexibility and flux. Social scientists have described the last seventy years as a period of increasing social fragmentation in which institutions—such as family, employment, and community structures—have undergone rapid transformation or dissolution in many parts of the planet. Amplified capitalist arrangements, global relations, and disruptive transport and communication technologies have contributed to creating a "liquid modernity" (Bauman 2000) wherein self and identity become reflexive projects in need of constant revision (Lifton 1999; Giddens 1991). Services and social movements that promote individualism thrive in such contexts—including among new mental health therapies (Kirmayer 2007) and religious and spirituality practices (Brown 1997; Heelas 1996; Gearin and Calavia Sáez 2021; Labate 2014). The ability of psychedelic therapies and ayahuasca healing modalities to promote psychological flexibility make them highly relevant to the increasing demands that people sense in modern societies.

The evidence for therapeutic individualism, however, is certainly not equal in all parts of the world. Until recent decades, mental illness in modern China has been highly stigmatized and hidden under social norms of shame and avoidance (Kleinman 1982). Although these norms are still prevalent today, the country experienced a burgeoning in psychological services (Huang 2014; Zhang 2017)—which sometimes overlap with New Age spirituality (Iskra 2022). In *Anxious China: Inner Revolution and the Politics of Psychotherapy*, Li Zhang (2020) examined the boom in talk therapies and argued that analyses of the neoliberalization of subjectivity overlooked how the therapies in China can aim at disentangling traditional, socialist, and neoliberal tensions of selfhood. She illustrated how psychotherapy provided spaces for Chinese selves to navigate the anxious contradictions of socialist worlds that have been rapidly transformed by market-economy reforms, wherein traditional values of family, community, and state come up against neoliberal values, desires, and sentiments.

This situated perspective of entangled tensions of cultural selfhood appear to shape parts of Chao's ayahuasca practices. Drinking ayahuasca helped him come to terms with the contradictions of family commitments, capitalist subjectivity, and ecological doom. It helped him adapt to the need to pursue intense financial growth in his company while balancing his family life and transcendent moral vision of humanity. The flexibility and faith that ayahuasca gave him rest upon a paradox: one of the most wondrous and significant aspects of Chao's ayahuasca visions, he explained, appeared with a strange feeling of familiarity in the face of what were unfamiliar worlds. In the visions, he felt like he was returning to something or somewhere he had already been. "It felt impossible. How could I know this already?" he stated. In that moment, he encountered a noetic opening of unbound truth while returning to an eternal cosmic home.

> We are not making this shit up. When we do the plants and we meditate and we see those things, it makes sense. When I see what I saw, it could have just been a psychological projection of what I thought it is, but for me it felt, at its core, the closest thing to the truth that I could see without my brain exploding.

The sense of epistemic return that many ayahuasca drinkers have described lends a special significance to their experiences. The sense of familiarity makes the wondrous appear closer and realer than it might without it. For Chao, the uncanny familiarity helped him overcome contradictions of motivation and meaninglessness, eternal paradise and destructive growth, and peace and suffering. Feeling the need to remember the truth of the otherworld that he experienced, Chao encountered an integration challenge that ayahuasca gave him to make the world better.

Ayahuasca integration and psychedelic integration, I argue, share a curious resemblance to religious conversion, particularly with regard to the element of psychological flexibility. Scholars recently raised concern that the therapeutic efficacy of psychedelic therapies may act as a "double-edged sword" (Timmerman, Watts, and Dupuis 2022) by covertly turning the wheels of religious conversion to Christianity, Buddhism, or neoshamanism without fair consent given by the patient (see also Dupuis 2021a). Mystical experience and belief change appear to have a long past together. As Lewis Rambo (1993) elucidated, many have viewed mystical experience as the prototypical dynamo of religious conversion with its "sudden and traumatic burst of insight, induced by visions, voices, or other paranormal experience" (15). Many religious traditions illustrate how "the purpose of conversion is to bring people into relationship with the divine and provide them a new sense of meaning and purpose" (10). However, the abrupt event of mystical experience is usually not enough to ensure an ongoing transformation in meaning and purpose in the person.

Religious conversion typically involves a gradual and incomplete transformation of beliefs, customs, and attitudes, which often takes years to achieve (Baer 2014). It does not "involve a simple and absolute break," but rather, it "proceeds over time and requires a process of *integrating* knowledge and experience" [italics added] (Austin-Broos 2003:2). Importantly, culture and society shape this integration challenge of religious conversion. Proselytizing religions like Christianity and Islam have long preached creeds that helped incorporate foreign populations into political economies of empire (Baer 2014; Gooren 2014), including capitalist relations in the "colonization of consciousness" (John 1989).

The concept of religious conversion, however, is too crude for psychedelic therapies. Psychedelic patients and global ayahuasca drinkers—who experience mystical ego dissolutions and neoshamanic visions of plant spirits—are not necessarily shifting their social affiliations to a new group, religion, or creed. The psychedelic ecosystem is marked by a radical, egalitarianist cosmology in this regard, which involves transformations in perceptions of self and the world. It is more about *transformation* than about *conversion* in a religious sense, but the abrupt changes in perception and attitude of psychedelic use reflect the flexibility required for integrating mystical experiences into everyday life. This flexibility necessarily hinges on the social and cultural contexts of integration. Commercial ayahuasca use, in its current forms, can help socialize individuals into a late modernization of consciousness that rewards being protean to the neoliberal adjustments of society (Gearin and Devenot 2021). There is a possibility that integration achievements could become a barometer for the patient's level of flexible adjustment into social and political regimes of power or work. Whatever becomes of psychedelic integration practices and ideas, their processual nature resembles those aspects of religious conversion that slowly consolidate spiritual experiences into new and enduring views of the world.

As noted, Chao does not discuss his ayahuasca visions or practices with his family members or work colleagues, but he does share them with Luke, his ayahuasca coach, and with some of his close confidants. He also communicates them to himself in various ways. His visions are stories of *and* for the self.

A particularly meaningful way he keeps this conversation active is through visual art. Chao is an avid painter and daubs the ineffable on canvases in an attempt to ground them in his ordinary reality. The paintings are like a portal that also appears to feed into his ayahuasca experiences.

> When I paint, I mainly deal with mythologies . . . when I was tripping on ayahuasca, it really made me feel like I was in my artworks. I was in the world of idols, gods. I heard them speak through the native American music Luke played. I was surrounded by them. Gods of nature, ancient, ancient gods. For some reason, I was very at peace with it. It's very much my story. It's for sure not the absolute truth but is something that I just took on very well.

Although Chao participates in ayahuasca sharing round circles and coaching sessions where he narrates his visions to others, he ultimately prefers to show them through his actions rather than words. This means attempting to be more flexible and impactful in workplace life yet also more sensitive, present, and loving with his family. It means trying to create a sustainable ecological world in a capitalist environment fixed on growth and numbers. It means trying to emanate eternal ideals of an impossibly familiar otherworld into the rigid and challenging terrain of this one. It means being flexible in a world pulling contradictory values this way and that.

When people drink ayahuasca, they travel and converse between worlds or between layers and dimensions of the world. This includes not just visionary and metaphysical worlds, but also moral domains that bring into focus tensions, fears, and hopes. Ayahuasca integration practices both mirror society and inject it with possibilities for change, given that the person is not outside society and their inner worlds cannot be adequately understood outside it. While Mother Ayahuasca may offer healing rays descending from the Great Beyond for many, it is the trials and tribulations of daily life that make her presence meaningful. These aspects make ayahuasca worthy of stories and worship and lend the plants the status of healer, deity, or fierce guardian spirit. Ayahuasca experiences, when turned into integration materials, are measured by their weight in ordinary life.

Ayahuasca visions and purging can be the preconditions of the person changing in some capacities. This includes whether someone is purging the pain of familial life and reinvigorating positive attitudes or overcoming workplace obstacles and boosting success in capitalist environments. Stories and ayahuasca visions entangle themselves into the enmeshment of social fields that are historical and changing. Stories and ayahuasca can become so close and entangled that they can resemble each other at deeper levels. Similar to ayahuasca visions, "narratives often reveal more about what can make life worth living than about how it is routinely lived" (Rosaldo 1986:98). Again, like ayahuasca visions, "narratives never simply mirror lived experience or an ideational cosmos, nor is a story a clear window through which the world, or some chunk of it, may be seen" (Garro and Mattingly 2000:22). The stories of ayahuasca experiences wrestle with psychedelic sensations of inner flux that can empower transformative kinds of social and cultural projects as much as they can reinforce and stabilize them. In this social way, visions and narratives are not just compatible and reinforcing to each other but overlapping and perhaps analogical.

The narrative aspects of integration, which have become central to many psychedelic therapies, show how ayahuasca experiences can be remarkably personal and cultural. Ido Hartogsohn (2020) drew upon Durkheim's sociological theory of the "sacred" and "profane" to help theorize psychedelic integration. The sacred, for Durkheim, refers to special objects, persons, or experiences that bind social groups together in a unified system of belief, whereas the profane refers to that which is not sacred and includes the everyday practices of individual persons and their mundane activities of work and domestic life. "The difficulty of integrating the psychedelic experience back into 'profane' everyday life," Hartogsohn suggested, mirrored "the inherent difficulty of integrating the unusual and extraordinary into the usual and mundane" (211). This is an important idea for theorizing psychedelic integration and is part of a larger argument Hartogsohn develops on the cultural and historical grounds of psychedelic experience in the twentieth-century United States.

The pervasiveness of this Durkheimian structure of psychedelic integration—that is, integrating sacred visions against the profane realities of ordinary life—is socially specific. For Indigenous uses of ayahuasca, we see other configurations. The Shipibo healers I met in the Peruvian Amazon drink large doses of ayahuasca in shamanic tourism settings approximately 130 nights per year, but they do not appear to be occupied with "integrating" even their most profound ceremonial experiences. This is because ayahuasca visions and ordinary or sober perception are not subject to such an ontological rift. Shipibo adepts experience ayahuasca visions not only as imaginary, reflective, or representational, but as real albeit non-ordinary channels of everyday affairs.

Importantly, this lack of ontological distinction between the seen and unseen covers broader aspects of Amazonian lifeworlds. Elements of what scholars of religion have termed the supernatural, religious, or sacred have not been separated from the "mundane" practices and ideas of work or labor for Indigenous Amazonian groups (Griffiths 2001), partly because the "invisible aspects of the world are as much part of the phenomenal world as the visible parts" (Rivière 2010:4). As various anthropologists have argued in response to Durkheim, there are many social groups that operate in a world in which the distinction between "sacred" and "profane" is simply inappropriate. The distinction has been traced to histories of European modernity and the dynamics of religion, the state, science, and capitalism (Asad 2003; Foucault 1994). This would suggest that the concept and possibly the therapeutic efficacy of psychedelic integration, which appears in debt to the sacred and profane, cannot be separated from the cultural and historical conditions of the societies that champion it.

CONCLUSION

VISIONARY CONTEXTS

Broadly speaking, the visionary experiences that ayahuasca inspires can include so many things, including not only plant spirits and otherworldly encounters, but also mundane impressions that appear like memories or animated pictures. Examples of mundane impressions include a person seeing the garden in their previous home or a manager observing the layout of their workplace settings. Other examples of the everyday would be those Indigenous visions that translocate sight to neighboring towns and distant cities. These are important for thinking about how social contexts entangle ayahuasca in direct and obvious ways. However, other strange dimensions and unbelievable worlds are so frequent in high-dose experiences that whatever relation they may have to immediate social contexts, they compel ayahuasca drinkers far beyond the here and now.

Considering this experiential spectrum—from the mundane to the ineffable—I observed a crude but striking global difference in my data, which can help to unpack an idea at the heart of the psychedelic renaissance. When consuming psychedelics, the experience of time, including being oriented in a present that is distinct from the past and future, can become untethered and reformed. My ethnographic research suggests some trends in the temporal orientations of ayahuasca experiences when comparing key Indigenous and non-Indigenous perspectives. For those in Australia, or on neoshamanic retreat in Peru, or clients in corporate Chinese contexts, all of these non-Indigenous approaches emphasized trauma dynamics in their visionary and bodily experiences with the brew. Many perceived or reexperienced troubled aspects of their pasts during the sessions.

This temporal orientation mirrors psychedelic-assisted therapies in North America and elsewhere that treat psychological and spiritual trauma. Rick Doblin, founder of the Multidisciplinary Association for Psychedelic Studies in the United States, recently set a nebulous goal of achieving what he called "net-zero trauma" by 2070, through the global rollout of psychedelic clinics. This was announced at the Psychedelic Science conference in 2023 in Denver, an event that attracted over twelve thousand punters and more than four hundred speakers—including myself speaking on a small stage about the limits of wonder in neoshamanic tourism in Shipibo contexts. At the beginning of the conference, Former Texas governor Rick Perry took to the main stage to charismatically describe the promise of psychedelic treatments for helping US veterans heal their war trauma. As also seen in many other talks at the conference, the past had become a dominant temporal and therapeutic register of psychedelic experiences across the US, and also likely beyond in many other countries where trauma healing is popular.

This encountering of the past through psychedelic experiences contrasts

FIGURE C.1 Opening talks at Psychedelic Science 2023 conference, Denver, Colorado. (Photo: Alex Gearin)

with widespread Indigenous approaches that see the future when consuming ayahuasca (Harner 1973; Luna and Amaringo 1999; Gearin and Calavia Sáez 2021). During the 1980s, Michael Brown (1986:166–168) explained that the Aguaruna he lived among did not believe everyone has a destiny or fated life plan that ayahuasca visions of the future displayed. A person's ability to see the future was based on their shamanistic abilities. These practitioners, in essence, could generate futures through dieting and training with special plants that lend the power of clear psychospiritual sight. In Amazonia, this has included seeing a successful hunt, observing outsiders coming to visit or the aggressive plans of the whites, and perceiving a prognosis for a patient. Shipibo healer Jose Lopez Sanchez envisioned an intergenerational future that is "fully situated in the present" and supported by shamanistic dieting and caring for special plants (2023). Anthropologists Emilia Sanabria and Silvia Mesturini Cappo described this as a "phytofuture" practice that involves "speculative gestures of bringing forth, growing, and multiplying" with plants through "collective imaginative practices" (2023). Speaking with a group of international guests at Pachamama Temple during a dedicated "educational class," Shipibo healer Maestro Juan shared concerns about ayahuasca practices that focus on the past.

> For a lot of the people that come here, ayahuasca shows them previous parts of their life. But this is where they block themselves, because healing is about going forward, not backwards. What we want is to be another kind of person, to be free. There are a lot of passengers [visitors] that say "no, in my life, this thing happened, to my dad, a lot of things," and they forget what it is they want. Then when the ayahuasca shows them the things they're thinking about, they move backwards. If they think, "I want to change my life. Those bad things that happened, I will put that behind me," then ayahuasca makes some kind of program towards whatever is there if you move forward in your life.

It is an open question why many global psychedelic therapies focus on the past, especially the traumatic past, as *the* royal road to healing and spiritually flourishing with ayahuasca and other psychedelics. Alternate approaches, including across Amazonia, focus on the capacity to see possible futures when consuming the brew.

In Amazonian ethnography, the meaning people ascribe to the source of sickness has typically not been a "traumatic" event, like in the psychedelic United States and elsewhere. Amazonia appears more ecological in the view that sickness can upset widespread social values of tranquillity and personal autonomy (Walker 2012; Rivière 1984; Rodd 2018). Healers may attempt to return the sick person—and their family members or others involved—to a state of tranquillity, while also juggling injustices, inequalities, and social tensions. In this way, the golden radiance of tranquillity in Amazonia is both an ideal and an affective atmosphere (Anderson 2009) that entangles everyday life with ayahuasca curing practices. Seeing the future or past with ayahuasca can help to consolidate, or even to upset, the affective atmosphere of human and nonhuman tranquillity.

In his ethnography among Shuar settlements in Amazonia, Steven Rubenstein (2012) explored the curious absence of trauma among their warriors, which he compared with US war veterans. Despite sentiment training to prepare World War II American soldiers for killing, the Americans were traumatized primarily by the horror of shooting others, not the fear of being shot at. Rubenstein argued that this trauma is part of a symbolic emasculation of the soldiers in response to struggling to sufficiently embody the warfare attitudes of their commanders and the state (65). This he contrasted with the psychoactive enculturation of Shuar warriors during the mid-twentieth century. As part of a stateless society that valued personal autonomy highly, Shuar had drunk ayahuasca for various purposes, including to help young men gain the courage to commit homicide (Harner 1972; Rubenstein 2012). Boys would encounter a terrifying monster spirit in their ayahuasca experiences. Their objective was to receive its power by touching it. Shuar, as savvy fighters, managed to avoid working in the rubber and other industries of the European colonists, while living relatively remotely until the mid-twentieth century. Their propensity for violence towards their enemies, while seemingly avoiding population-level trauma, sheds light on how distress may be embodied or absent across different social worlds.

This global distinction in temporal orientations of ayahuasca experiences that I have presented is crude and located among other temporal registers. Another major orientation in Amazonia would be a "present moment" state of the visions: what I called the "ambient present." This includes when immediate social issues and everyday challenges appear in visionary experience and the lyrics of ayahuasca-drinking songs—including themes of finding lost objects, seeing inside people's houses, and sorcery issues or recent episodes of social antagonism. Second, there are plenty of past-dimensional aspects too, including in cosmogenic myths of the origins of life, plants, people, and animals. Reichel-Dolmatoff (1997) described a Tukano *yagé* initiation in the 1970s during which the neophyte drank ayahuasca and transformed his body-perception backwards in time, undergoing a kind of reverse bodily and foetal development, shrinking down to finally pierce through his mother's body and enter the world of the ancestors.

There are clearly some biological and mental aspects to trauma, as found in epigenetic research and psychological symptomologies. But it appears there is also a dynamic social, historical, and narrative foundation to this. Memory work and enduring visual and auditory media have probably inspired, or at least reinforced, some of the past-looking tendencies of those who identify psychological trauma as the core targets of existential transformation. The urban, neoshamanic cosmology of evoking an archaic and primordial world of the Indigenous rainforest has also likely helped to cast the experiences as past-oriented or as windows onto a prior condition, whether of the self, humanity, or the planet. By contrast, the ambient-present and forward-looking orientations among Indigenous ayahuasca practices speak to how the future could also address the past by orienting distress, hope, and healing variably in time and space. Realizing that other approaches to healing with ayahuasca have not, or have barely, involved "trauma" should not diminish the relevance of trauma-based therapies, but it should encourage wider views of the possible temporal orientations within ayahuasca and its psychedelic sibling compounds.

Many ayahuasca researchers came to the conclusion, while possibly starting with the assumption, that universally shared aspects of the experiences were not only common but paramount to understanding the brew. The attempts by psychologists and others to empirically map ayahuasca visions as if they were like flora and fauna might have helped to legitimize ayahuasca to some scientific juries, but only at the expense of diminishing attention to the vast mass of differences in experience. If it could be shown that ayahuasca is shared, molecular, biological, and relatively predictable—and therefore more like naturalistic phenomena—then the visions would be less bizarre, less irrational, and more normal than scientific paradigms had previously granted altered states or psychoactive drug experiences.

These universalist efforts dovetail neatly with the psychedelic science of the twentieth century and today. Nicolas Langlitz examined perennial ambitions within a neuroscience laboratory in Switzerland that conducted experiments with psychedelics on human subjects. The scientists appeared to convert the perennialist views of Aldous Huxley and others into "biomystical" perspectives and a kind of *"neurobiologia perennis"* (Langlitz 2013:249). The mystical notion had endured through scientists searching in drug experiences and brain signals for objective truths and unifying knowledge. Although Huxley's *The Perennial Philosophy* was first published in 1945—eight years before he had ever tried a psychedelic—his early focus on unitive mysticism came to reflect psychedelic science and clinical trial participants in studies sixty to eighty years later. Huxley had championed the "unitive knowledge of the divine Ground . . . that can come only to those who are prepared to 'Die to self' and so make room, as it were, for God" (1945). When psychedelic trials reemerged in the early twenty-first century, Johns Hopkins University pioneered the new wave by illuminating how the substances could inspire mystical experiences and psychological benefits. Emerging from this and related clinical contexts, the advice to "surrender" and "let go" and the expectation to experience "ego death" and "become one with everything" are now common tropes in psychedelic therapy (Richards 2016). It has been secularized into "unity" and "oneness" for some of the scientists measuring psychedelic experiences. Yet, at its core, the perennialist message remains the same.

The messy social worlds of psychedelic healing that occur beyond research clinics and laboratories, that is, in natural settings and everyday life, present some challenges to the philosophical assumptions of perennialism. Across the whole ocean of humanity's oral understandings of psychedelic use there are likely some perennial and shared truths, but these are unlikely to animate effective healing practices in ways comparable to the impacts of local beliefs and perspectives, whether they involve plant spirits, an evil eye, or spiritual trauma, to name a few. Narratives of healing with ayahuasca in countercultural Australia, neoshamanic tourism Peru, and corporate China, have included widespread genres of biographical visions that aim less at the universal than at obscure narratives of the self and its unraveling and reordering. Amazonian healers, by contrast, tend to experience ayahuasca in a more social and porous way, where the realms they enter are shared and public to other shamans, persons, and creatures (See also Gearin and Calavia Sáez 2021:148–49). Psychedelic experiences of a perennialist nature might turn out to be more healing for scientists than for others, or they might go down in the annals of history as formal elitist codes that clashed against the informal knowledge worlds of ordinary people.

The perennialist ambitions of prior research into ayahuasca experiences were destined for trouble given the need to account for the overwhelming variety of experience reports. When psychologist Claudio Naranjo interviewed urban Chileans who had consumed ayahuasca in his clinical settings, one participant wrote a forty-page eclectic account of a single experience (Naranjo 1973). Psychologist Benny Shanon described a mind-boggling array of visions in his masterful research, yet strangely concluded that the "topology" of visions is overwhelmingly defined by "one coherent picture" of the "fantastic, the enchanted, and the marvellous" (2002:431). Such visions, he argued, are not "dependent upon [social] context" and are overly represented "in reports furnished by persons who are unrelated, come from different places, and have varied personal and social-cultural backgrounds" (431). Analyzing 154 reports of ayahuasca experiences described by Indigenous and non-Indigenous drinkers, Shanon ranked the frequency of experience reports into a quantitative table (427). On the least frequent side, across all reports, are visions of insects, personal biography, history, and household objects, and on the most frequent side are serpents, felines, angels and transparent figures. Regarding the lack of biographical visions, Shanon argued,

> While some aspects of the Ayahuasca experience may be related to the individual's biography and personal concerns, most often this is not the case. Significantly, items of personal and autobiographical nature were common only in the reports of first-timers, both indigenous and non-indigenous. *With experience, it seems, such content becomes increasingly less frequent.* [italics added] (432)

Whereas personal biography ranked very low in his data, the common reports in *Global Ayahuasca* of people perceiving vivid aspects of their biographies in ayahuasca experiences paints a different picture. In my research, it was clear that many in Australia did not see fewer biographical visions the more they drank the brew. Some had increasingly fewer visions in general, over many years or sometimes decades of practice. Others moved from marvelous to fantastical to otherworldly experiences each month. Yet some drinkers increasingly experienced biographical visions and found themselves seeing ordinary situations, objects, and persons. As described earlier, many Australian and Chinese drinkers pursued biographical visions in an attempt to uncover the conditions of their psychological malaise or to help overcome challenges or gain new perspectives on old problems.

While there are probably some perennial and universally shared aspects in the biographical visions of people from Sydney, Beijing, and Pucallpa, their differences are surely more important for the tasks of living (and healing, for that matter). Biographical meaning derived from ayahuasca experiences can become more meaningful when it speaks to the realities of the participant's life and not simply or primarily to lofty theological postulates like "All is One" or the experience of "melting into the godhead." Integration of the mystical and the mundane has become the mission for many psychedelic enthusiasts, drawing heavily upon psychological frameworks and talking cures to help users make meaning about their experiences and to live better lives with psychedelics. As ayahuasca spread across the planet in recent decades, it absorbed psychotherapeutic modes of understanding that aimed psychedelic experiences squarely at the narrative self. Bia Labate (2014) described how ayahuasca became more psychologized as it left Amazonia. She also argued that Shanon's theories about cross-cultural commonalities in ayahuasca visions are symptomatic of a historical Western tendency to prioritize sight over other senses. By contrast, in Amazonia "ayahuasca visions are not taken as 'things unto themselves' (either psychological or universal) but are placed within certain cosmologies and values that have culturally specific attributes" (Labate 2014:186). Ayahuasca takes on the cosmological possibilities of the social worlds it enters. This includes when it meets a marketplace filled with psychology and trauma service. Trauma-based approaches that emphasize the past and the biographical have helped to generate a particular cosmolog-

228 GLOBAL AYAHUASCA

ical perspective with psychedelics. Elsewhere, I have looked at this cosmology as a kind of social individualism given its emphasis on the autonomy and the self (Gearin 2015; Gearin and Calavia Sáez 2021). Biology research has taken another angle on this. Scientists recently illustrated how an area of the brain associated with the "self" exhibited changes in cortical thickness among long-term ayahuasca users (Piot, Bouso, de Araujo, and Skipper 2023), which raised the question of whether the embodied, biographical, and narrative self, that is so crucial to identity, healing, and self-awareness, may also change with repeated psychedelic treatments (see also Dupuis 2022b; Devenot et al. 2022; Letheby 2021). If the new ayahuasca drinking practices around the globe are shaped by a biographical focus of trauma theories and psychology to produce more visionary experiences of the past—including seeing more mundane, memory-like phenomena—then this could help explain why Shanon's (2002) perennialist theories contrast sharply with the many ethnographic examples examined here.

In addition to the issue of biographical visions, another discrepancy appears in Shanon's extremely low rank for insects in ayahuasca experiences (2002:427). Insectoid motifs appeared regularly in my data, particularly in Australia (see also Desmond Tramacchi 2006 on insects in Australian DMT visions). The global proliferation of multicolored insectoid visions seems to share a legacy with American authors William Burroughs (1914–1997) and Terence McKenna (1946–2000). The dreamlike Interzone of Burroughs' popular 1959 novel *Naked Lunch*—and film adaptation of the same name, released in 1991—is swarming with insectoid persons and qualities, while also including references to ayahuasca as *yagé*. When American psychologist and countercultural icon Timothy Leary consumed DMT in the 1960s, he encountered "a band of radar-antennae, elf-like insects merrily working away" (1966). However, it was Terence McKenna, who Leary himself once called the Timothy Leary of the 1990s, who was perhaps most influential in propagating an insectoid psychedelia.

In the 1960s, long before he was a celebrity among psychedelic Westerners and others, McKenna was a young assistant in the Entomology Department at the University of California. After studying at university, he traveled across continents and countries while earning money capturing and selling exotic insects, mainly butterflies, to buyers in Singapore and the United States. Then, in 1971, McKenna, his brother Dennis, and their friends encountered when consuming psilocybin mushrooms in remote parts of the Colombian Amazon an "insectoid intelligence" from the future. They had been searching for ayahuasca, but after failing to locate the bitter brew, they instead grazed on local psychedelic mushrooms for days or longer in what Erik Davis called a "blast of high weirdness" (2019:111) that pushed the McKennas' ontological limits into overdrive. During the 1980s and 1990s, the mantis and other insects became key motifs in Terence McKenna's popular narratives of tryptamine drug use. Insects not only colored his ayahuasca experiences but appeared frequently across visions Australians and others were having. It remains an open question why Shanon's large dataset, which showed an overwhelming lack of insect beings and motifs, contrasts sharply with these contexts.

Insects featured in the ayahuasca experiences of some Shipibo healers I interviewed in Peru. Maestra Mama Maria, the most esteemed healer at Pachamama Temple, told me that when she was a child, master healers could cure through a mosquito-shamanic perspective.

> Before the *onanya* [healers] and the *meraya* [master healers] existed, people commented and said "those people know so much about the medicine and cure so many sick." People were surprised. But not anymore. The healers are not as good now. That's why I say that there were people that did really know, like the masters who cured from inside a mosquito and transported to other places.

The lack of insects in Shanon's book is not reflective of the pure, biological, and cognitive nature of the brew, but is related to the particular social worlds that his data represents. Contextual worlds of meaning and social life entangle ayahuasca, including sometimes with an insectoid affective atmosphere.

Reaching towards the universal, Shanon concluded that ayahuasca experiences were most commonly populated by serpents and felines, while adding that the more someone drinks ayahuasca, the less likely they will see visions of serpents. In my survey and interview data from Australia, serpents were also a leading category of nonhuman persons encountered, but descriptions of plant persons were more popular. In addition, jaguars and other felines were less common than angels or extraterrestrials. Importantly, many of my interlocutors from across the planet described seeing a huge variety of switching persons, scenes, animals, objects, and places when drinking ayahuasca. It appears that what parts they chose to share with others were typically those that were more meaningful to them. Therefore, it would make less sense to describe these expressions as narratives of drug effects; rather, and more accurately, they are social meaning worlds mediated and enhanced by psychedelic and plant practices.

The question of whether the visionary realms of ayahuasca can be quantitatively mapped in some ultimate global coherence is less interesting to me than examining what drives the search for coherence. When drinkers in Australia described seeing a similar or identical vision during a ceremony, it imbued the vision with a sacred power and enhanced meaning, partly because such an occurrence is rare. Whether or not this shared vision validates any truth for the drinkers, it brings a sense of shared experience that can reverberate through social relations. In a Durkheimian sense, seeing the same gods and animal spirits provides an existential glue that binds the social with shared meaning. But what about when scientists collectively see the *same things* in their phenomenological data on ayahuasca experiences or find patterns in their psychometric studies on mystical psychedelic experiences in clinics in Europe or North America? Within scientific and shamanic cases, when the visions align or coherence emerges respective to each context, there is social agreement and even truth. But given that not all ayahuasca visions or contexts do or will ultimately align across all social diversity, then the visionary realms are intrinsically contested, partial, and unfolding. They are not just (selective) perennial truths from world religions. The psychedelic academic ecosystem, including its knowledge about the experiences of others, should be viewed among cognate social traditions that have engaged psychedelic plants and molecules, such as in Amazonian shamanism or elsewhere.

When considering the social nature of scientific work on ayahuasca experiences along these lines, then the scholarly drive to perennialize ayahuasca visions can be situated among those Indigenous uses that emphasized ayahuasca's social and political networking dimensions. Ayahuasca has long been associated with foreigners, strangers, and social networking in Amazonia. Before the brew had international appeal, the esteem of a specialist was sometimes equivalent to the distance they had traveled (Barbira Freedman 2014; Calavia Sáez 2011). Collective drinking sessions were undertaken to ease the encounter and forge alliances between groups (Virtanen 2014:67). Ayahuasca masters would travel far to exchange vines and other plant inebriates, and to acquire songs, visions, and knowledge (Harner 1972; Langdon 1981; Calavia Sáez 2011). They would trade and seek particular vision-songs from specialists renowned for particular skills, including visions for healing, hunting, and warfare. Receiving a new vision from another shaman required meeting them to drink a particular brew and master a particular song until a particular vision was vividly perceived (Langdon 1981). This ties ayahuasca to other kinds of shamanism across the planet that focus on the cultivation of vivid mental imagery and the ability to manipulate and control it (Noll 1985). Mastering the special brews and their mysterious realms could help with mastering the social edges and political horizons of Amazonian life, including those aspects linked to social mobility across vast rivers and high mountains.

The enduring fascination of scholars with finding perennial psychedelic experiences comes from its own intellectual and scientific histories in Europe that date back centuries (Langlitz 2013). During the mid-twentieth century and until recently, psychedelics found themselves at odds with science and stigmatized by medical and scientific institutions. Following the recent revival in clinical psychedelic research, the substances have now carved a niche across various academic disciplines, while still sitting rather peripheral in the academy. In a competitive intellectual labor market in a historical context of psychedelic stigma, the scholarly effort to locate global types of quantitative coherence in the shapeshifting narratives of psychedelic experiences could bring a level of legitimacy to the experiences by labeling them as more patterned, objective, and scientific (less irrational and more amenable to science) despite that high-dose psychedelic experiences tend to be messy, contingent, and sometimes ungraspable. Social and political life, part of scientific practice, are also messy and unpredictable, which makes them particularly amenable to these attributes of psychedelic experiences. The role of clinical psychedelic science and practice in the reproduction and transmission of particular kinds of meaningful and ecstatic experiences in society is an important topic for future researchers.

Also relevant to this critique would be the theme of researchers and therapists self-experimenting with the substances, given that so many of them appear to dabble. Do the psychedelic experiences of scientists and therapists, in their private lives, have an impact on their research and theories on the phenomenology of the experiences of others (including clinical trial participants)? Do therapists and their patients in North America tend to have the same kinds of psychedelic experiences? How are these different from the ayahuasca experiences of Shipibo healers and the local patients they treat? I hope that *Global Ayahuasca* will help shift the theorization of psychedelic experience away from searching for absolutes or perennial truths that hold constant across all social contexts to appreciating the diversity and wondrous unpredictability of the experiences and the historical and social contexts that infuse them.

Given the vastly different ayahuasca experiences I have heard narrated across the planet, I now perceive scientific endeavors aimed at charting what are deemed the most important, true, or shared ayahuasca experiences as social and therapeutic enterprises rather than purely phenomenological efforts. From visions of a disenchanted and dull society in Australia to corporate visions of fast-food restaurants in China and visionary encounters with flying piranha teeth by Shipibo sorcerers in Peru, the enigma of ayahuasca appears undeniably enmeshed in the human social worlds that it can reflect and help address. Something I am still left considering, at the end of writing this book, is how much a person's positionality within the unequal webs of modernity influences how ayahuasca becomes healing for them and what the brew shows them. Whether modernity is encountered with wonder or anti-wonder, interest or indifference, or malaise or meaning, indicates a dynamic that has shaped ayahuasca experiences in contradictory ways. Although the three ethnographic sites analyzed in this book sharply contrast with each other, they also revolve around a common meta-axis, namely capitalism. This is partly because all the sites are commercial groups and exist within broader wellness and spirituality marketplaces aimed at healing and transforming clients. But it is also because capitalism is pervasive and extends to the subjective realms of life, including for those countercultural enthusiasts who attempt to envision something else.

Answering the ontological question of what ayahuasca experiences might be across their totality of renditions is problematized by the general issue of coming to terms with the contradictions that reside between cultural variation. This is because, echoing Clifford Geertz (Olson 1991:260), cultural worlds are not heading towards some omega point of ultimate coherence but appear to have inbuilt diversifying tendencies. The same could be said about ayahuasca, not least because the brew temporarily perturbs consciousness by inspiring what neuroscientists called relaxed mental models and states of mental entropy (Carhart-Harris et al. 2014) but also because it has a special legacy of cultural shapeshifting. As Des Tramacchi (2009) explained, psychoactive substances are like chameleons that take on the characteristics of the societies that consume them. This is perhaps especially true for substances like ayahuasca that inspire bodily-perceptual transformations. Many global enthusiasts consider the brew as an elixir to take them beyond their everyday lived experience and see something ancient, primordial, otherworldly, and marvelous. Such experiences can purify and triangulate the here and now by transcending it, thus allowing the person to encounter vastly amplified or different renditions of themselves, their societies, and their modernities.

What it means to be modern and break from the past can inform wildly different ayahuasca experiences. The brew has become a visionary vehicle of Indigenous modernization at the center of a shamanic tourism industry and, paradoxically, a visionary space beyond the vicissitudes of modern life for the global enthusiasts it attracts. It has helped Chinese managers optimize their business goals and strategies while also motivating some of them to challenge a neoliberal erosion of human nature. Ayahuasca discloses wondrous opportunities for encountering other worlds, perceiving things from different perspectives, and revitalizing what is deeply familiar. This has helped the plant brew take many visionary forms across the different social and cultural worlds it entangles.

EPILOGUE

Among the hundreds of ayahuasca drinkers I spoke with from across the planet, it was relatively common to hear people describe a few personal experiences with the brew that were especially significant to them. The craft of storytelling has an affinity with ayahuasca, and even those who drank the brew many dozens of times tended to narrate just a few wondrous experiences that left them particularly astonished. I am probably no different in that regard.

One of the personal stories I could share involved encountering the spirit of my grandmother overlaid with Shipibo songs at Pachamama Temple in Peru. My strong response to these ceremonies was somewhat surprising, given that I had gone to the retreat without the inflated expectations that many foreigners bring to ayahuasca. After reading the anthropology of primitivist tourism, I arrived from my academic life in China to the edges of the Amazon rainforest having primed a skeptical imagination. I had imagined an intercultural shamanic spectacle designed to suit the expectations of the wealthy international tourists. I still cherished ayahuasca at the time and held the brew in high esteem, as I do now, yet almost a decade of researching drinkers in Australia, and reading the vast literature on Amazonian shamanism, had eroded a great deal of romanticism. Despite all this, my experiences drinking ayahuasca at Pachamama Temple were truly marvelous.

The caliber of the ayahuasca sessions became clear shortly after an episode of disillusionment. On the third day of the retreat, just before the second

GLOBAL AYAHUASCA

ayahuasca ceremony began at 7:00 p.m., five Shipibo healers entered the large thatched-roof hut whistling ceremonial songs and jovially chatting to each other. As they had done hundreds of times before, they lay down in the center of the space with the international guests sitting silently on dedicated mattresses around the perimeter. It was a Friday night and the music from a stereo could be heard coming from a neighbor's house, about one hundred meters away. The music pounded in my mind like a fusion between a Spanish rodeo and a reggaeton circus. It was the last thing I wanted to hear during an ayahuasca session.

We all drank the thick brown brew, including all of the healers, and I lay down on my mattress, staring up at the darkness in anticipation. Typically, we all sat in silence for around forty minutes and listened to the soothing symphony of insects, frogs, and birds that surrounded the *maloca*. But that night, the sonic intrusion from the neighborhood stereo created a different atmosphere. After a few radio songs, the channel changed to a fiery religious oration with an angry masculine, Spanish voice warning of the dangers of not following the path of Jesus. The preacher was passionately hectoring the community about the need for imminent salvation. The healers in the ceremony waited, as usual, for their plant and animal helpers to arrive, remaining silent apart from occasional sighs of frustration. The nature sounds could not compete with the preacher. As the fluid, corporeal sensations that ayahuasca inspires started to overtake my embodied mind, it was impossible to not feel drowned in the afflictive tones of the loud preacher. I began to see faint imagery of angry and ugly faces moving in unison across the darkness above me.

After forty minutes of spiritual propaganda, I felt less indoctrinated than frustrated, tired, and angry. "Where are my headphones?" I thought to myself. "*Icaros, icaros, icaros*, where are the *icaros*?" I begged inside my head while waiting for the healers to start singing. At this stage, Maestro Ricardo seemed to be sleeping and slightly snoring. I started to lose hope in the ceremony and felt disappointed with the organizers and healers for allowing this psychological torment.

Slowly but surely, however, a soft *icaro* coming from Maestro Juan in the middle of the *maloca* emerged and started to permeate me. The sinuous vocalizations became imagery and appeared as beautiful blue and white tapestry cracking through the faint monstrous faces and patterns that I had been attempting to avoid. The *icaro* moved in cycles and inspired ornate designs that glowed with vibratory layers which soothed my mind and impressed my inner eyes. Soon this was joined by another *icaro*, whistled this time, by Maestro Ricardo, who had awakened from his nap. Even this was not enough, however, to dispel my feelings of cynicism as the preacher continued to kick venomous dust in my eyes.

Once the healers welcomed the plant spirits in their visions, the special molecules in the syrupy brew had passed through our empty stomachs into the bloodstream. That is when the main structure of the ceremonies begin. Maestro Ricardo was the first healer to come to me. I was relatively sober but still provoked by the dregs of cynicism and discomfort. We sat, cross-legged, facing each other, our knees almost touching. His song was loud enough to banish the preacher's voice. I decided to try my hardest to relax and allow the *icaro* to penetrate my softening embodied mind. I found myself attuning my chest with a magnetic sensation of openness. As the *icaro* gained energy and momentum, I felt my body filling with an electric fluid. It seemed as though the more the healer realized I was receiving the song openly, the stronger the song and psychic fluid became. A feeling of salubrious vitality permeated me. My senses expanded brighter and clearer. My mind was filled with faint ornamental visions and glowing sensations. Within moments, the monsters, afflictive feelings, and worries had gone. I could then shape and interact with the visions purely with conviction and intuition. Each time an *icaro* finished and the healer left me to attend to the next guest, I could sense how much my embodied mind had changed. It felt emptier but stronger, flexible but firm; open, curious, and sensitive.

My visions then started to take on an exploratory and biographical nature. The seventy-eight-year-old matriarch of Pachamama Temple, Mama Maria, came to me and sang a delicate and high-pitched *icaro*. My grandmother appeared, animated and alive, in her face: old, wise, and with a similar firmness or even grumpiness to her. I was filled with awe. It did not matter in the slightest that my deceased grandmother—a white woman with European ancestry who had lived her whole life in outback Australia—was now transposed onto a Shipibo healer's face and voice in Amazonia. Time stood still and somehow everything made sense at that moment. A vivid mutual recognition was unfolding. It was a similar feeling to when we had farewelled each other, several years prior, in a palliative care unit in a rural hospital in Australia. At the time, I had to leave town briefly, and we both sensed that when I returned later in the week, she would no longer be alive. To finally see and feel her presence again, this time directed at me during the ayahuasca session, was precious. I closed my eyes and traveled back at my own pace and witnessed beautiful and animated faces of younger versions of my family members. The biographical impressions were carried by the tenderness of the *icaro* and were accompanied by elongated feelings, including gratitude, happiness, grief, reverence.

The next morning, I felt elated, yet at peace and relaxed, with an inspirited buzzing energy, mainly in my chest, but also in my head and arms. My memory faculties were sharper. I could travel at will in my mind (sober, without visions) and remember experiences from childhood with more clarity than usual. I spent hours after the ceremony lying in bed exploring the past and recuperating memories long abandoned in my busy life.

The biographical, however, is only one aspect of the ayahuasca experiences I have had over the years. Others include being swept away by textbook mysticism. This includes feeling myself dissolve into a great cosmic ocean, having vivid sensations of becoming every person on earth, and embodying a graceful and radiating unity with all life. Yet such mystical encounters only happened to me occasionally across dozens of sessions. More often, my experiences with the brew have been visionary and ecological and involved interactions with plant and animal persons in marvelous worlds made of geometric light. An evening ceremony of multiple cups of ayahuasca can last a long time—not least because the sense of time itself may be skewed. I usually find myself appreciating and examining my past at some point during an evening of ayahuasca. This biographical focus may be especially significant and perhaps even therapeutic shortly after the more profound episodes, when the brew is still permeating consciousness yet at a lower intensity. Many personal layers may unfold in close proximity to the extraordinary, the mystical, and the seemingly impossible.

This ceremony left me filled with gratitude. It helped open me to other ways of life among Shipibo healers, while also retrieving buried parts of myself. These existential and moral dimensions refer to what Claude Lévi-Strauss (1977) called the emotional geography of shamanistic flight. The true nature of this geography is less interesting to me than the journey and the consequences of traveling within it. But I am still grappling with this simple adage, even after fifteen years of attending ayahuasca sessions. It is tested by a cognitive itch I have, which comes from my tendency to research and get swept away in comprehending, explaining, and measuring. Wonder can become part of this compulsion, but it is more of a trickster than a master and it ultimately transcends our need to know.

The visionary marvels of drinking ayahuasca tend to elicit an empowering humility in me similar to the sense of wonder that Rachel Carson described after gazing at an illuminated night sky. "An experience like that," she explained, "when one's thoughts are released to roam through the lonely spaces of the universe, can be shared with a child even if you don't know the name of a single star. You can still drink in the beauty, and think and wonder at the meaning of what you see" (1998: 69). Part of this empowering humility comes from an appreciation that my relationship with ayahuasca is shaped by the idiosyncrasies of my own social, historical, and biological lineages, and that the brew entangles itself with the plight of human affairs in a wide variety of ways.

REFERENCES

Abramson, A., and M. Holbraad, eds. 2014. *Framing Cosmologies: The Anthropology of Worlds*. Manchester, UK: Manchester University Press.

Alexiades, Miguel N., and Didier Lacaze. 1996. "FENAMAD's Program in Traditional Medicine: An Integrated Approach to Health Care in the Peruvian Amazon." In *Medicinal Resources of the Tropical Forest: Biodiversity and Its Importance to Human Health*, ed. M. J. Balick, E. Elisabetsky, and S. Laird , 341–365. New York: Columbia University Press.

Anderson, B. 2009. "Affective Atmosphere." *Emotion, Space and Society* 2:77–81.

Århem, K. 1996. "The Cosmic Food Web: Human-Nature Relatedness in Northwest Amazon." In *Nature and Society: Anthropological Perspectives*, ed. P. Descola and G. Pálsson, 185–204. London, Routledge.

Arora, D. 2008. "Xiao Ren Ren: The 'Little People' of Yunnan." *Economic Botany* 62(3): 540–544.

Asad, T. 2003. *Formations of the Secular: Christianity, Islam, Modernity*. Stanford, CA: Stanford University Press.

Austin-Broos, D. 2003. "The Anthropology of Conversion: An Introduction." In *The Anthropology of Religious Conversion*, ed. A. Buckser and S. Glazier. New York: Rowman & Littlefield.

Baer, M. D., 2014. "History and Religious Conversion." In *The Oxford Handbook of Religious Conversion*, ed. L. Rambo and C. Farhadian. Oxford, UK: Oxford University Press.

Barbira Freedman, F. B. 2016. "The Jaguar Who Would Not Say Her Prayers: Changing Polarities in Upper Amazonian Shamanism." In *Ayahuasca Reader: Encounters with the Amazon's Sacred Vine*, 2nd ed., ed. L. E. Luna and S. F. White. Santa Fe: Synergetic Press.

———. 2014. "Shamans' Networks in Western Amazonia: The Iquitos-Nauta Road." In *Ayahuasca Shamanism in the Amazon and Beyond*, ed. B. C. Labate and C. Cavnar, 130–158. New York: Oxford University Press.

———. 2010. "Shamanic Plants and Gender in the Healing Forest." In *Plants, Health and Healing: On the Interface of Ethnobotany and Medical Anthropology*, ed. E. Hsu and S. Harris, 135–178. Oxford, UK: Berghahn Books.

Barnard, G. W. 2022. *Liquid Light: Ayahuasca Spirituality and the Santo Daime Tradition*. New York: Columbia University Press.

Baud, M., and A. Ypeij. 2009. "Cultural Tourism in Latin America: An Introduction." In *Cultural Tourism in Latin America*, 1–22. Leiden, Netherlands: Brill.

Bauman, Z. 2000. *Liquid Modernity*. Cambridge, UK; Malden, MA: Polity Press.

———. 1997. *Postmodernity and Its Discontents*. London: Polity Press.

Becker, G. 1997. *Disrupted Lives: How People Create Meaning in a Chaotic World*. Berkeley: University of California Press.

Bellah, R., R. Madsen, W. M. Sullivan, A. Swidler, and S. M. Tipton. 1996. *Habits of the Heart: Individualism and Commitment in American Life*. Berkeley, CA: University of California Press.

Bennett, J. 2001. *The Enchantment of Modern Life: Attachments, Crossings, and Ethics*. Princeton, NJ: Princeton University Press.

Berquist, E. S. 2014. *The Bishop's Utopia: Envisioning Improvement in Colonial Peru*. Philadelphia: University of Pennsylvania Press.

Beyer, S. 2009. *Singing to the Plants: A Guide to Mestizo Shamanism in the Upper Amazon*. Albuquerque: University of New Mexico Press.

———. 2007. "The Telepathic Meme." Singing to the Plants Website. https://sing ingtotheplants.com/2007/12/the-telepathy-meme/, (accessed January 2023).

Biehl, J., and P. Locke, eds. 2017. *Unfinished: The Anthropology of Becoming*. London: Duke University Press.

Boschemeier, A. G., and C. K. Carew. 2018. " 'Men,' 'Shaman,' and 'Ayahuasca' as Overlapping Cliches in the Peruvian Vegetalismo." In *The Expanding World Ayahuasca Diaspora: Appropriation, Integration, Legislation*, ed. B. Labate and C. Cavnar. London: Routledge.

Bouso, J. C., Ó Andión, J. J. Sarris, M. Scheidegger, L. F. Tófoli, E. S. Opaleye, V. Schubert, and D. Perkins. 2022. "Adverse Effects of Ayahuasca: Results from the Global Ayahuasca Survey." *PLOS Global Public Health* 16:2(11): e0000438.

Bouso, J. C., D. González, S. Fondevila, M. Cutchet, X. Fernández, P.C.R. Barbosa, M. A. Alcázar-Córcoles, W. S. Araújo, M. J. Barbanoj, J. M. Fábregas, and J. Riba. 2012. "Personality, Psychopathology, Life Attitudes and Neuropsychological Performance Among Ritual Users of Ayahuasca: A Longitudinal Study." *PLOS One* 7(8): e42421.

Bowler, D. E., L. M. Buyung-Ali, T. M. Knight, and A. S. Pullin. "A Systematic

Review of Evidence for the Added Benefits to Health of Exposure to Natural Environments." *BMC Public Health* 10(1): 456.

Brabec de Mori, B. 2014. "From the Native's Point of View: How Shipibo-Konibo Experience and Interpret Ayahuasca Drinking with 'Gringos.'" In *Ayahuasca Shamanism in the Amazon and Beyond*, ed. B. Labate and C. Cavnar. Oxford, UK: Oxford University Press.

———. 2012. "About Magical Singing, Sonic Perspectives, Ambient Multinatures, and the Conscious Experience." *Indiana* 29:73–101.

———. 2011. "Tracing Hallucinations: Contributing to a Critical Ethnohistory of Ayahuasca Usage in the Peruvian Amazon." In *The Internationalisation of Ayahuasca*, ed. B. C. Labate and H. Jungaberle, 23–47. Zürich: Lit Verlag.

Brabec de Mori, B., and L. Mori Silvano de Brabec. 2009. "Shipibo-Konibo Art and Healing Concepts: A Critical View on the 'Aesthetic Therapy.'" *Viennese Ethnomedicine Newsletter* 6:18–26.

Brouwer, A., and R. L. Carhart-Harris. 2021. "Pivotal Mental States." *Journal of Psychopharmacology* 35(4): 319–352.

Brown, M. 2002. "Moving Towards the Light: Self, Other, and the Politics of Experience in New Age Narratives." In *Stories of Change: Narrative and Social Movements* ed. J. E. Davis. Albany: State University of New York Press.

———. 1997. *The Channeling Zone: American Spirituality in an Anxious Age*. Cambridge, MA: Harvard University Press.

———. 1991. "Beyond Resistance: A Comparative Study of Utopian Renewal in Amazona." *Ethnohistory* 38(4): 388–413.

———. 1988. "Shamanism and Its Discontents." *Medical Anthropology Quarterly* 2(2): 102–120.

———. 1986. *Tsewa's Gift: Magic and Meaning in an Amazonia Society*. London: Smithsonian Institute.

Burroughs, W. S. 1994. *The Letters of William S. Burroughs, 1945–1959*, ed. O. Harris. New York: Penguin.

Burroughs, W. S., and A. Ginsberg. 2006 [1963]. *The Yagé Letters Redux*, ed. O. Harris. San Francisco: City Lights Books.

Calabrese, J. D. 2013. *A Different Medicine: Postcolonial Healing in the Native American Church*. Oxford, UK: Oxford University Press.

Calavia Sáez, O. 2014. "Foreword: Authentic Ayahuasca." In *Ayahuasca Shamanism in the Amazon and Beyond*, ed. B. Labate and C. Cavnar. Oxford, UK: Oxford University Press.

———. 2011. "A Vine Network." In *The Internationalization of Ayahuasca*, ed. B. C. Labate and H. Jungaberle, 131–144. Zürich: Lit Verlag.

Candiotto, L. 2019. "Epistemic Emotions: The Case of Wonder." *Journal of Philosophy Aurora* 31(54): 848–863.

Carhart-Harris, R. L. 2018. "The Entropic Brain—Revisited." *Neuropharmacology* 142:167–178.

Carhart-Harris, R. L., R. Leech, P. J. Hellyer, M. Shanahan, A. Feilding, E. Tagliazucchi, D. R. Chialvo, and D. Nutt. 2014. "The Entropic Brain: A Theory of Conscious States Informed by Neuroimaging Research with Psychedelic Drugs." *Frontiers of Human Neuroscience* 3:8:–20.

Carneiro, R. L. 1980. "Chimera of the Upper Amazon." In *The Don Juan Papers*, ed. R. de Mille. Lincoln: iUniverse.

Carson, R. 1998 [1965]. *The Sense of Wonder*. New York: HarperCollins.

Carter, D. J. 2017. "Bush Legends and Pastoral Landscapes." In *Teaching Australian and New Zealand Literature*, ed. N. Birns, N. Moore, and S. Shieff. New York: Modern Language Association of America.

Charing, H. G., P. Cloudsley, and P. Amaringo. 2011. *The Ayahuasca Visions of Pablo Amaringo*. Rochester, VT: Inner Traditions.

Chau, A. 2006. *Miraculous Response: Doing Popular Religion in Contemporary China*. Stanford, CA: Stanford University Press.

Chaumeil, J-P. 1992. "Varieties of Amazonian Shamanism." *Diogenes* 40:101–113.

Chen, F.P.L. 2021. "Hallucinogens Use in China." *Sino-Platonic Papers* 318:1–39. Department of East Asian Languages and Civilizations.

Clement, C., W. Denevan, M. J. Heckenberger, A. B. Junbqueira, E. G. Nevas, W. G. Teixeira, and W. I. Woods. 2015. "The Domestication of Amazonia Before European Conquest." *Proceedings of the Royal Society B* 282:1–9.

Close, J. B., E. C. Haijen, R. Watts, and L. Roseman. 2020. "Psychedelics and Psychological Flexibility: Results of a Prospective Web-Survey Using the Acceptance in Action Questionnaire II." *Journal of Contextual Behavioral Science* 16:37–44.

Cohen, S. 1965. *Drugs of Hallucination: The Uses and Misuses of Lysergic Acid Diethylamide*. London: Martin Secker & Warburg Limited.

Cole-Adams, K. 2021. "Love and Fear: Towards an Australian Model of Psychedelic Mental Health." *Griffith Review* 72:63–77.

Colpron, A-M. 2013. "Contact Crisis: Shamanic Explorations of Virtual and Possible Worlds." *Anthropologica* 55(2): 373–383.

Comaroff, J., and J. L. Comaroff. 2001. "Millennial Capitalism: First Thoughts on a Second Coming." In *Millennial Capitalism and the Culture of Neoliberalism*, ed. J. Comaroff and J. L. Comaroff. London: Duke University Press.

Córdova-Ríos, M., and F. Bruce Lamb. 1974. *Wizard of the Upper Amazon: The Story of Manuel Córdova-Rios*. 3d ed. Berkeley, CA: North Atlantic.

Davidov, V. M., 2010. "Shamans and Shams: The Discursive Effects of Ethnotourism in Ecuador." *The Journal of Latin American Caribbean Anthropology* 15(2): 387–410.

Davis, E. 2019. *High Weirdness: Drugs, Esoterica, and Visionary Experience in the Seventies*. London: Strange Attractor / MIT Press.

Desmond, J. 1999. *Staging Tourism: Bodies on Display from Waikiki to Sea World*. Chicago: University of Chicago Press.

Dev, L. 2019. "Healing in the Chthulucene: Becoming Beyond Human with Medicinal Plants." *Dialogue and Universalism* 3:151–162.

———. 2018. "Plant Knowledges: Indigenous Approaches and Interspecies Listening Toward Decolonizing Ayahuasca Research." In *Plant Medicines, Healing and Psychedelic Science*, ed. B. C. Labate and C. Cavnar, 185–204. Cham, Switzerland: Springer.

Devenot, N., S.-F. Aidan, S. Elyse, N. Tehseen, G.-R. Albert, and W. J. Matthew. 2022. "Psychedelic Identity Shift: A Critical Approach to Set and Setting." *Kennedy Institute of Ethics Journal* 32(4): 359–399.

Dobkin de Rios, M. 1994. "Drug Tourism in the Amazon." *Anthropology of Consciousness* 5(1): 16–19.

———. 1972. *Visionary Vine: Hallucinogenic Healing in the Peruvian Amazon*. Prospect Heights, IL: Waveland Press.

Dobkin de Rios, M., and R. Rumrrill. 2008. *A Hallucinogenic Tea Laced with Controversy*. Westport, CT: Greenwood.

Dupuis, D. 2022a. "The Socialization of Hallucination: Cultural Priors, Social Interactions, and Contextual Factors in the Use of Psychedelics." *Transcultural Psychiatry* 59(5): 625–637.

———. 2022b. "The Psychedelic Ritual as a Technique of the Self: Identity Reconfiguration and Narrative Reframing in the Therapeutic Efficacy of Ayahuasca." *HAU: Journal of Ethnographic Theory* 12(1): 198–216.

———. 2021a. "Psychedelics as Tools for Belief Transmission: Set, Setting, Suggestibility, and Persuasion in the Ritual Use of Hallucinogens." *Frontiers in Psychology* 12: Article 730031.

———. 2021b. "Learning to Navigate Hallucinations. Comparing Voice Control Ability During Psychosis and in Ritual Use of Ayahuasca." In *Voices in Psychosis: Interdisciplinary Perspectives*, ed. B. Alderson-Day, C. Fernyhough, and A. Woods. Oxford, UK: Oxford University Press.

Durkheim, E. 2001 [1911]. *The Elementary Forms of Religious Life*. Oxford, UK: Oxford University Press.

Earleywine, M., F. Low, C. Lau, and J. De Leo. 2022. "Integration in Psychedelic-Assisted Treatments: Recurring Themes in Current Providers' Definitions, Challenges, and Concerns." *Journal of Humanistic Psychology* [Early View]: 1–18.

Eisner, B. G. 2002. *Remembrances of LSD Therapy Past*. Unpublished manuscript. https://bibliography.maps.org/citation/9758 (accessed April 19, 2022).

246 REFERENCES

EntheonGaia. 2012. Website. Retrieved September 2012 from http://entheongaia .com.au/.

Espinosa, O. 2012. "To Be Shipibo Nowadays: The Shipibo-Konibo Youth Organisations as a Strategy for Dealing with Cultural Change in the Peruvian Amazon Region." *The Journal of Latin American and Caribbean Anthropology* 17(3): 451–471.

Estala, P. 1798. *El viagero universal o Noticia del mundo antiguo y nuevo / obra recopilada de los mejores viageros por D.P.E.P. ; tomo XVI.* Madrid: Imprenta de Cillalpando.

Fabian, J. 2014 (1983). *Time and the Other: How Anthropology Makes Its Object.* New York: Columbia University Press.

Farrelly, P. J. 2017. *Spiritual Revolutions: A History of New Age Religion in Taiwan.* PhD diss. Canberra: Australian National University.

Fausto, C. 2004. "A Blend of Tobacco: Shamans and Jaguars Among Parakaná of Eastern Amazonia." In *In Darkness and Secrecy: The Anthropology of Assault Sorcery and Witchcraft in Amazonia,* ed. N. Whitehead and R. Wright. London: Duke University Press.

Fernandez, J. W. 1982. *Bwiti: An Ethnography of the Religious Imagining in Africa.* Princeton, NJ: Princeton University Press.

Fish, S. 1997. "Boutique Multiculturalism, or Why Liberals Are Incapable of Thinking About Hate Speech." *Critical Inquiry* 23(2): 378–395.

Follér, M. 1989. "A New Approach to Community Health." *Social Science & Medicine* 28(8): 811–818.

Foster, G. 1972. "The Anatomy of Envy: A Study in Symbolic Behavior." *Current Anthropology* 13:165–202.

Fotiou, E. 2020. "Shamanic Tourism in the Peruvian Lowlands: Critical and Ethical Considerations." *The Journal of Latin American and Carribbean Anthropology* 25(3): 374–396.

———. 2016. "The Globalization of Ayahuasca Shamanism and the Erasure of Indigenous Shamanism." *Anthropology of Consciousness* 27(2): 151–179.

———. 2014. "On the Uneasiness of Tourism: Considerations on Shamanic Tourism in Western Amazonia." In *Ayahuasca Shamanism in the Amazon and Beyond,* ed. B. Labate and C. Cavnar. Oxford, UK: Oxford University Press.

———. 2010. *From Medicine Men to Day Trippers: Shamanic Tourism in Iquitos.* PhD diss. University of Wisconsin.

Foucault, M. 1994. *The Order of Things.* 2nd ed. London: Routledge.

Frecska, E., P. Bokor, and M. Winkelman.. 2016. "The Therapeutic Potentials of Ayahuasca: Possible Effects Against Various Diseases of Civilization." *Frontiers in Pharmacology* 7(35).

Fuller, R. 2001. *Spiritual But Not Religious: Understanding Unchurched America.* Oxford, UK: Oxford University Press.

Gandy, S., M. Forstmann, R. L. Carhart-Harris, C. Timmermann, D. Luke, and R. Watts. 2020. "The Potential Synergistic Effects Between Psychedelic Administration and Nature Contact for the Improvement of Mental Health." *Health Psychology Open* 6;7(2): 1–21.

Garro, L. C., and C. Mattingly. 2000. "Narrative as Construct and Construction." In *Narrative and the Cultural Construction of Illness and Healing,* ed. C. Mattingly and L. Garro. Berkeley, CA: University of California Press.

Gearin, A. K. 2023a. "On the Ambiguity of Psychedelic Awe in China." *Anthropology Today* 39(6):18–20.

———. 2023b. "Moving Beyond a Figurative Psychedelic Literacy: Metaphors of Psychiatric Symptoms in Ayahuasca Narratives." *Social Science & Medicine* 334(116171):1–9.

———. 2019. "Ayahuasca Joined the Parliament of the World's Religions." Kahpi. net. https://kahpi.net/ayahuasca-joined-parliament-worlds-religions-toronto/ (accessed April 18, 2002).

———. 2017. "Ayahuasca Neoshamanism as Cultural Critique in Australia." In *The World Ayahuasca Diaspora: Reinventions and Controversies,* ed. B. Labate, C. Cavnar, and A. Gearin. 123–141. London: Routledge.

———. 2015. "'Whatever You Want to Believe': Kaleidoscopic Individualism and Ayahuasca Healing in Australia," *The Australian Journal of Anthropology* 26(3): 442–455.

Gearin, A. K., and O. Calavia Sáez. 2021. "Altered Visions: Sensory Individualism and Ayahuasca Shamanism." *Current Anthropology* 62(2): 138–163.

Gearin, A. K., and N. Devenot. 2021. "Psychedelic Medicalization, Public Discourse, and the Morality of Ego Dissolution." *International Journal of Cultural Studies* 24(6): 917–935.

Gearin, A. K., and B. Labate. 2018. "'La Dieta': Ayahuasca and the Western Reinvention of Indigenous Amazonian Food Shamanism." In *The Expanding World Ayahuasca Diaspora: Appropriation, Integration, Legislation,* ed. B. Labate and C. Cavnar, 179–197. London: Routledge.

Gebhart-Sayer, A. 2016. "Design Therapy." In *Ayahuasca Reader: Encounters with the Amazon's Sacred Vine,* 2nd ed., ed. L. E. Luna and S. F. White. Santa Fe, NM: Synergetic Press.

———. 1985. "The Geometric Designs of the Shipibo-Conibo in Ritual Context." *Journal of Latin American Lore* 11(2): 143–175.

Geertz, C. 2000. *Available Light: Anthropological Reflections on Philosophical Topics.* Princeton, NJ: Princeton University Press.

Giddens, A. 1991. *Modernity and Self-Identity: Self and Society in the Late Modern Age*. Stanford, CA: Stanford University Press.

Goldberger, A. 1996. "Fractals and the Birth of Gothic: Reflections on the Biologic Basis of Creativity." *Molecular Psychiatry* 1(2): 99–104.

Goldfried, M., P. Pachankis, and A. Bell. 2005. "A History of Psychotherapy Integration." In *Handbook of Psychotherapy Integration*, ed. J. Norcross and M. Goldfried, 24–64. Oxford, UK: Oxford University Press.

Golub, A. 1982. "The Upper Amazon in Historical Perspective. PhD diss. City University of New York.

Gonzales, D., M. Carvalho, J. Cantillo, M. Aixala, and M. Farre. 2019. "Potential Use of Ayahuasca in Grief Therapy." *Omega (Westport)* 79(3): 260–285.

Gooren, H. 2014. "Anthropology of Religious Conversion." In *The Oxford Handbook of Religious Conversion*, ed. L. Rambo and C. Farhadian. Oxford, UK: Oxford University Press.

Goossaert, V., and D. Palmer. 2011. *The Religious Question in Modern China*. Chicago: University of Chicago Press.

Gow, P. 2012. "Sueño, embriaguez, alucinación. Alterando los estados corporales a través del consumo en la Amazonía Peruana. In *Ayahuasca y Salud*, ed. B. C. Labate and J. C. Bouso. Barcelona: Los Libros de La Liebre de Marzo.

———. 1994. "River People: Shamanism and History in Western Amazonia. In *Shamanism, History, & the State*, ed. N. Thomas and C. Humphrey. Ann Arbor: University of Michigan Press.

———. 1993. "Gringos and Wild Indians: Images of History in Western Amazonia. *L'Homme* 126/128:327–347.

Greene, S. 1998. "The Shaman's Needle: Development, Shamanic Agency, and Intermedicality in Aguaruna Lands, Peru." *American Ethnologist* 25(4): 634–654.

Griffiths, T. 2001. "Finding One's Body: Relationships Between Cosmology and Works in Northwest Amazonia." In *Beyond the Visible and the Material: The Amerindianization of Society in the Work of Peter Riviere*, ed. L. Rival and N. Whitehead, 247–262. Oxford, UK: Oxford University Press.

Grob, C. 2013. "Forward: Ancient Medicine and the Modern World." In *The Therapeutic Use of Ayahuasca*, ed. B. C. Labate and C. Cavnar. Berlin: Springer-Verlag.

Grob, C. S., D. J. McKenna, J. C. Callaway, G. S. Brito, E. S. Neves, G. Oberlaender, O. L. Saide, E. Labigalini, C. Lacla, C. R. Miranda, R. J. Strassman, and K. B. Boone. 1996. "Human Psychopharmacology of Hoasca, a Plant Hallucinogen Used in Ritual Context in Brazil." *The Journal of Nervous and Mental Disease* 184(2): 86–94.

Grof, S. 2008 [1980]. *LSD Psychotherapy*, 4th ed. San Jose, CA: Multidisciplinary Association for Psychedelic Studies.

Haebich, A., and J. Taylor. 2007. "Modern Primitives Leaping and Stomping the Earth: From Ballet to Bush Doofs." *Aboriginal History* 31:63–84.

Hanegraaff, W. 2012. "'Entheogenic esotericism.'" In *Contemporary Esotericism*, ed. E. Asprem and K. Granholm. Bristol, UK: Equinox.

———. 2010. "'And End History. And Go to the Stars': Terence McKenna and 2012." In *Religion and Retributive Logic: Essays in Honour of Professor Garry W. Trompf*, ed. C. M. Cusack and C. Hartney. Danvers, MA: Brill.

———. 1996. *New Age Religion and Western Culture: Esotericism in the Mirror of Secular Thought*. New York: SUNY Press.

Hannerz, U. 1996. *Transnational Connections: Culture, People, Places*. London and New York: Routledge.

Harner, M., ed. 1973. *Hallucinogens and Shamanism*. New York: Oxford University Press.

———. 1972. *The Jivaro: People of the Sacred Waterfalls*. New York: Natural History Press.

Harrington, A. 2008. *The Cure Within: A History of Mind-Body Medicine*. New York: W.W. Norton.

Harris, O. 2017. "Introduction." In *Everything Lost: The Latin American Notebook of William S. Burroughs. By William S. Burroughs*, ed. O. Harris, G. D. Smith, and J. M. Bennett, ix-xxvi. Columbus: Ohio State University Press.

Hartig, T., R. Mitchell, S. De Vries, and H. Frumkin. 2014. "Nature and Health. *Annual Review of Public Health* 35:207–228.

Hartogsohn, I. 2020. *American Trip: Set, Setting, and the Psychedelic Experience in the Twentieth Century*. Cambridge, MA: MIT Press.

———. 2018. "The meaning-Enhancing Properties of Psychedelics and Their Mediator Role in Psychedelic Therapy, Spirituality, and Creativity." *Frontiers in Neuroscience* 12:129.

———. 2016. "Set and Setting, Psychedelics and the Placebo Response: An Extra-Pharmacological Perspective on Psychopharmacology." *Journal of Psychopharmacology* 30:1259–1267.

Heelas, P. 1996. *The New Age Movement: The Celebration of the Self and the Sacralization of Modernity*. Oxford, UK: Blackwell.

Hendricks, P. S. 2018. "Awe: A Putative Mechanism Underlying the Effects of Classic Psychedelic-Assisted Psychotherapy." *International review of Psychiatry* 30(4): 331–342.

Hern, W. M. 1992. "The Impact of Cultural Change and Population Growth on the Shipibo of the Peruvian Amazon." *Journal of Latin American Anthropology* 4(1): 3–8.

Highpine, G. 2018. "Is It Cultural Appropriation for White People to Drink Ayahuasca?" Kahpi.net. https://kahpi.net/cultural-appropriation-ayahuasca-tourism/ (accessed January 2023).

Hilario, M. W. 2010. "Political Participation of Indigenous Amazonians in Peru: The Case of the Shipibo-Konibo." PhD diss. Stanford University.

Homan, J. 2017. "Disentangling the Ayahuasca Boom: Local Impacts in Western Peruvian Amazon." In *The World Ayahuasca Diaspora: Reinventions and Controversies*, ed. B. Labate, C. Cavnar, and A. K. Gearin, 165–181. London: Routledge.

Huang, H. 2014. "The Emergence of the Psycho-Boom in Contemporary Urban China." In *Psychiatry and Chinese History*, ed. Howard Chiang. New York: Cambridge University Press.

Huggan, G. 2001. *The Post-Colonial Exotic: Marketing the Margins*. London: Routledge.

Hughes-Warrington, M. 2018. *History as Wonder: Beginning with Historiography*. London: Routledge.

Hugh-Jones, S. 1996. "Shamans, Prophets, Priests and Pastors." In *Shamanism, History and the State*, ed. N. Thomas and C. Humphrey, 32–75. Ann Arbor: University of Michigan Press.

Huxley, A. 1954. *The Doors of Perception*. New York: Harper & Brothers.

———. 1945. *The Perennial Philosophy*. New York: Harper & Brothers.

Illius, B. 1992. "The Concept of Nihue Among the Shipibo-Conibo of Eastern Peru." In *Portals of Power: Shamanism in South America*, ed. E. Langdon and G. Baer, 63–78. Albuquerque: University of New Mexico Press.

Iskra, A. 2022. "Navigating the Owl's Gaze: The Chinese Mind-Body-Spirit Milieu and Circulation of New Age Teachings in the Sinosphere." *Nova Religio* 25(4): 5–31.

———. 2021. "Chinese New Age Milieu and the Emergence of Homo *Sentimentalis* in the People's Republic." *China Information* 35(1): 89–108.

Izquierdo, C., and A. Johnson. 2007. "Desire, Envy, and Punishment: A Matsigenka Emotion Schema in Illness Narratives and Folk Stories." *Culture, Medicine, and Psychiatry* 31:419–444.

Izquierdo, C., A. Johnson, and G. H. Shepard Jr. 2008. "Revenge, Envy and Cultural Change in an Amazonian Society." In *Revenge in the Cultures of Lowland South America*, ed. S. Berkerman and P. Valentine, 162–186. Gainesville, FL: University of Florida Press.

Jackson, M. 2021. *Coincidences: Synchronicity, Verisimilitude, and Storytelling*. Oakland: University of California Press.

Jay, M. 2019. *Mescaline: A Global History of the First Psychedelic*. London: Yale University Press.

John, L. 1989. "The Colonization of Consciousness in South Africa." *Economy and Society* 18(3): 267–296.

Josephson Storm, J. 2017. *The Myth of Disenchantment: Magic, Modernity and the Birth of the Human Sciences*. Chicago: Chicago University Press.

Kalberg, S. 2005. "Introduction—Max Weber: The Confrontation with Modernity." In *Max Weber Readings and Commentary on Modernity*, ed. S. Kalberg. Oxford, UK: Blackwell.

Kanelli, A. A., P. G. Dimitrakopoulos, N. M. Fyllas, G. P. Chrousos, and O.-I. Kalantzi. 2021. "Engaging the Senses: The Association of Urban Space with General Health and Well-Being in Urban Residents." *Sustainability* 13(13): 7322.

Kaplan, C. 2011. "Forward: Ayahuasca and the Coming Transformation of the International Drug Control System." In *The Internationalization of Ayahuasca*, ed. B. C. Labate and H. Jungaberle, 15–19. Zürich: Lit Verlag.

Keltner, D. 2023. *Awe: The New Science of Everyday Wonder and How It Can Transform Your Life*. New York: Penguin Press.

Keltner, D., and J. Haidt. 2003. "Approaching Awe, a Moral, Spiritual, and Aesthetic Emotion." *Cognition and Emotion* 17(2): 297–314.

Keomany, M. 2016. "Burrough's Postcolonial Visions in The Yage Letters." *CLCWeb: Comparative Literature and Culture* 18(5): 1–8.

King, M. L. 1968. "The Role of the Behavioral Scientist in the Civil Rights Movement." *Journal of Social Issues* 24:1–12.

Kipnis, A. B. 2012. "Introduction: Chinese Modernity and the Individual Psyche. In *Chinese Modernity and the Individual Psyche*, ed. A. Kipnis. New York: Palgrave.

Kirmayer, L. 2007. "Psychotherapy and the Cultural Concept of the Person." *Transcultural Psychiatry* 44(2): 232–257.

Kleinman, A. 2011. "Quests for Meaning." In *Deep China: The Moral Life of the Person*, ed. A. Kleinman, Y. Yan, J. Jun, S. Lee, E. Zhang, P. Tianshu, W. Fei, and G. Jinhua. Berkeley: University of California Press.

———. 1982. "Neurasthenia and Depression: A Study of Somatization and Culture in China." *Culture, Medicine, and Psychiatry* 6:117–190.

Kohn, E. 2013. *How Forests Think: Toward an Anthropology Beyond the Human*. Berkeley: University of California Press.

Kondo, M. C., K. O. Oyekanmi, A. Gibson, E. C. South, J. Bocarro, and J. A. Hipp. 2020. "Nature Prescriptions for Health: A Review of Evidence and Research Opportunities." *International Journal of Environmental Research and Public Health* 17(12): 4213.

Kripal, J. J. 2007. *Esalen: America and the Religion of No Religion*. Chicago: The University of Chicago Press.

Kusel, H. 1965. "Ayahuasca Drinkers Among the Chama Indians of Northeast Peru." *Psychedelic Review* 6:58–66.

Kuypers, K.P.C., J. Riba, M. de la Fuente Revenga, S. Barker, E. L. Theunissen, and J. G. Ramaekers. 2016. "Ayahuasca Enhances Creative Divergent Think-

252 REFERENCES

ing While Decreasing Conventional Convergent Thinking." *Psychopharmacology* 223:3395–3403.

Labate, B. 2014. "The Internationalization of Peruvian Vegetalismo." In *Ayahuasca Shamanism in the Amazon and Beyond*, ed. B. Labate and C. Cavnar. Oxford, UK: Oxford University Press.

Labate, B., and C. Cavnar,eds. 2014. *Ayahuasca Shamanism in the Amazon and Beyond*. Oxford, UK: Oxford University Press.

Labate, B., C. Cavnar, and A. Gearin, eds. 2017. *The World Ayahuasca Diaspora: Reinventions and Controversies*. London: Routledge.

Labate, B., and E. MacRae, eds. 2010. *Ayahuasca, Ritual and Religion in Brazil*. London: Equinox.

La Condamine, C-M. 1808. "Abridged Narrative of Travels Through the Interior of South America from the Shores of the Pacific Ocean to the Coasts of Brazil and Guyana, Descending the River of Amazons." *A General Collection of the Best and Most Interesting Voyages and Travels*. 28 X 21 Cm. V. 14 (1813) p. [211]–257. Plates.

Langdon, E. J. M. 1992. "Dau: Shamanic Power in Siona Religion and Medicine." In *Portals of Power: Shamanism in South America*, ed. E. Langdon and G. Baer, 63–78. Albuquerque: University of New Mexico Press.

———. 1981. "Cultural Bases for Trading of Visions and Spiritual Knowledge in the Colombian and Ecuadorian Montaña." In *Networks of the Past: Regional Interaction in Archaeology: Proceedings of the 12th Annual Conference of the Archaeological Association of the University of Calgary*. Calgary, Alberta: Department of Archaeology, University of Calgary, 101–116.

———. 1979. "Yage Among the Siona: Cultural Patterns in Visions." In *Spirits, Shamans, and Stars: Perspectives from South America*, ed. D. L. Browman and R. A. Schwarz. The Hague: Mouton.

Langlitz, N. 2013. *Neuropsychedelia: The Revival of Hallucinogen Research Since the Decade of the Brain*. Berkeley: University of California Press.

Langlitz, N., E. Dyck, M. Scheidegger, and D. Repantis. 2021. "Moral Psychopharmacology Needs Moral Inquiry: The Case of Psychedelics." *Frontiers in Psychiatry* 2(12): 680064.

Lathrap, D. 1970. *The Upper Amazon*. New York: Praeger.

Leary, T. 1966. "Programmed Communication During Experiences with DMT (dimethyltryptamine). *Psychedelic Review* 8:83–95.

Leary, T., R. Metzner, and R. Alpert. 1964. *The Psychedelic Experience: A Manual Based on the Tibetan Book of the Dead*. New York: University Books.

Lees, A. J. 2017. *Mentored by a Madman: The William Burroughs Experiment*. London: Notting Hill Editions.

Letheby, C. 2021. *Philosophy of Psychedelics*. Oxford, UK: Oxford University Press.

REFERENCES 253

Lévi-Strauss, C. 1977. "The Effectiveness of Symbols." In *Structural Anthropology*. Harmondsworth: Penguin.

Li, Hui-Lin. 1975. "Hallucinogenic Plants in Chinese Herbals." *Botanical Museum Leaflets* 25(6): 161–181.

Lifshitz, M., M. van Elk, and T. Luhrmann. 2019. "Absorption and Spiritual Experience: A Review of Evidence and Potential Mechanisms." *Consciousness and Cognition* 73:102760.

Lifton, R. J. 1999. *The Protean Self: Human Resilience in an Age of Fragmentation*. Chicago: University of Chicago Press.

Londono Sulkin, C. 2005. "Inhuman Beings: Morality and Perspectivism Among Muinane People (Colombian Amazon)." *Ethnos* 70(1): 7–39.

Lopez Sanchez, J., 2023. "Planting the Future." *American Anthropologist* 125(3): 701–706.

Losonczy, A-M., and S. Mesturini Cappo. 2014. "Ritualised Misunderstanding Between Uncertainty, Agreement and Rupture: Communication Patterns in Euro-American Ayahuasca Ritual Interactions." In *Ayahuasca Shamanism in the Amazon and Beyond*, ed. B. Labate and C. Cavnar. Oxford, UK: Oxford University Press.

Loureiro Dias, C. 2012. "Jesuit Maps and Political Discourse: The Amazon River of Father Samuel Fritz." *The Americas* 69(1): 95–116.

Lovejoy, A., and G. Boas. 1935. *Primitivism and Related Ideas in Antiquity*. Baltimore: John Hopkins University Press.

Luckman, S. 2003. "Going Bush and Finding One's 'Tribe': Raving, Escape and the Bush Doof." *Continuum: Journal of Media & Cultural Studies* 17(3): 318–332.

Luhrmann, T. M. 2020. "Thinking About Thinking: The Mind's Porosity and the Presence of Gods." *Journal of the Royal Anthropological Institute* 26(S1): 148–162.

Luna, L. E. 2016. "Some Observations on the Phenomenology of the Ayahuasca Experience." In *Ayahuasca Reader: Encounters with the Amazon's Sacred Vine*, ed. L. E. Luna and S. F. White, 251. London: Synergetic Press.

———. 2011. "Some Reflection on the Global Expansion of Ayahuasca." In *The Internationalization of Ayahuasca*, ed. B. C. Labate and H. Jungaberle. Berlin: Lit Verlag.

———. 1986. *Vegetalismo: Shamanism Among the Mestizo Population of the Peruvian Amazon*. Stockholm: Almqvistand Wicksel.

———. 1984. "The Concept of Plants as Teachers Among Four Mestizo Shamans in Iquitos Northeastern Peru." *Journal of Ethnopharmacology* 11(2):135–156.

Luna, L. E., and P. Amaringo. 1999 [1991]. *Ayahuasca Visions: The Religious Iconography of a Peruvian Shaman*. Berkeley, CA: North Atlantic Books.

Luna, L. E., and S. F. White. eds. 2016. *Ayahuasca Reader: Encounters with the Amazon's Sacred Vine*. London: Synergetic Press.

REFERENCES

Maccormack, S. 1985. "'The Heart Has Its Reasons': Predicaments of Missionary Christianity in Early Colonial Peru." *The Hispanic American Historical Review* 65(3): 443–466.

Mazarrasa, J. 2019. "Ayahuasca: Tourism vs Tradition. Talk presented at Breaking Conventions, London, United Kingdom. https://youtu.be/TX4mDDeo8Kg (accessed January 2021).

McCarraher, E. 2019. *The Enchantments of Mammon: How Capitalism Became the Religion of Modernity.* Cambridge, MA: Harvard University Press.

Mckenna, D. 2005. "Ayahuasca and Human Destiny." *Journal of Psychoactive Drugs* 37(2): 231–234.

———. 1999. "Ayahuasca: An Ethnopharmacologic History." In *Ayahuasca: Human Consciousness and the Spirits of Nature,* ed. R. Metzner, 187–213. New York: Thunder's Mouth Press.

McKenna, D., L. Luna, and G. Towers. 1995. "Biodynamic Constituents in Ayahuasca Admixture Plants: An Uninvestigated Folk Pharmacopoeia." *Ethnobotany: Evolution of a Discipline,* 349–361.

McKenna, T. 1993. *Food of the Gods: The Search for the Original Tree of Knowledge: A Radical History of Plants, Drugs, and Human Evolution.* New York: Bantam Books.

McKenna, T., D. McKenna. 1993 [1975]. *The Invisible Landscape: Mind, Hallucinogens and the I Ching.* New York: HarperCollins.

Mead, M. 1977. *Sex and Temperament in Three Primitive Societies.* London and Henley, UK: Routledge & Kegan Paul.

Mesturini Cappo, S. 2018. "What Ayahuasca Wants: Notes for the Study and Preservation of an Entangled Ayahuasca." In *The Expanding World Ayahuasca Diaspora: Appropriation, Integration, Legislation,* ed. B. Labate and C. Cavnar. London: Routledge.

Metzner, R. 1999. *Ayahuasca: Human Consciousness and the Spirits of Nature.* New York: Thunder's Mouth Press

Meyer, B., and P. Pels. 2003. *Magic and Modernity: Interfaces of Revelation and Concealment.* Stanford, CA: Stanford University Press.

Minca, C., and T. Oakes. 2006. *Travels in Paradox: Remapping Tourism.* Lanham, Md: Rowman & Littlefield.

Mowforth, M., and I. Munt. 2003. *Tourism and Sustainability. Development and New Tourism in the Third World,* 2nd ed. New York: Routledge.

Muraresku, B., 2020. *The Immortality Key: The Secret History of the Religion with No Name.* New York: Palgrave Macmillan.

Myers, T. 1974. "Spanish Contacts and Social Change on the Ucayali River, Peru." *Ethnohistory* 21(2): 135–157.

Naranjo, C. 1973. "Psychological Aspects of the Yage Experience in an Experimental Setting." In *Hallucinogens and Shamanism*, ed. M. Harner. New York: Oxford University Press.

Naranjo, P. 1986. "El ayahuasca en la arqueología ecuatoriana." *América Indígena* 46(1): 117–127.

Narby, J. 2019. "My life as a White Vampire: Gringos, Amazonians and the Antidote of Reciprocity." Talk at The World Ayahuasca Conference, Girona, Spain. https://youtu.be/jAGdBhi1pZw (accessed March 2020).

———. 1998. *The Cosmic Serpent: DNA and the Origins of Knowledge*. New York: Putnam.

Needham, J., and G. Lu. 1974. *Science and Civilisation in China. Volume 5: Chemistry and Chemical Technology*. Cambridge, UK: Cambridge University Press.

Noll, R. 1985. "Mental Imagery Cultivation as a Cultural Phenomenon: The Role of Visions in Shamanism." *Current Anthropology* 26(4): 443–461.

Nugent, S. 2007. *Scoping the Amazon: Image, Icon, Ethnography*. London: Routledge.

Olson, G. A. 1991. "The Social Scientist as Author: Clifford Geertz on Ethnography and Social Construction." *Journal of Advanced Composition* 11(2): 245–268.

Ortner, S. 1972. "Is Female to Male as Nature Is to Culture? *Feminist Studies* 1(2): 5–31.

Ott, J. 1996. *Pharmacotheon: Entheogenic Drugs, Their Plant Sources and History*. Kennewick, WA: Natural Products Co.

Otto, R., 1958. *The Idea of the Holy: An Inquiry into the Non-Rational Factor in the Idea of the Divine and Its Relation to the Rational*. London: Oxford University Press.

Oyarce-Cruz, J., M. Medina Paredes, and M. Maier. 2019. "Indigenous Amazonians on Air: Shipibo-Konibo Radio Broadcasters and Their Social Influence in Peru." *AlterNative* 15(2): 93–100.

Padoch, C., A. Steward, P. Pinedo-Vasquez, L. Putzel, and M. Miranda Ruiz. 2014. "Urban Residence, Rural Employment, and the Future of Amazonian Forests." In *The Social Lives of Forests: Past, Present, and Future of Woodland Resurgence*, ed. S. Hecht, K. Morrison, and C. Padoch, 322–335. Chicago: University of Chicago Press.

Palmer, D. 2021. "Isomorphic or Poly-Ontological Pluralism? The Implications of Chinese Religion for Poly-Ontological Pluralism: The Implications of Chinese Religion for Covenantal Pluralism." In *The Routledge Handbook of Religious Literacy, Pluralism, and Global Engagement*, ed. C. Seiple and D. R. Hoover. London: Routledge.

———. 2012. "Dao and Nation: Li Yujie—May Fourth Activist, Daoist Cultivator, and Redemptive Society Patriarch in Mainland China and Taiwan." In *Daoism in the Twentieth Century: Between Eternity and Modernity*, ed. D. Palmer and X. Lui. Berkeley: University of California Press.

Parsons, H. L. 1969. "A Philosophy of Wonder." *Philosophy and Phenomenological Research* 30(1):84–101.

Partridge, C. 2018. *High Culture: Drugs, Mysticism and the Pursuit of Transcendence in the Modern World.* New York: Oxford University Press.

———. 2005. *The Re-Enchantment of the West*, Vol. 2. New York: T&T Clark International.

Patiño, V. M. 1968. "Guayusa, a Neglected Stimulant from the Eastern Andean Foothills." *Economic Botany* 22(4): 310–316.

Paulson, S., L. Sideris, J. Stellar, and P. Valdesolo. 2021. "Beyond Oneself: The Ethics and Psychology of Awe." *Annals of the New York Academy of Sciences* 1501:30–47.

Peluso, D. 2022. "Gendered Geographies of Care: Women as Health Workers in an Indigenous Health Project in the Peruvian Amazon." *Tipiti: Journal of the Society for the Anthropology of Lowland South America* 18(1): 25–56.

———. 2017. "Global Ayahuasca: An Entrepreneurial Ecosystem." In *The World Ayahuasca Diaspora: Reinventions and Controversies*, ed. B. Labate, C. Cavnar, and A. K. Gearin, 203–221. London: Routledge.

———. 2014. "Ayahuasca's Attractions and Distractions: Examining Sexual Seduction in Shaman-Participant Interactions." In *Ayahuasca Shamanism in the Amazon and Beyond*, ed. B. C. Labate and C. Cavnar, 231–255. Oxford, UK: Oxford University Press.

Peluso, D., and M. Alexiades. 2006. "For Export Only: 'Ayahuasca' Tourism and Hyper-Traditionalism." *Traditional Dwellings and Settlements Review* 18(1): 73–74.

Piot, A. C., J. C. Bouso, D. de Araujo, and J. I. Skipper. 2023. "Repeated Ayahuasca Use Increases Structural Covariance in Networks Associated with 'Self' Processing." Paper presented at the 29th Annual Meeting of the Organization for Human Brain Mapping, Montreal, Canada.

Pollan, M. 2018. *How to Change Your Mind: The New Science of Psychedelics.* New York: Allen Lane.

Plevin, J. 2018. "From Hauiki to Shinrin-Yoku. A Brief History of Forest Bathing." *Forest History Today* 3:17–19.

Puls, M. 2017. "Negotiated Christianity: Between the 17th and 18th Centuries, Jesuit Missions in the Spanish Amazon Had to Deal with Indigenous Versions of Catholicism." http://revistapesquisa.fapesp.br/en/2017/08/22/negotiated-christianity-2/.

Putsche, L. 2000. "A Reassessment of Resource Depletion, Market Dependency, and Culture Change on a Shipibo Reserve in the Peruvian Amazon." *Human Ecology* 28(1): 131–140.

Qing, L. 2018. *Forest Bathing: How Trees Can Help You Find Health and Happiness.* New York: Penguin Random House.

Rambo, L. 1993. *Understanding Religious Conversion*. New Haven: Yale University Press.

Rappaport, R. 1999. *Ritual and Religion in the Making of Humanity*. Cambridge, UK: Cambridge University Press.

Razam, R. 2014. *The Ayahuasca Sessions: Conversations with Amazonian Curanderos and Western Shamans*. Berkeley, CA: North Atlantic Books.

———. 2009. *Aya: A Shamanic Odyssey*. Melbourne, Australia: Icaro.

Reichel-Dolmatoff, G. 1997. *Rainforest Shamans: Essays on the Tukano Indians of the Northwest Amazon*. London: Themis Books.

———. 1972. "The Cultural Context of an Aboriginal Hallucinogen: Banisteriopsis Caapi." In *Flesh of the Gods: The Ritual Use of Hallucinogens*, ed. P. Furst. Long Grove, IL: Waveland Press.

Richards, W. A. 2016. *Sacred Knowledge: Psychedelics and Religious Experiences*. New York: Columbia University Press.

Rivière, P. 2010. "Ambiguous Environments." *Tipiti: Journal of the Society for the Anthropology of Lowland South America* 8(2):1–13.

———. 1984. *Individual and Society in Guiana*. Cambridge, UK: Cambridge University Press.

Robb, E. M. 2009. "Violence and Recreation: Vacationing in the Realm of Dark Tourism." *Anthropology and Humanism* 34(1): 51–60.

Rodd, R. 2018. "Piaroa Shamanic Ethics and Ethos: Living by the Law and the Good Life of Tranquillity." *International Journal of Latin American Religions* 2(2): 315–333.

Roe, P. G. 1982. "The Cosmic Zygote." In *Myth, Cosmos, and Ceremony Among the Shipibos*. New Brunswick, NJ: eHRAF World Cultures.

Rosaldo, R. 1986. "Ilongot Hunting as Story and Experience." In *The Anthropology of Experience*, ed. V. Turner and E. Bruner, 97–138. Champaign: University of Illinois Press.

Roseman, L., K. Preller, E. Fotiou, and M. Winkelman. 2022. "Editorial: Psychedelic Sociality: Pharmacological and Extra Pharmacological Perspectives." *Frontiers in Pharmacology* 13.

Roseman L., Y. Ron, A. Saca, N. Ginsberg, L. Luna, N. Karkabi, R. Doblin, and R. Carhart-Harris. 2021. "Relational Processes in Ayahuasca Groups of Palestinians and Israelis." *Frontiers in Pharmacology* 12:607529.

Roy, A., and A. Ong, eds. 2011. *Worlding Cities: Asian Experiments and the Art of Being Global*. Malden, MA: Wiley-Blackwell.

Rubenstein, M-J. 2008. *Strange Wonder: The Closure of Metaphysics and the Opening of Awe*. New York: Columbia University Press.

Rubenstein, S. L. 2012. "On the Importance of Visions Among the Amazonian Shuar." *Current Anthropology* 53(1): 39–79.

258 REFERENCES

Salazar, N. B., and H. H. Graburn, eds. 2014. *Tourism Imaginaries: Anthropological Approaches*. New York: Berghahn.

Salomon, F. 1983. "Shamanism and Politics in Late-Colonial Ecuador." *American Ethnologist* 10(3): 413–428.

Sanabria, E., and S. Mesturini Cappo. 2023. "Introduction: Plot-ing Phytofutures." *American Anthropologist* 125(3): 673–678.

Santos-Granero, F. 2006. "Sensual Vitalities: Noncorporeal Models of Sensing and Knowing in Native Amazonia." *Tipiti: Journal of the Society for the Anthropology of Lowland South America* 4(1):57–80.

Schultes, R. E., and R. F. Raffauf. 1992. *Vine of Souls: Medicine Men, Their Plants and Rituals in the Colombian Amazonia*. Tucson, AZ: Synergetic Press.

Scott, M. W. 2017. "Getting More Real with Wonder: An Afterword." *Journal of Religious and Political Practice* 3(3):212–229.

———. 2016. "To Be Makiran Is to See Like Mr Parrot: The Anthropology of Wonder in Solomon Islands." *Journal of the Royal Anthropological Institute* 22:474–495.

———. 2014. "To Be a Wonder: Anthropology, Cosmology, and Alterity." In *Framing Cosmologies: The Anthropology of Worlds*, ed. A. Abramson and M. Holbraad, 31–54. Manchester, UK: Manchester University Press.

Shanon, B. 2002. *The Antipodes of the Mind: Chartering the Phenomenology of the Ayahuasca Experience*. New York: Oxford University Press.

Sheldrake, M. 2020. "The 'Enigma' of Richard Schultes, Amazonian Hallucinogenic Plants, and the Limits of Ethnobotany." *Social Studies in Science* 50(3): 345–376.

Shepard, G. H. 2017. "Foreword: Ayahuasca in the 21st Century: Having It Both Ways." In *The World Ayahuasca Diaspora: Reinventions and Controversies*, ed. B. C. Labate, C. Cavnar, and A. K. Gearin, xv–xix. London: Routledge.

———. 2014. "Will the Real Shaman Please Stand Up? The Recent Adoption of Ayahuasca Among Indigenous Groups of the Peruvian Amazon." In *Ayahuasca Shamanism in the Amazon and Beyond*, ed. B. Labate and C. Cavnar, 16–39. Oxford, UK: Oxford University Press.

———. 2004. "A Sensory Ecology of Medicinal Plant Therapy in Two Amazonian Societies." *American Anthropologist* 102(2): 252–266.

Sherry, P. 2013. "The Varieties of Wonder." *Philosophical Investigations* 36(4):340–354.

Shiota, M. N. 2021. "Awe, Wonder, and the Human Mind." *Annals of the New York Academic of Science* 1501:85–89.

Sloshower, J., J. Guss, R. Krause, R. M. Wallace, M. T. Williams, S. Reed, and M. D. Skinta. 2020. "Psilocybin-Assisted Therapy of Major Depressive Disorder Using Acceptance and Commitment Therapy as a Therapeutic Frame." *Journal of Contextual Behavioral Science* 15:12–19.

Spruce, R., and A. R. Wallace. 1908. *Notes of a Botanist on the Amazon & Andes: Being Records of Travel on the Amazon and Its Tributaries, the Trombetas, Rio Negro, Uaupés, Casiquiari, Pacimoni, Huallaga and Pastasa : As Also to the Cataracts of the Orinoco, Along the Eastern Side of the Andes of Peru and Ecuador, and the Shores of the Pacific, During the Years 1849–1864.* London: Macmillan.

Srinivas, T. 2018. *The Cow in the Elevator: An Anthropology of Wonder.* London: Duke University Press.

Stafford, P. 1992. *Psychedelics Encyclopedia,* 3rd expanded ed. Berkeley, CA: Ronin.

Stasch, R. 2016. "Dramas of Otherness: 'First Contact' Tourism in New Guinea." *HAU: Journal of Ethnographic Theory* 6(3):7–27.

———. 2015. "Introduction: Double Signs and Intrasocietal Heterogeneity in Primitivist Tourism Encounters." *Ethnos* 80(4): 433–447.

———. 2014. "Primitivist Tourism and the Romantic Individualism: On the Values in Exotic Stereotypy About Cultural Others." *Anthropological Theory* 14(2): 191–214.

Stellar, J. E. 2021. "Awe Helps Us Remember Why It Is Important to Forget the Self." *Annals of the New York Academy of Science* 1501:81–84.

Stern, S. J., ed. 1998. *Shining and Other Paths: War and Society in Peru, 1980–1995.* Durham, NC: Duke University Press.

Sternberg, E. M. 2009. *Healing Spaces: The Science of Place and Well-Being.* Cambridge, MA: Harvard University Press.

St John, G. 2024. *Strange Attractor: Terence McKenna & the Hyperspace Age.* Cambridge, MA: MIT Press.

———. 2017. "Aussiewaska: A Cultural History of Changa and Ayahuasca Analogues in Australia." In *The World Ayahuasca Diaspora: Reinventions and Controversies,* ed. B. Labate, C. Cavnar, and A. Gearin, 144–162. London: Routledge.

———. 2015. *Mystery School in Hyperspace: A Cultural History of DMT.* Berkeley, CA: Evolver Editions.

———. 2012. *Global Tribe: Technology, Spirituality & Psytrance.* Sheffield, UK: Equinox.

———. 2001. "Doof! Australian Post Rave Culture." In *FreeNRG: Notes from the Edge of the Dance Floor,* ed. G St John. Melbourne, Australia: Commonground.

Stoller, P. 1984. "Horrific Comedy: Cultural Resistance and the *Hauka* Movement in Niger." *Ethos* 12(2): 559–570.

Strassman, R. 2001. *DMT: The Spirit Molecule: A Doctor's Revolutionary Research into the Biology of Near-Death and Mystical Experiences.* Rochester, VT: Park Street Press.

Suárez Álvarez, C. 2023. "Ayahuasca, Global Consumption & Reported Deaths in the Media." ICEERS website. https://www.iceers.org/ayahuasca-global-con sumption-deaths/ (accessed September 2023).

———. 2019. "Reciprocity and the Impacts of Ayahuasca Tourism." Presentation given at The 2019 World Ayahuasca Conference, Girona, Spain. ICEERS. https://youtu.be/Y9Wh24kB8yU (accessed September 2020).

Taussig. M. 2010 [1980]. *The Devil and Commodity Fetishism in South America.* Chapel Hill: University of North Carolina Press.

———. 1993. *Mimesis and Alterity: A Particular History of the Senses.* London: Rout ledge.

———. 1987. *Shamanism, Colonialism, and the Wild Man: A Study in Terror and Heal ing.* Chicago: University of Chicago Press.

Taussig, M., and P. Lamborn Wilson. 2002. *Shamanism and Ayahuasca: Michael Taussig Interviewed by Peter Lamborn Wilson.* Brooklyn, NY: Automedia.

Taylor, A. C. 2018. "Individualism in the Wild: Oneness in Jivaroan Culture." *Lecture, The Marett Memorial Lecture,* University of Cambridge, Cambridge, UK, April 27, 2018. https://podcasts.ox.ac.uk/marett-memorial-lecture-2018 -individualism-wild-oneness-jivaroan-culture. (accessed April 2022).

———. 1993. "Remembering to Forget: Identity, Mourning and Memory Among the Jivaro." *Man* 28(4): 653–678.

Taylor, C. 2007. *A Secular Age.* Cambridge, MA: Harvard University Press.

Theodossopoulos, D. 2014. "Scorn of Idealisation? Tourism Imaginaries, Exoti cization, and Ambivalence in Embera Indigenous Tourism." In *Tourism Imagi naries: Anthropological Approaches,* ed. N. B. Salazar and H. H. Graburn, 57–79. New York: Berghahn.

Timmerman, C., R. Watts, and D. Dupuis. 2022. "Towards Psychedelic Ap prenticeship: Developing a Gentle Touch for the Mediation and Validation of Psychedelic-Induced Insights and Revelations." *Transcultural Psychiatry* 59(5): 691–704.

Torgovnick, M. 1990. *Gone Primitive: Savage Intellects, Modern Lives.* Chicago: Uni versity of Chicago Press.

Torres, C. M. 2018. "The Origins of the Ayahuasca/Yagé Concept: An Enquiry into the Synergy Between Dimethyltryptamine and Beta-Carbolines." In *An cient Psychoactive Substances,* ed. S. Fitzpatrick. Gainesville: University Press of Florida.

Torres, C. M., and D. Repke, 2006. *Anadenanthera: Visionary Plant of Ancient South America.* New York: Hawthorn Press.

Townsley, G. 1993. "Song Paths: The Way and Means of Yaminahua Shamanic Knowledge." *L'Homme* 33:449–468.

Townsley, G., and H. Reid. 1989. "The Shaman and His Apprentice." London: British Broadcasting Corp.

Tramacchi, D. 2017. "Ayahuasca, World Spiritualities, and Psychonautics." Online video course at Kahpi: The Ayahuasca Hub. Kahpi.net. https://courses .kahpi.net/courses/ayahuasca-world-spiritualities-psychonautics (accessed December 2023).

———. 2009. "Entheogens and the Disincarnate." *Entheogenesis Australis EGA Journal* 1:6–9.

———. 2006. *Vapours and Visions: Religious Dimensions of DMT Use*. PhD diss. Brisbane, Australia: University of Queensland.

———. 2001. "Chaos Engines: Doofs, Psychedelics and Religious Experience." In *FreeNRG: Notes from the Edge of the Dancefloor*, ed. G. St John Altona, Australia: Common Ground.

Tsing, A. 2015. *The Mushroom at the End of the World: On the Possibility of Life in Capitalist Ruins*. Princeton, NJ: Princeton University Press.

Tukano, D. 2022. "A Medicine Heritage of 160 Indigenous Peoples: The Origins of Ayahuasca Before Globalization." *Chacruna.net*. https://chacruna.net /indigenous-peoples-medicine-heritage-ayahuasca-globalization/ (accessed April 8, 2022).

Tupper, K. 2014. "Entheogenic Education: Psychedelics as Tools of Wonder and Awe." *MAPS Bulletin* 24(1): 14–19.

———. 2009. "Ayahuasca Healing Beyond the Amazon: The Globalisation of a Traditional Indigenous Entheogenic Practice." *Global Networks: A Journal of Transnational Affairs* 9(1): 117–136.

Turner, V. 1995 [1969]. *The Ritual Process: Structure and Anti-Structure*. New York: Aldine.

UNWTO. 2010. "Global Report on Women in Tourism." *United Nations World Tourism Organization*.

Van Kuelen, E., D. Tramacchi, and K. Williamson, eds. 2010. *Entheogenesis Australis. Journal 1*. https://www.scribd.com/document/189824664/Entheogenesis -Australis-Journal-One (accessed April 19, 2022).

Veigl, F. X. 1798. *Noticias detalladas sobre el estado de la Provincia de Maynas en América meridional hasta el año de 1768*. Iquitos, Peru: CETA.

Villavicencio, M. 1858. *Geografía de la República del Ecuador*. New York: Craighead.

Vincent, E. 2017. "Fear and Wonder Out Bush: Engaging a Critical Anthropological Perspective on Indigenous Alterity." *Journal of Religious and Political Practice* 3:152–167.

Virtanen, P. K. 2014. "Materializing Alliances: Ayahuasca Shamanism in and

262 REFERENCES

Beyond Western Amazonian Indigenous Communities." In *Ayahuasca Shamanism in the Amazon and Beyond*, ed. B. Labate and C. Cavnar. Oxford, UK: Oxford University Press.

Viveiros de Castro, E. 1998. "Cosmological Deixis and Amerindian Perspectivism." *Journal of the Royal Anthropological Institute* 4(3): 469–488.

———. 1996. "Images of Nature and Society in Amazonian Ethnology." *Annual Review of Anthropology* 25:179–200.

Voogelbreinder, S. 2009. *Garden of Eden: The Shamanic Use of Psychoactive Flora and Fauna, and the Study of Consciousness*. Self-published with Black Rainbow.

Walker, H. 2012. *Under a Watchful Eye: Self, Power, and Intimacy in Amazonia*. Berkeley, CA: University of California Press.

Wallace, A.F.C. 1959. "Cultural Determinants of Response to Hallucinatory Experience." *JAMA Psychiatry* 1(1): 58–69.

Walsh, R. 2012. "From State to Trait: The Challenge of Transforming Transient Insights into Enduring Change." In *Spiritual Growth with Entheogens: Psychoactive Sacramentals and Human Transformation*. ed. T. Roberts, 24–30. Rochester, VT: Park Street Press.

Watts, F., and L. Turner, eds. 2014. *Evolution, Religion, and Cognitive Sciences: Critical and Constructive Essays*. Oxford, UK: Oxford University Press.

Watts, R., and J. Luoma. 2020. "The Use of the Psychological Flexibility Model to Support Psychedelic Assisted Therapy." *Journal of Contextual Behavioral Science* 15:92–102.

Weber, M. 2009 [1915]. "The Social Psychology of World Religion." In *From Max Weber: Essays in Sociology*, ed. C. W. Mills; B. S. Turner, and H. Gerth. London: Routledge.

———. 1992 [1905]. *The Protestant Ethic and the Spirit of Capitalism*. New York: Routledge.

Whitehead, N., and R. Wright, eds. 2004. *In Darkness and Secrecy: The Anthropology of Assault Sorcery and Witchcraft in Amazonia*. London: Duke University Press.

Wilkinson, I., and A. Kleinman. 2016. *A Passion for Society: How We Think About Human Suffering*. Berkeley: University of California Press.

Williams, J. 2015. "Investigating a Century-Long Hole in History: The Untold Story of Ayahuasca from 1755–1865." Masters thesis, Department of Anthropology, University of Boulder, Colorado.

Wilson, E. O. 1984. *Biophilia*. Cambridge, MA: Harvard University Press.

Winkelman, M. 2005. "Drug Tourism or Spiritual Healing? Ayahuasca Seekers in Amazonia." *Journal of Psychoactive Drugs* 37(2): 209–218.

Wright, I., and L. Ross. 2021. "That's an Old Story." *Power Trip. Cover Story. New York Magazine* podcast. https://podcasts.apple.com/us/podcast/cover-story/id 1594675355 (accessed February 27, 2022).

REFERENCES 263

Wright, R., and J. Hill. 1986. "History, Ritual, and Myth: Nineteenth Century Millenarian Movements in the Northwest Amazon." *Ethnohistory* 33(1): 31–54.

Yang, M. 2008. "Introduction." In *Chinese Religiosities: Afflictions of Modernity and State Formation*, ed. M. Yang. Berkeley: University of California Press.

Zelenietz, M. 1981. "Sorcery and Social Change: An Introduction." *Social Analysis* 8:3–14.

Zhang, L. 2020. *Anxious China: Inner Revolution and Politics of Psychotherapy.* Oakland: University of California Press.

———. 2017. "The Rise of Therapeutic Governing in Postsocialist China." *Medical Anthropology* 36(1): 6–18.

Zheng Mahler. 2019. *Psychedelic Technics.* Hong Kong: Small Tune Press.

Znamenski, A. 2007. *The Beauty of the Primitive: Shamanism and the Western Imagination.* New York: Oxford University Press.

INDEX

Aboriginal Dreamtime cosmology, 145
Abramson, Allen, 21
acacia trees, xi, 130, 157; DMT in, 133
adverse reactions, to ayahuasca, 57–58
agency, 94, 187, 192–93; plant agency, 22, 66
agnosticism, in Bridging the Gap, 189
Agua de Florida, 154, 180
alcohol, 56, 88, 101, 148, 205
Alexiades, Miguel N., on tourism, 83
alienation, 144, 207
allopathic medicine, 126–27, 128, 166, 191
Amaringo, Pablo, 8, 22–24, 58; boutique multiculturalism and, 60
Amazonia, 22, 72, 75, 227, 230; ethnography in, 222; inequalities in, 77; metaphysics in, 65; music in, 24–25; *quiqui* in, 19; rubber industry in, 139; Shuar people in, 97, 110, 190, 222–23; tourism economy in, 30. *See also* shamanism

ambient present, in visions, 223
AMETRA, 69
angels, in visions, 27, 56, 145, 156, 205, 226–29
anger, 183
anthropology: Indigenous medicine relation to, 94–95; psychology compared to, 5–6, 10–11
The Antipodes of the Mind (Shanon), 6, 17–18, 226–28
anxiety: of international guests, 109; in modern life, 94
Anxious China (Zhang), 214
Apokyn, 107
apomorphine, 107
"Arbol Magico" (painting), 22
Århem, Kaj, 87
arutam spirit, 87
Asociación de Onanyabo Médicos Ancestrales Shipibo Konibo (ASOMASHK), 69–70, 73
attitudes, 23; in Australia, 15, 99–100; of Bridging the Gap, 186; toward capitalism, 29; in China, 170; colonial, 55–56; countercultural,

265

266 INDEX

attitudes (*continued*)
142–43; emotional barriers and,
12; management skills and, 187;
Mother Ayahuasca and, 165–66;
religious conversion and, 216; of
Shipibo healers, 100–102; warfare, 223
Australia, 13–14, 16–17, 137; attitudes
in, 15, 99–100; Ayahuasca Australiana in, 146; bush doofs in, 145–
46; counterculture in, 29, 194,
225; drugs in, 33–34; "Entheon-
Gaia" in, 143–44; healing in, 134,
136; integration in, 193, 194, 197,
199, 201, 202–3; McKenna, T., in,
132; Mother Ayahuasca in, 158;
New Age spirituality in, 31; New
South Wales, 135; psychonauts in,
133–34, 146–47; public opinion in,
203–4
authority, 52, 73, 204; shamanism
and, 53
awe, 6–7, 20, 25, 83–84, 104, 109–
10; counterculture and, 165; DMT
and, 146; entheogens and, 67; in
ontological crisis, 124, 125; at Pachamama Temple, 121–22; at plant
spirits, 129; in psychedelic therapy,
17–19; Shipibo lifeworlds relation
to, 97; in visions, 96; wonder compared to, 193–94. *See also* wonder
ayahuasca. *See specific topics*
Ayahuasca Australiana, 146
ayahuasca churches, 30, 152. *See also*
Santo Daime, Uniao de Vegetal
Ayahuasca Visions (Luna), 8

Banisteriopsis caapi, 38, 47
Bateson, Gregory, 199
Bauman, Zygmunt, 29–30

B-carbolines, 5
Becker, Gay, 192
Berquist, Emily, 44–45
"Beyond the Brain" (1997), 133
biographical materials, in visions, 6–7,
155, 226–27, 237–38
Body-Heart-Spirit (*shen xin ling*), 171
boundaries, 149, 193, 202–3
boutique multiculturalism, 60
Brabec de Mori, Bernd, 53, 61; on
humor, 101; on *kené* designs, 73; on
perspective, 66; on tourism, 82
Brazil, 46, 136, 190; ayahuasca
churches in, 30, 152; Darpan in,
132; Luke in, 12, 176; World Ayahuasca Conference in, 58
Bridging the Gap, 12, 177–78, 209;
agnosticism in, 189; capitalism
and, 186–87; intention and, 183,
184; modernity and, 187–88; Ting
Ting and, 182
Brown, Michael, 104–5, 222
brujeria, 4, 64, 94
Burroughs, William, 23, 55; *Naked
Lunch*, 56, 107, 228
bush doofs, 141, 145–46

Calavia Sáez, Oscar, 37, 86
capital, 22, 29, 37, 54, 91; of healers, 99; in occult economies, 92–
93; *onanya joni* and, 83; for social
change, 94; tourism and, 75,
86–87
capitalism, 13, 209–12, 219; Bridging
the Gap and, 186–87; in China,
28–29, 169; disenchantment with,
137; fashion, 58–59, 60; Indigenous cosmologies relation to, 21;
onanya joni and, 93; as religion,
139; shamanism and, 54, 91; social

fragmentation relation to, 214; sorcery and, 64; spirituality and, 29–30, 232
Cappo, Silvia Mesturini, 22–23, 28, 222
career development, 11, 16, 171, 174, 177, 208
Carlos (guide), 114–15, 116, 118, 119
Carneiro, Robert L., 56
Carson, Rachel, 239
Carter, David, 144
Catholic ideology, 9
ceremonial order, 100
ceremonies, 41, 127–28, 135, 206, 235–38; at Ayahuasca Australiana, 146; healers at, 104; *maloca* for, 80, 81; music in, 156–57; traditional, 108–9. *See also* facilitators; Pachamama Temple, Pucallpa; retreats
chaman. See shamanism
chaman's healing utensils, 81
Channel 7 News, 204
Chantre y Herrera, Jose, 40–42
Chao, ayahuasca and, 208–12, 214–15, 216–17
chaos, 192, 199, 213
Chau, Adam, 169–70, 187
childhood trauma, 142
China, 11, 16–17, 31; attitudes in, 170; capitalism in, 28–29, 169; corruption in, 185; disenchantment in, 169–70; drug policies in, 33, 168–69, 173–74; individualism in, 188; integration in, 193, 194; mental health in, 214; neoliberal values in, 171; psychedelics in, 167–69, 171–72; secularism in, 12–13, 186–87; shamanism in, 168, 171
Chinese culture, 167, 186

Chinese Nationalist Party, 168
Christianity, 169, 199, 216; culture of, 39–40; shamanism relation to, 43
chronic pain, 160
cinematic theory, 51–52
cities: envy in, 82; nature compared to, 140; in visions, 5, 6, 17, 23–24, 47, 118, 158, 220
civilization, 14. *See also* cities
civil unrest, in Peru, 27
cleanliness, 148–49
cognitive psychology, 6, 10
Cohen, Sidney, 196
collective trauma, 23
Colombia, Putumayo, 49–50
colonial attitudes, 55–56
colonialism, 35, 37, 55–56, 192; ASOMASHK relation to, 69–70; in consciousness, 216; Indigenous cosmologies relation to, 21; missionaries and, 37; shamanism relation to, 49, 52–53; sorcery relation to, 49–50
colonial violence, 50
Colpron, Anne-Marie, 71
commercial spaces, retreats as, 29
communist uprising, in Peru, 116
Compañón, Martínez, 44–45
competition, 29, 87; shamanism and, 91–92
Conibo people, 40
consciousness, 28–29, 52, 111–12, 162, 163, 199–200; in China, 188; colonialism in, 216; healing of, 136; mirror and, 26; of plants, 66; sovereignty and, 152
context, 20, 89–90, 127, 187, 191; of ayahuasca tourism, 64–65, 72; cultural, 109, 138; integration and, 197, 201; money in, 16; in set and

context (*continued*)
setting theory, 172, 173; social, 35, 112, 192, 226; urban, 16; visions relation to, 28, 226, 230; wonder relation to, 21
Córdova-Rios, Manuel, 56–57
corruption, in China, 185
cosmologies, 224, 227; Aboriginal Dreamtime, 145; of ego dissolution, 56; environmental, 145; Indigenous, 21–22; of international guests, 64; secular, 173; shamanic, 138; among Shipibo healers, 87–88; of tourism, 89; in visions, 7
counterculture, 57, 132, 165, 171, 173; attitudes, 142–43; in Australia, 29, 194, 225; capitalism and, 232; New Age spirituality and, 144. *See also* culture; Leary, Timothy; McKenna, Terence
courage: suffering and, 20
co-workers, 181–82
creative thinking, 110
crisis, 63, 82, 97, 160, 170, 213; of meaning, 16, 170, 186–87; ontological, 124, 125; wonder and, 20
cultural context, 109, 138
cultural integration, 203–5
cultural meaning, 109–10
culture, 6, 15, 23, 151, 216; boutique multiculturalism and, 60; Chinese, 167, 186; of Christianity, 39–40; Indigenous, 118, 127; McKenna, T., on, 15, 131; popular, 58, 72; religious conversion and, 216; of Shipibo people, 63, 78, 90, 106, 108; visions relation to, 7, 8–9; wonder relation to, 109
Cuna curing songs, 192
curanderismo, otherness and, 89
curiosity, 34, 60, 98–99

dark determinism, 192
Darpan, 7, 14–15, 132–34, 197–99; on diet, 148; on integration, 201–2; Joseph relation to, 151; McKenna, D., relation to, 143; on music, 156; on nature, 136
Davis, Erik, 25, 228
demonization, of ayahuasca, 40–43, 49, 203
depression, 205–6
diet, 66, 157; plant, 2, 32, 63, 66, 151; for preparation, 84, 148–49; shamanism and, 71, 222; of Shipibo healers, 67–68
Discoteque Pescadoras, 108
disenchantment, 189; with capitalism, 137; in China, 169–70; neo-shamanism relation to, 170; with society, 16, 138–39, 143, 167, 188, 207; Suited Monk and, 187; transcendence of, 14
distress, 2–3, 4, 97, 157, 223; of healers, 129
disturbing experiences, 4
DMT, 132, 146, 228; in acacia trees, 133. *See also* psychedelics
DMT (Strassman), 171–72
Doblin, Rick, 221
domination, 72, 73; Jesuit priests relation to, 40; in rubber industry, 71; in sorcery, 64; of visions, 3, 4, 80, 91, 104, 114, 119
The Doors of Perception (Huxley), 111
Doré, Gustave, 2
drawings, 178; intention in, 179
dreams, 9, 40, 68, 149, 174; and intuition, 107. *See also* visions
drug policies, in China, 33, 168–69, 173–74
drugs, 158, 196; in Australia, 33–34; ayahuasca compared to, 30, 188,

204–5; Burroughs relation to, 55–56; mysticism and, 224–25; recreational, 101, 204; tourism for, 75–76

Dupuis, David, 9–10

Durkheim, E., 218–19

eclecticism, 112

economy, tourism, 30

ecstatic dance, 12, 33, 180

Ecuador, Rio Napo Basin, 47

education, psychedelics and, 67

ego death, 183, 225; purging and, 4

ego dissolution, 7, 200, 203, 216; cosmologies of, 56

egoism, 190

Eisner, Betty, 196

Ejército Guerrillero Popular (The People's Guerrilla Army), 116

Elle (magazine), 59

Embrace of the Serpent (film), 51–52

emotional barriers, 12

emotional pain, 126, 142

enchantment, in modernity, 139

Entheogenesis Australis, 133

entheogens, 146; awe and, 67

"EntheonGaia," 143–44

entrepreneurism, 77, 177, 187; ecosystem in Peru, 60

environmental cosmology, 145

environmentalism, 22

envy: among healers, 89–90; sorcery and, 91–92

Espinosa, Oscar, 63, 83

Estala, Pedro, 42–43

ethnography: in Amazonia, 222; wonder in, 33–34

European perception, 37, 49

existential transformation, 224

expectations, 129, 195; psychedelics relation to, 149

facilitators, 78, 120, 144, 150–51, 154–55; at EntheonGaia, 143; Indigenous specialists and, 134; money of, 13–14; music and, 156–57, 163; salary of, 14; at World Ayahuasca Conference, 145. *See also* Darpan; Luke (pseudonym)

faith, 39, 40, 211–12, 214

familiarity, in visions, 214–15

family, 82–83, 167, 181, 205, 209, 214; healers as, 32, 63; relationships with, 163–64; trauma and, 11, 84–86, 92, 141; visions of, 6, 161, 180, 182, 208, 237–38

Farmer, Paul, 69

Farrelly, Paul, 171

fashion capitalism, 58–59; otherness in, 60

felines, in visions, 229

Fischer Cárdenas, Guillermo, 113

Fish, Stanley, 60

flower bath activity, 85

food accumulation, shamanism and, 87

Food of the Gods (McKenna), 132

foreign civilizations, in visions, 23–24

foreign-owned retreats, 76–77

forests, 22; shamanism and, 53. *See also* nature

Foster, George, 90

Fotiou, Evgenia, 9, 73

fractals, 141–43

Franciscan missionaries, 40; Shipibo people relation to, 70–71

Freedman, Françoise Barbira, 72–73, 173

Fujimori, Alberto, 117

galactic entities, 165

Geertz, Clifford, 10, 232

Ge Hong, 168

gender, 150; Shipibo healers and, 71, 72, 73

Geography of the Republic of Ecuador (Villavicencio), 47

Ginsberg, Allen, 55

Global Ayahuasca Project, 57

globalization, 30; of mindfulness, 198

gnosis, 150; of visions, 186, 188; in Western spirituality, 18

Goldberger, Ary, 141

Gow, Peter, 52–53, 205; on shamanism, 54

grace, 197, 199–200

grief, 124, 126, 128, 209, 238

Grof, Stanislav, 132; on integration, 195, 196; on psychedelics, 192

Guerra, Ciro, 51–52

guilt, 121, 128, 181; purging of, 209

hallucinations, 9–10

Han Dynasty, 168

Hanegraaff, Wouter, 18

happiness, 100–102, 173, 177, 180

Harner, Michael, 5

Harrington, Anne, 198

Hartogsohn, Ido, 111, 138, 218

healers: capital of, 99; distress of, 129; envy among, 89–90; as family, 32, 63; money and, 3–4; poverty of, 119; social environment of, 120; sorcery and, 114. *See also* Shipibo healers

healing, 84–85, 122–24, 147–48; in Australia, 134, 136; fractals relation to, 141; integration and, 206–8; meaning and, 134; modernity relation to, 232; from Mother Ayahuasca, 217; narratives of, 225; nature relation to, 22, 73, 136, 139–40, 142; transformation and,

153, 180; of trauma, 123–24, 134, 144, 149, 191; wonder relation to, 97–98

"held well," 150, 157

hierarchies, social, 87

Holdbraad, Martin, 21

Holy Mountain (film), 172

Hu, Terry, 171

Huggan, Graham, 60

humility, 6–7

humor, 20, 101–2

Huni Kuin, Ibã, 58

Huxley, Aldous, 25–26, 140–41; *The Doors of Perception*, 111; *The Perennial Philosophy*, 225

hyper-traditionalism, tourism and, 83

icaro (songs), 1–3, 79; of Juan, 68, 101, 102–4, 236–37; as medicine, 123; of Shipibo healers, 129; visions relation to, 127; wonder in, 102–3, 104

ICEERS. *See* International Center for Ethnobotanical Education, Research, and Service

identity, 104, 185–86; of healers, 66, 67; social fragmentation relation to, 214

Illius, Bruno, 87–88

The Immortality Key (Muraresku), 98

"In A Perfect World" (podcast), 14

Indigenous cosmologies, 21–22

Indigenous culture, 118, 127

Indigenous medicine, 94–95

Indigenous patients, international guests compared to, 104–5

Indigenous peoples, 38–39; Conibo, 40; neoshamanism relation to, 145; racism toward, 44; Shuar, 97,

190, 222–23; tourism relation to, 74, 75–76. *See also* Shipibo healers; Shipibo people
Indigenous specialists, 122–23, 126, 150; culture of, 127; facilitators and, 134
Indigenous visions, 5, 6
individualism, 150, 203, 227; in China, 188; in neoshamanism, 158; social fragmentation relation to, 213–14
inequalities, 77; sorcery relation to, 89–91; tourism relation to, 93
initiation, 152–53
insects, in visions, 228–29
integration, 194–96, 213, 216; boundaries and, 202–3; in ceremonies, 157; cultural, 203–5; healing and, 206–8; intrapsychic, 197, 199, 200; modernity relation to, 193; Mother Ayahuasca relation to, 201–2; narratives and, 191–92, 193, 203, 205, 218; psychological flexibility and, 215; relational, 200–201; in sharing circles, 199, 202; Shipibo healers relation to, 219; society and, 217
integrative holism, 199
intention, 195; Bridging the Gap and, 183, 184; diet and, 149; in drawings, 179; for retreats, 153–54; in set and setting theory, 172, 173; in visions, 112–13
intercultural relations, 109
International Center for Ethnobotanical Education, Research, and Service (ICEERS), 57
international guests: anxiety of, 109; cosmologies of, 64; Indigenous patients compared to, 104–5; restlessness of, 107; suffering of, 120;

visions of, 123; wonder of, 105, 114, 129–30
interpretation, 96–97; of visions, 11–12
intrapsychic integration, 197, 199; neoshamanism and, 200
intuition, and dreams, 107
Iquitos, Peru, 39, 72–73; retreats in, 70
Iskra, Anna, 171
Islam, 216
Izquierdo, Carolina, 89–90

Jackson, Michael, 107, 110
James, William, 197, 199, 200
Jesuit priests, 40–41, 43; Shipibo people relation to, 70–71. *See also* missionaries
Jodorowsky, Alejandro, 172
Johns Hopkins University, 225
Johnson, Allen, 89–90
Jordan, 120–22
Joseph (facilitator), 150–51, 154–55; initiation of, 152–53
Josephson-Storm, Jason, 138–39, 170
Juan (Maestro), 1–5, 91–92; *icaro* of, 68, 101, 102–4, 236–37; as *onanya joni*, 16; on visions, 112–13, 114
Jung, Carl, 197
Junky (Burroughs), 55

Kabat-Zinn, Jon, 198
Kalberg, Stephen, 137
Kate, ayahuasca and, 160–63, 201
Keltner, Dacher, 19
kené designs, 73
Kenzo show, 58, 60
King, Martin Luther, 213
Kirmayer, Laurence, 202
Kleinman, Arthur, 169
Kounen, Jan, 58

272 INDEX

Kripal, Jeffrey, 112
Kusel, Heinz, 47

Labate, Bia, 227
La Condamine, Charles-Marie de, 44
Lamb, Frank Bruce, 56
Langdon, Esther Jean, 8
Langlitz, Nicolas, 8, 112, 224
Leary, Timothy, 98, 228; "The Psy-
    chedelic Experience," 165
Lees, Andrew, 107
Letheby, Chris, 7
Lévi-Strauss, Claude, 192, 238
lifeworlds: Shipibo, 97; Shuar, 110
literary shamanism, 52
Lomas, Olivia Arevalo, 69
Lopez Sanchez, Jose, 222
Losonczy, Anne-Marie, 28
The Lost City of Z (film), 100
LSD, 98; ayahuasca compared to,
    165; integration for, 196. *See also*
    psychedelics
Lucero, Juan Lorenzo, 39
Luhrmann, Tanya, 96
Luke (pseudonym), 12–14, 174, 176;
    retreats of, 177–80
Luna, Luis Eduardo, 17, 24; *Ayahuasca
    Visions*, 8; on humor, 101; on mis-
    sionaries, 42; on *Wizard of the Upper
    Amazon*, 57

magical arts, 87. *See also* shamanism;
    sorcery
Magnin (Father), 44
The Making of a Counter Culture
    (Roszak), 131
maloca, at Pachamama Temple, 80, 81
Mama Maria, 63, 229; diet of, 66–67;
    icaro of, 237; *Sendero Luminoso* and,
    116–17; sorcery and, 80, 82

management skills, 184, 187
Manuel (Maestro), 117
Mao Zedong, 169
Marquez Lopez, Adelina, 72
Marquez Pinedo, Feliciano, 72
Marquez Pinedo, Genaro, 72
Marquez Pinedo, Luis, 78
Marquez Sanchez, Sandro, 32
materialism, 14, 86; capitalistic, 169
Maynas, Mateo Arvalo, 54
Maynas mission, 44
Mazarrasa, Jerónimo, 94
McKenna, Dennis, 29, 228; Darpan
    relation to, 143
McKenna, Terence, 15, 133, 143, 228;
    psychedelics relation to, 131–32
Mead, Margaret, 34
meaning, 34–35, 67, 76, 110, 184;
    crisis of, 16, 170, 186–87; cultural,
    109–10; healing and, 134; narra-
    tives for, 192; in neoshamanism,
    137–38; religious conversion and,
    215–16; of visions, 8, 112–14, 191,
    203
medicina, 67–68
medicine, 143, 147–48, 161, 180; allo-
    pathic, 126–27; Apokyn, 107; *icaro*
    as, 123; Indigenous, 94–95; for
    mental health, 213; plant, 52, 62,
    66–67, 69, 78; primitivism as, 76;
    social, 205–6; transbodied, 67–68
memory work, 223–24
mental health, 57, 95, 158; in China,
    214; integration and, 196; medicine
    for, 213; nature relation to, 140
mescaline, 111
mestizo, 53, 73, 117,
metaphysics, Amazonian, 65
Metzner, Ralph, 138
Meyer, Birgit, 188

Michael, ayahuasca and, 163–66
military, in visions, 27, 117; veterans 151
militias, 115, 116–17
mindfulness, 198; insights from 128; meditation 78, 153, 180
mirror, 26–27
misfortune, sorcery relation to, 87–88
missionaries: ayahuasca relation to, 39, 41–43; colonialism and, 37; Franciscan, 40, 70–71; primitivism and, 86
modernity, 29, 129, 219; Bridging the Gap and, 187–88; in China, 170; enchantment in, 139; healing relation to, 232; integration relation to, 193; meaning and, 138; neo-shamanism relation to, 166; social fragmentation relation to, 214; in sorcery, 21
modern life, 15, 28, 85, 139; anxiety in, 94; in China, 173, 186–87; primitivism relation to, 90–91; stress of, 13, 28–29, 198; transcendence of, 1, 4, 57, 74, 99
modern society, suffering of, 136–37
money, 88, 120–21, 123, 129; of facilitators, 13–14; healers and, 3–4; sorcery relation to, 16
moral ambiguity complex, 87
moral beauty, 19; in visions, 20–21
Mother Ayahuasca, 145, 200, 207; attitudes and, 165–66; in Australia, 158; healing from, 217; integration relation to, 201–2; intentions and, 153; Mother Nature and, 22; society and, 165
Mother Earth, 161
Mother Nature, 22, 72; fractals and, 142. *See also* nature

Mowforth, Martin, 77
MRTA. *See* Túpac Amaru Revolutionary Movement
multisensory perception, 25, 65. *See also* synesthesia, 25
mundane impressions, in visions, 220
Muraresku, Brian, 98
mushrooms: psilocybin, 228; spirit, 168
music, 25, 155, 179–80, 211; facilitators and, 156–57, 163; shamanism and, 24. *See also icaro*
musical ability, 155
mystery, 17–18, 20, 130, 143, 171; humility toward, 6–7; of plant medicine, 52; of visions, 18, 109; wonder and, 98
mystical experience, 186; religious conversion and, 215–16
mysticism, 238; drugs and, 224–25

Naked Lunch (Burroughs), 56, 107, 228
Naranjo, Claudio, 226
Narby, Jeremy, 94, 105
narratives, 190; of Chao, 208–12, 215, 217; of Fei Fei, 184–86; of healing, 225; integration and, 191–92, 193, 203, 205, 218; of Kate, 160–63, 201; for meaning, 192; of Michael, 163–66; in relational integration, 200–201; in sharing circles, 158, 205; visions compared to, 218; of Wang, 183–84, 187
National Geographic, 119
Native American Church, 205
nature, 74–75, 139, 143–44, 158, 186; civilization compared to, 14; culture relation to, 72; fractals in, 141; healing relation to, 22, 73, 136, 139–40, 142; modern life relation

274   INDEX

nature (*continued*)
to, 15; for psychedelic therapy,
140–41; retreats and, 16–17; Shipibo healers and, 70; society division with, 137; spirits of, 207–8;
tourism and, 119
neoliberal values, 214, 233; in China,
171
neoshamanism, 13, 28; counterculture
and, 142–43; disenchantment relation to, 170; Indigenous peoples
relation to, 145; individualism in,
158; intrapsychic integration and,
200; meaning in, 137–38; modernity relation to, 166; Shipibo healers and, 79. *See also* shamanism
neural plasticity, 213
neuroscience research, psychedelics
and, 110–11
New Age spirituality, 13–14, 28; in
Australia, 31; in China, 214; *shen
xin ling* and, 171; Western society
relation to, 144
New Amazonian Art movement, 22
New Rain Publishers, 171
New South Wales, Australia, 135
nihue, 3, 65; capital and, 93; shamanism relation to, 88–89; Shipibo
healers and, 112
noa jonikon ("The Real People"), 66
Norzi, Mateo, 32
noya rao medicine plant, 1

occult economies, capital in, 92–93
ocular perception, 25
"*Omeco Machacuai*" (painting), 45
onanya joni (wise person), 3; capitalism
and, 93; Juan as, 16; shamanism
and, 82–83
ontological crisis, 124, 125

Osho, 132
otherness, 28; *curanderismo and*, 89; in
fashion capitalism, 60; primitivism
and, 74; visions relation to, 97
Ott, Jonathan, 75, 101–2
Otto, Rudolf, 83

Pachamama Temple, Pucallpa, 32,
63–64, 77–80, 108, 122–24, 235–
38; happiness at, 100–101; *onanya
joni* and, 83; poverty at, 86; psychotic episode at, 120–21; social
media of, 105–6; sorcery and, 68,
80, 92
pain, 11–12, 20, 106, 129, 144;
chronic, 160; ego death and, 4;
emotional, 126, 142; purging of,
218
Panure, 46
Parliament of the World's Religions,
58
Parsons, Howard, 19
past experiences: in psychedelic therapy, 222; in visions, 160, 221
Pegnaum harmala, 113
Peluso, Daniela, 30; on entrepreneurism, 77; on tourism, 60–61, 83
The People's Guerrilla Army. *See Ejército Guerrillero Popular*
perception, 50, 96, 107, 129, 149, 188;
European, 37, 49; of meaning, 138;
multisensory, 65; ocular, 25; primitivist, 83, 136–37; public, 204;
social, 9; of society, 188; transformation of, 216; in urban life, 82; of
workplace relations, 182
perennialism, 112, 225; in visions,
226–28, 231–32
The Perennial Philosophy (Huxley),
224–25

INDEX 275

Perkins, Daniel, 57
Perry, Rick, 221
personality, 196, 197; transformation
  of, 213–14
perspective, 65–66, 233
Peru, 193; civil unrest in, 27; communist uprising in, 116; Iquitos,
  39, 70, 72–73; missionaries in, 40;
  tourism in, 30, 31, 53–54, 60–61.
  See also Pucallpa, Peru
peyote, 205
Picota Lopez, Gilberto, 72
Pinedo Vasquez, Rosa, 72
pintas. See visions
Pitt-Rivers, Augustus, 24
plant diet, 2, 32, 63, 66, 151
plant life, 66
plant medicine, 52, 62, 66–67, 69,
  78
Plants of the Gods (Schultes and
  Hofmann), 171, 172
plant spirits, 129–30, 138, 204, 237
popular culture, 58, 72
The Post-Colonial Exotic (Huggan), 60
post-industrial societies, psychedelics in, 21
pottery, 73, 115
poverty, 62–63; of healers, 119; at Pachamama Temple, 86; primitivism
  and, 90–91; of Shipibo people, 69
pre-ceremony activities, 179
preparation, 195; diet for, 84, 148–49
present, ambient, 223
primitive-civilized schema, 37–38, 49;
  in visions, 50
primitivism, 84; as medicine, 76; missionaries and, 86; otherness and,
  74; poverty and, 90–91; at retreats,
  85–86; shamanism and, 151; therapy in, 94, 137–38

primitivist tourism, 74–75, 83–84, 235
profane, and sacred, 218–19
propaganda, 173–74, 175
psilocybin mushrooms, 168, 228
"The Psychedelic Experience"
  (Leary), 165
psychedelics, 192; in China, 167–69,
  171–72; education and, 67; expectations relation to, 149; fractals
  and, 142; humor and, 101–2; Mc-
  Kenna, T., relation to, 131–32;
  neuroscience research and, 110–
  11; ontological crisis and, 124, 125;
  in post-industrial societies, 21; self-
  experimentation with, 231; time relation to, 220–21, 222; wonder and,
  98–99
Psychedelic Science conference, 221
psychedelic therapy, 4; awe in, 18–19;
  capitalism and, 29–30; integration
  for, 191, 195–96; nature for, 140–
  41; past experiences in, 222; perennialism and, 225; for psychological
  flexibility, 212–13; public opinion on, 203–4; religious conversion
  compared to, 216; retreats compared to, 194–95
psychological flexibility: integration
  and, 215; psychedelic therapy for,
  212–13; social fragmentation relation to, 214
psychology, anthropology compared
  to, 5–6, 10–11
psychonauts, 15, 25; in Australia,
  133–34, 146–47
psychotherapy, 195
psychotic episode, 120–21
Psychotria viridis, 38
public opinion, on psychedelic therapy, 203–4

INDEX

Pucallpa, Peru, 32; poverty in, 62–63. *See also* Pachamama Temple, Pucallpa

purging, 155, 180, 205–6; Bridging the Gap and, 182; ego death and, 4; of guilt, 209; of pain, 218; synesthesia and, 25

Putumayo, Colombia, 49

Quechua language, 38

quiqui, 19

racism, 44, 49, 63, 120, 213

Rambo, Lewis, 215

Rappaport, Roy, 197, 199

Razam, Rak, 14, 199

reality, 159, 197–98;

"The Real People." *See noa jonikon*

recreational drugs, 101, 204

Reichel-Dolmatoff, Gerardo, 20, 223

relational integration, 200–201

relationships, 163–64, 165; with co-workers, 181–82. *See also* family

religion, 8, 219; ayahuasca compared to, 208–9; capitalism as, 139; in China, 169; integration relation to, 200; psychological flexibility and, 215; spirituality compared to, 151–52; visions relation to, 9

religious conversion, 215–16

religious pilgrimage, tourism compared to, 76

restlessness, of international guests, 107

Retreat Guru, 54

retreats, 31, 63–64, 84; as commercial spaces, 29; foreign-owned, 76–77; integration at, 191; intention for, 153–54; in Iquitos, 70; of Luke, 177–80; primitivism at, 85–

86; psychedelic therapy compared to, 194–95

Ricardo (Maestro), 92, 117, 119; *icaro* of, 236–37

Rio Napo Basin, Ecuador, 47

Roe, Peter, 73

Roszak, Theodore, 131

rubber industry, 71, 139. *See also* colonialism

Rubenstein, Mary-Jane, 19

Rubenstein, Steven, 223

rules, 108; of ceremonies, 157

sacred, and profane, 218–19

salary: of facilitators, 14. *See also* money

Sanabria, Emilia, 222

San Francisco de Yarinacocha, 71

San Pedro cactus, 39; missionaries relation to, 40

Santo Daime, 190

Santos-Granero, Fernando, 65

Schultes, Richard Evans, 55

Scott, Michael, 97; on wonder, 104

A Secular Age (Taylor), 137

secular cosmology, 173

secularism, 176–77; in China, 12–13, 186–87

self-experimentation, with psychedelics, 231

selfhood, 202

Sendero Luminoso (Shining Path), 115, 116–17, 118

sensory experience, in visions, 24–25

serpents, in visions, 229

set and setting theory, 111–12, 172, 173, 195

sexual abuse, 130, 136

shadow self, 197–99, 205

shamanic cosmologies, 138

shamanic tourism, 30, 31, 71, 233
shamanism, 22, 39; capitalism and, 54, 91; in China, 168, 171; Christianity relation to, 43; colonialism relation to, 49, 52–53; competition and, 91–92; diet and, 222; food accumulation and, 87; gender and, 72–73; literary, 52; music and, 24; *nihue* relation to, 88–89; *onanya joni* and, 82–83; primitivism and, 151; songs in, 230; sorcery and, 64
Shamanism, Colonialism, and the Wild Man (Taussig), 49–50
Shangzhou Press, 171
Shanon, Benny, 26; *The Antipodes of the Mind*, 6, 17–18; on diet, 148–49; on meaning, 110, 138; on visions, 96, 226, 227–28, 229
shared visions, 229–30
sharing circles: in Australia, 134, 136; in China, 33, 185; integration in, 199, 202; intention in, 154; narratives in, 158, 205
shen xin ling (Body-Heart-Spirit), 171
Shining Path. *See Sendero Luminoso*
Shipibo healers, 78, 80; attitudes of, 100–102; cosmologies among, 87–88; gender and, 71, 72, 73; integration relation to, 219; *medicina* and, 67–68; militias relation to, 117; nature and, 70; neoshamanism and, 79; *nihue* and, 112; perspective and, 65–66; social welfare and, 70; tourism relation to, 77, 82; visions relation to, 128–29; wonder and, 102
Shipibo people: culture of, 63, 78, 90, 106, 108; humor of, 101; Jesuit priests relation to, 70–71; poverty of, 69

Shipibo sorcery, 1–3, 17, 64–65, 79, 93
Shuar people, 97, 110, 190, 222–23
soberness, 99–100
social change, 64, 83, 192; capital for, 94
social context, 35, 112, 192, 226
social environment: of healers, 120; visions relation to, 118
social fragmentation, 213–14
social hierarchies, 87
social media, of Pachamama Temple, 105–6
social medicine, 205–6
social perception, 9
social structures, 192
social suffering, 119
social welfare, Shipibo healers and, 70
society: disenchantment with, 16, 138–39, 143, 167, 188, 207; integration and, 217; Mother Ayahuasca and, 165; nature division with, 137; perception of, 188; religious conversion and, 216; Western, 136–37, 144
sociocultural background, visions relation to, 28
songs: Cuna curing, 192; in shamanism, 230. *See also icaro*; music
sorcery: colonialism relation to, 49–50; envy and, 91–92; healers and, 114; inequalities relation to, 89–91; Mama Maria and, 80, 82; misfortune relation to, 87–88; modernity in, 21; money relation to, 16; Pachamama Temple and, 68, 80, 92; Shipibo, 1–3, 17, 64–65, 79, 93; tourism and, 64–65, 70, 92–93, 94
sovereignty, 152

278 INDEX

Spanish empire, witchcraft trials in, 49

specialists, Indigenous, 122–23

spirit mushrooms, 168

spirits: of nature, 207–8; plant, 130, 204; in visions, 125–26. *See also* visions

spirituality, 8, 137, 159; capitalism and, 29–30, 232; in China, 170; New Age, 13–14, 28, 31, 144, 171, 214; religion compared to, 151–52; Western, 18. *See also* neoshamanism; shamanism

spiritual minimalism, 86

Spruce, Richard, 46–47

staff performance, psychedelics for, 167–68

Stasch, Rupert, 74–75

St. John, Graham, 55

Strassman, Rick, 171–72

stress, 183, 184; mindfulness for, 198; of modern life, 13, 28–29, 198

St. Vincent Hospital, 204

Suárez Álvarez, Carlos, 70

suffering, 30, 84, 139, 192, 200, 205; disenchantment and, 139; of healers, 129; of international guests, 120; of modern society, 136–37; social, 119; trauma and, 92

Suited Monk, 177–78, 180, 186; disenchantment and, 187

synchronicities, 107; visions and, 110

synesthesia, 24–25, 46, 58, 141

Taiwan, 171

Tango Lopez, Pedro, 100

Taussig, Michael, 26, 27, 100, 192; *Shamanism, Colonialism, and the Wild Man*, 49–50; on visions, 51, 52

Taylor, Anne Christine, 87

Taylor, Charles, 137

textiles, 73

therapy: in China, 214; in primitivism, 94, 137–38. *See also* psychedelic therapy

Tiananmen Square massacre, 185

time, 220–21, 222, 238

Ting Ting, 11–12, 16, 174, 181–82, 187

tourism, 28; capital and, 86–87; cosmologies of, 89; economy, 30; hyper-traditionalism and, 83; Indigenous peoples relation to, 74, 75–76; inequalities relation to, 93; nature and, 119; in Peru, 30, 31, 53–54, 60–61; primitivist, 74–75, 83–84, 235; religious pilgrimage compared to, 76; shamanic, 30, 31, 71, 233; Shipibo healers relation to, 77, 82; sorcery and, 64–65, 70, 92–93, 94; wonder and, 118, 129

Tramacchi, Des, 21, 145, 232; *Vapours and Visions*, 146

transbodied medicine, 67–68

transcendence, 93, 155, 164; of disenchantment, 14; of modern life, 1, 4, 57, 74, 99; of transbodied medicines, 68

transformation, 97, 122, 128, 185, 215–16, 232; existential, 224; healing and, 153, 180; of perception, 216; of personality, 213–14; social, 49

trauma, 80, 117, 197, 220–21, 222–24, 227; childhood, 142; collective, 23; family and, 11, 84–86, 92, 141; healing of, 123–24, 134, 144, 149, 191

travel restrictions, of Australia, 14

Tsing, Anna, 129
Tukano shamans, 26, 46, 223
Túpac Amaru Revolutionary Movement (MRTA), 115
Tupper, Kenneth, 67

unethical acts, 130
Uniao de Vegetal, 190
unity, 114, 126, 225, 238, 267. *See also* perennialism
urban context, 16
urban life, 82
utopic primitivism, 85

Vapours and Visions (Tramacchi), 146
Vargas Fernández, Elisa, 73
Veigl, Franz Xavier, 43
El Viagero Universal (Estala), 42–43
Villavicencio, Manuel, 47–48
Vincent, Eve, 98
violence, 20, 117–18, 213, 223; colonial, 50; of materialism, 86; in visions, 183–84
visions, 103–4, 147, 189, 211, 224; ambient present in, 223; biographical materials in, 6–7, 155, 226–27, 237–38; of Burroughs, 56; cinematic theory and, 51–52; cities in, 5, 6, 17, 23–24, 47, 118, 158, 220; context relation to, 28, 226, 230; of co-workers, 181–82; culture relation to, 7, 8–9; domination of, 3, 4, 80, 91, 104, 114, 119; familiarity in, 214–15; of family, 161, 180, 182, 208, 237–38; foreign civilizations in, 23–24; fractals in, 141–42; gnosis of, 186, 188; *icaro* relation to, 127; Indigenous, 5, 6; insects in, 228–29; integration relation to,

191–92; intention in, 112–13; of international guests, 123; interpretation of, 11–12; of Kate, 161–63; meaning of, 8, 112–14, 191, 203; mirror relation to, 26–27; moral beauty in, 20–21; mundane impressions in, 220; music and, 156–57; mystery of, 18, 109; narratives compared to, 218; otherness relation to, 97; past experiences in, 160, 221; perennialism in, 226–28, 231–32; primitive-civilized schema in, 50; sensory experience in, 24–25; shared, 229–30; Shipibo healers relation to, 128–29; social environment relation to, 118; spirits in, 125–26; synchronicities and, 110; violence in, 183–84; in visual art, 217; wonder in, 96
visual art, 217
Viveiros de Castro, E., 65

Wallace, Alfred, 46–47
Wang, ayahuasca and, 183–84, 187
Wang, CC, 171
warfare attitudes, 223
Weber, Max, 137, 138, 186
wellness services, 30
Western society, 136–37, 144
Western spirituality, gnosis in, 18
White, S. F.: on missionaries, 42; on *Wizard of the Upper Amazon*, 57
Williams, Justin, 43; on Villavicencio, 48
Wilson, Edward, 140
wise person. *See onanya joni*
witchcraft trials, in Spanish empire, 49
Wizard of the Upper Amazon (Córdova-Rios and Lamb), 56–57

280 INDEX

wonder, 18–19, 106, 128, 239; awe compared to, 193–94; context relation to, 21; crisis and, 20; culture relation to, 109; in ethnography, 33–34; healing relation to, 97–98; in *icaro*, 102–3, 104; of international guests, 105, 114, 129–30; psychedelics and, 98–99; tourism and, 118, 129; in visions, 96
workplace relations, 182. *See also* co-workers

World Ayahuasca Conference, 58, 145
world peace, visions of, 161

Xiao Changming, 168

yagé. See ayahuasca
The Yagé Letters (Burroughs and Ginsberg), 55–56; *Wizard of the Upper Amazon* compared to, 57

Zhang, Li, 214

SPIRITUAL PHENOMENA
TANYA LUHRMANN and ANN TAVES, Series Editors

Spiritual Phenomena features investigations of events, experiences, and objects, both unusual and everyday, that people characterize as spiritual, paranormal, magical, occult and/or supernatural. Working from the presupposition that the status of such phenomena is contested, it seeks to understand how such determinations are made in a variety of historical and cultural contexts. Books in this series explore how such phenomena are identified, experienced, and understood; the role that spontaneity and cultivation play in the process; and the similarities and differences in the way phenomena are appraised and categorized across time and cultures. The editors encourage work that is ethnographic, historical, or psychological, and, in particular, work that uses more than one method to understand these complex phenomena, ranging from the qualitative to quantitative surveys and laboratory-based experiments.

Nathanael J. Homewood, *Seductive Spirits: Deliverance, Demons, and Sexual World-Making in Ghanaian Pentecostalism*

Hugh Turpin, *Unholy Catholic Ireland: Religious Hypocrisy, Secular Morality, and Irish Irreligion*

Alicia Puglionesi, *Common Phantoms: An American History of Psychic Science*

Yoram Bilu, *With Us More Than Ever: Making the Absent Rebbe Present in Messianic Chabad*

David J. Halperin, *Intimate Alien: The Hidden Story of the UFO*

J. Bradley Wigger, *Invisible Companions: Encounters with Imaginary Friends, Gods, Ancestors, and Angels*

Kelly Bulkeley, *Lucrecia the Dreamer: Prophecy, Cognitive Science, and the Spanish Inquisition*